Taking You Lion to the Max

Michael Grothaus

Steve Sande

Dave Caolo

Apress®

Taking Your OS X Lion to the Max

ISBN-13 (pbk): 978-1-4302-3668-9

ISBN-13 (electronic): 978-1-4302-3669-6

President and Publisher: Paul Manning
Lead Editor: Steve Anglin
Developmental Editor: Douglas Pundick and Richard Carey
Technical Reviewer: Jesse Cole Guthry
Editorial Board: Steve Anglin, Mark Beckner, Ewan Buckingham, Gary Cornell, Jonathan Gennick, Jonathan Hassell, Michelle Lowman, Matthew Moodie, Jeff Olson, Jeffrey Pepper, Frank Pohlmann, Douglas Pundick, Ben Renow-Clarke, Dominic Shakeshaft, Matt Wade, Tom Welsh
Coordinating Editor: Kelly Moritz
Copy Editor: Kim Wimpsett
Compositor: MacPS, LLC
Indexer: BIM Indexing & Proofreading Services
Artist: April Milne
Cover Designer: Anna Ishchenko

Distributed to the book trade worldwide by Springer Science+Business Media, LLC., 233 Spring Street, 6th Floor, New York, NY 10013. Phone 1-800-SPRINGER, fax (201) 348-4505, e-mail orders-ny@springer-sbm.com, or visit www.springeronline.com.

For information on translations, please e-mail rights@apress.com, or visit www.apress.com.

Apress and friends of ED books may be purchased in bulk for academic, corporate, or promotional use. eBook versions and licenses are also available for most titles. For more information, reference our Special Bulk Sales–eBook Licensing web page at www.apress.com/bulk-sales.

To Jerry Dresden and Hannah Kurylenko, your journey will soon be complete.

—Michael

To my high school English teacher David Faull, who I never properly thanked for teaching me how to write while attending W.C. Hinkley High School in the early 1970s. Thanks, Mr. Faull!

—Steve

To my wife, Mia, and children, Grace and William, who put up with the long days and late nights I spent tucked away writing and editing. Also, to Sr. Gail Cabral, IHM, Ph.D., and professor of psychology at Marywood University, who taught me the importance of writing well.

—Dave

Contents at a Glance

Contents

About the Authors

Michael Grothaus is an American novelist and journalist living in London. He was first introduced to Apple computers in film school and went on to use them for years to create award-winning films. However, after discovering many of Hollywood's dirty little secrets while working for 20th Century Fox, he left and spent five years with Apple as a consultant. He's since moved to London and earned his master's degree in creative writing. His first novel, *Epiphany Jones*, is a story about trafficking and America's addiction to celebrity. Currently, Michael is a staff writer at AOL's popular tech news site the Unofficial Apple Weblog (TUAW.com), where he writes about all things Mac. Additionally, Michael has written several other books for Apress, including *Taking Your iPad to the Max, Taking Your iPod touch to the Max, 2nd edition*, and *Taking Your iPhoto '11 to the Max*. When not writing, Michael spends his time traveling Europe, Northern Africa, and Asia. You can reach him at www.michaelgrothaus.com and www.twitter.com/michaelgrothaus.

Steve Sande has been a loyal fan of Apple technology since buying his first Mac in 1984. Originally trained as a civil engineer, Steve's career as an IT professional blossomed in the 1990s. A longtime blogger, Steve is the features editor at AOL's the Unofficial Apple Weblog (TUAW.com), the author of three books about Apple's iWeb application, and a collaborator on *Taking Your iPad 2 to the Max* and *Taking Your iPhone 4 to the Max*. You can join Steve every Wednesday for the popular TUAW TV Live show and follow his exploits at www.twitter.com/stevensande. He lives with Barb, his wife of 32 years, in Highlands Ranch, Colorado.

Dave Caolo is an author and the managing editor at the Unofficial Apple Weblog (TUAW.com). Previous to his career as a writer, Dave spent eight years as the IT director at a Mac-friendly residential school in Massachusetts. Today, Dave can be found geeking out with his Macs and spending time with his kids, wife, and Boston terrier, Batgirl. Learn more at http://davecaolo.com.

About the Technical Reviewer

 Originally from Owasso, Oklahoma, **Jesse Cole Guthery** moved to Phoenix, Arizona, to attend Collins College where he received a bachelor's degree in film/HDTV production in 2007. While working as an Apple technician at Collins College, he received a master's degree from Full Sail University in media design. Jesse currently works for the Salt River Project in Phoenix, Arizona, as an HD post-production coordinator. Jesse also is an Apple Certified Macintosh Technician and Apple Certified Final Cut 7 Professional.

Acknowledgments

Thanks to the wonderful staff at Apress for all of their hard work and assistance during the production of this book. We also want to send our gratitude to Apple's Mac OS X team for their phenomenal work on Lion, and to our families, friends, and colleagues for putting up with us during writing and editing. Last, but certainly not least, many thanks to all of you who are reading this book; we're glad you chose us as your companions on your knowledge quest.

—Michael, Steve, and Dave

Introduction

OS X Lion has arrived with a roar.

Lion is the latest addition to the proud lineage of Mac OS, the operating system that has powered Apple's Macintosh line since 1984. When the first Macs rolled off the assembly line, the point-and-click Mac OS and the introduction of the mouse as a pointing device revolutionized the personal computing industry. No longer did computer users need to remember and type arcane command-line instructions; instead, Mac OS brought a more visual paradigm to personal computing.

Fast-forward to 2001. Apple released Mac OS X, a new version of Mac OS written from the ground up around the venerable Unix operating system. Bringing a new level of power, security, and stability to the Mac platform, Mac OS X is the software core around which the renaissance of the Mac has happened.

In 2007, Apple introduced the first iPhone. The operating system used on the iPhone, iOS, is based on Mac OS X but is specifically designed to let owners interact with their phones through touch gestures. iOS is about to enter its fifth generation and is now being used on the iPhone, iPod touch, iPad, and the second-generation Apple TV.

With the introduction of Mac OS X 10.7 "Lion," Apple took many of the features first popularized in iOS and moved them to the Mac platform. Through the Mac App Store, Mac users can purchase, install, and upgrade software for their computers without ever handling a DVD. In fact, OS X Lion is the first major personal computer operating system to be distributed primarily through the Internet rather than through the traditional store/disc method.

Of course, there's more to OS X Lion than just a fast electronic distribution method, and that's what this book is all about. *Taking Your Mac OS X Lion to the Max* is your introduction to the many new features—almost 250 in total—that make this new operating system so compelling. This book is primarily targeted to those who have used Macs in the past and are familiar with much of the terminology associated with the platform. If you know how to launch applications from the Dock, are familiar with the location of the menu bar and Apple menu, and can navigate your way around the Finder, then you'll feel right at home as you read this book.

A look at the changes to the Finder in OS X Lion is your first destination in the book. The Spotlight search engine has new options and features to make looking for your files faster and more enjoyable. AirDrop is a new and easy way for you to wirelessly share files with others just by dragging and dropping them on an image of the recipient. Apple has recognized the mobile Mac user with the addition of new or improved security features in OS X Lion, including improved FileVault encryption, Find My Mac, and remote wipe capabilities.

The Mac App Store debuted in Mac OS X 10.6 "Snow Leopard," but the virtual software store has really hit its stride in OS X Lion. You'll learn how to discover the latest software for Mac, buy and install it, and keep it up-to-date. Many apps are being rewritten to take advantage of OS X Lion's autosave capabilities and versions, a way of keeping a virtual audit trail of all changes made to documents that you create on your Mac.

While a discussion of Launchpad, Spaces, and Mission Control might seem to be more at home in a book about NASA, these are OS X Lion features that provide new methods of launching and organizing apps on a screen. Fans of Dashboard, which was added to Mac OS X in version 10.4 "Tiger," will rejoice when they find out how Apple has revitalized the world of widgets.

Most Mac owners use their computers to send and receive e-mail, and Apple has changed the look, feel, and functionality of the Mail app significantly in OS X Lion. It now more closely resembles the Mail apps on iPad, iPhone, and iPod touch, and it takes advantage of another Lion feature—full-screen mode. We'll guide you through the new features of other apps included with OS X Lion, including iCal, Address Book, Image Capture, Preview, Photo Booth, and FaceTime.

If some of Lion's features have you wishing you'd never upgraded your Mac, there's a chapter in this book highlighting the many ways that System Preferences can bring back your happy thoughts.

Finally, we cap off the discussion of Lion with a look at OS X Lion Server. Whether you want to set up an office file server, share a calendar or address book with the Macs and devices in your home, or just want to learn more about the inner workings of OS X Lion Server, the final chapter of this book details how the Server application is used to configure and maintain a useful shared computing environment.

To get the most out of OS X Lion, we recommend reading the book from cover to cover to pick up all the details. But we also encourage you to experiment hands-on with Lion, and when you have a question or concern, the book is here to help you. Most of all, have fun while you're learning how Lion is going to change your computing life. We had a blast trying the new operating system during its development, and we sincerely hope that our enthusiasm shines through in every chapter. Thanks for letting us show you OS X Lion.

Chapter 1

Finder Basics

Mac OS X 10.7 Lion introduces another major revision to Finder, the Macintosh's default file system. After decades of refinement and revisions, Finder scarcely resembles its early incarnation. What is unchanged, however, is that Finder is the first thing a person interacts with when using a Mac. In many ways, it's a Macintosh's "first impression."

In this chapter, I'll explain what's new with Finder, from subtle changes in the preference panes to sweeping differences such as scroll behavior and a new method of window resizing.

First I'll explain how to acquire Lion, because Apple has moved to an all-new distribution system, and then I'll explain how to ensure that your Mac is ready for the transition. Let's begin with how and where to buy Mac OS 10.7 Lion.

Buying Lion

The sale of Lion marks a significant change for Apple. For the first time, the Macintosh operating system is being sold exclusively through the Mac App Store. Lion will not be available on DVD or other physical media.

To purchase Lion, launch the Mac App Store and find Lion. Click the price tag, and then click Buy Now. Enter your password when prompted, and the download will begin.

It's a large file, about 4GB. Once the download is complete, you'll be prompted through the installation.

System Requirements

As expected, Lion has specific system requirements. The following sections describe what you'll need to install Lion on your Mac.

A Compatible Mac

Mac OS X 10.7 Lion requires a Mac with an Intel Core 2 Duo, Core i3, Core i5, Core i7, or Xeon processor. You can identify your Mac's processor by selecting the Apple menu in the upper-left corner and choosing About This Mac. A new window will appear listing machine-specific information, including the processor.

Snow Leopard

Lion also requires the latest version of Mac OS X 10.6 Snow Leopard. Again, click the Apple menu and then select About This Mac to see what version of the operating system you have installed. Select Software Update to update to the latest version of Mac OS X 10.6.

The Up-to-Date Program

Apple's Up-to-Date Program lets customers who purchased a qualifying new Mac from Apple or an Apple Authorized Reseller within a certain date range receive a copy of Mac OS X Lion at no charge. See www.apple.com/macosx/uptodate/ to find out whether you qualify.

What's New in Lion's Finder

Apple has added several new features to Finder with Mac OS X 10.7 Lion, both big and small. For example, new window icons are minor in comparison to the sweeping support for Multi-Touch gestures. In the following section, I'll describe what's new in the Mac Finder under Lion, including the Finder windows (both in design and function), improvements to existing features such as Quick Look, all-new updates such as scroll bar overlays, and, of course, the extensive Multi-Touch support. Let's start with the login screen.

The Login Screen

As you can see in Figure 1–1, Mac OS X 10.7's login screen is quite different from previous iterations.

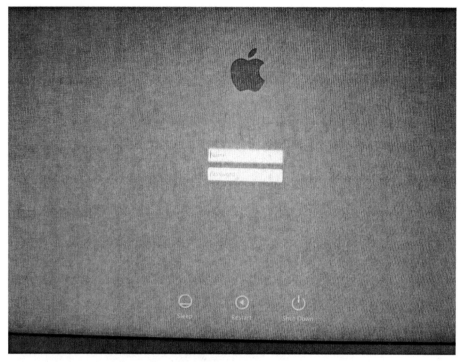

Figure 1–1. *Mac OS X Lion's minimalistic login screen*

Note that I've described the default settings. You can make some changes to the login screen's appearance and behavior via the Users and Groups system preference. (See the upcoming note.)

The most striking difference is the "gray linen" background, which is in keeping with a user interface theme used throughout the operating system. At the top of the screen is an Apple logo, and beneath that you'll find an icon for each user account.

To log in, click your desired account's icon, enter the password, and hit Return.

Three icons appear across the bottom of the screen: Sleep, Restart, and Shutdown. Clicking each does just what the name implies. In the upper-right corner you'll find a battery status indicator (if your Mac is a laptop), a Wi-Fi signal indicator (if connected), and the current time. The battery icon, Wi-Fi icon, and time are new additions.

There's also a lot missing. Snow Leopard's login screen, which consisted of a control panel above a starry image, offered more information. Below the Apple logo and title "Mac OS X," the screen displayed the administrator's name. By clicking it, you could cycle through the following information:

- The OS version

- The OS build number

- The machine's serial number

- The machine's IP address (if online)

- Any available network accounts

- The current date, time (in hours, minutes, and seconds), day of the week, and time zone

Lion's login screen offers a simplified view.

> **NOTE:** To alter the login screen's options, open System Preferences and then click Users & Groups. Next, click Login Options, and finally, authenticate with your administrator password. You'll find several—although limited—options for customizing your Mac's login screen. Other than some minor changes of wording and layout, these options are unchanged since Snow Leopard.

The Mac OS X Lion Desktop

For the most part, Lion's desktop is unchanged. However, a few minor yet notable additions are in place. See Figure 1–2.

Figure 1–2. *The default Finder desktop in Lion*

Lion's desktop features a new default background image, or *wallpaper*, consistent with the outer-space theme introduced with Leopard. A swirling galaxy greets new users.

You'll also find new items in the Dock. For example, Launchpad's icon, a black "rocket ship" on a round field of brushed metal, is on the far left. (Launchpad is discussed in detail in Chapter 5.) You'll also find icons for the Mac App Store (the familiar, stylized *A* on a field of blue) and FaceTime (a sliver camera). Of course, you can relocate or remove these icons as you have in previous versions of the Mac operating system.

The Apple Menu

In the upper-left corner of your Mac, you'll find the Apple menu. It offers a handy list of features and functions, such as one-click access to the Mac App Store, System Preferences, and the Sleep, Shutdown, and Restart commands.

As with previous versions of the Mac OS, Lion's Apple menu also provides a link to system information such as the amount and type of RAM installed, the processor's type and speed, and more. However, the System Profiler application (now called System Information) has been revamped in Lion. See Figure 1–3.

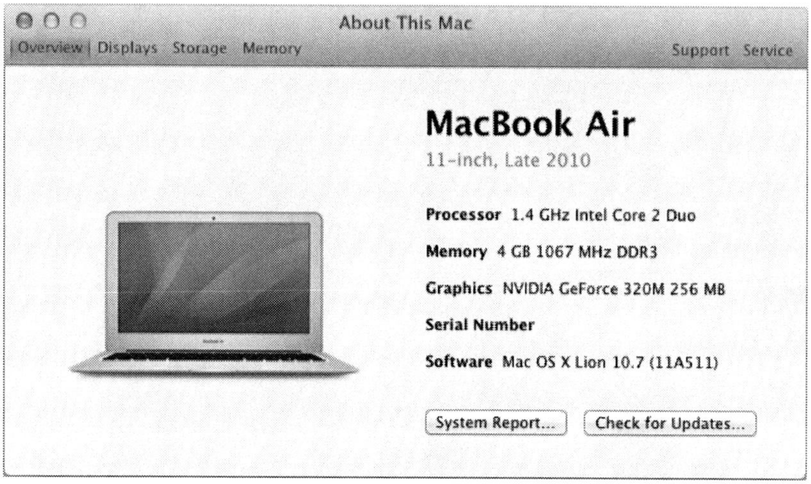

Figure 1–3. *The new About This Mac screen as shown in Lion*

To access System Information from the Apple menu, click it and then select About This Mac. A new window appears bearing the Apple logo and some general information. This is the same as it was in Snow Leopard. Next, click More Info... to launch the System Information application.

Right away you'll notice that its user interface has been completely rebuilt. Instead of the text-heavy lists of information that System Profiler offered in earlier versions of the Mac OS, System Information presents an elegant, tabbed window. You'll find details on System Information in Chapter 11.

New Finder Preferences

Apple has made several changes to Finder's list of preferences. To access these options, bring Finder to the front (click the desktop or Finder icon in the Dock, for example), and then select Preferences from Finder menu. The following sections describe what's new in the preferences list.

General Preferences

The General Preferences tab offers two minor changes. The first is a bit of wording; a line that read "New Finder windows open" in Snow Leopard is "New Finder Windows show" in Lion. The second change is a new default option in that list. Specifically, All My Files is the first choice (more on All My Files later in this chapter). See Figure 1–4.

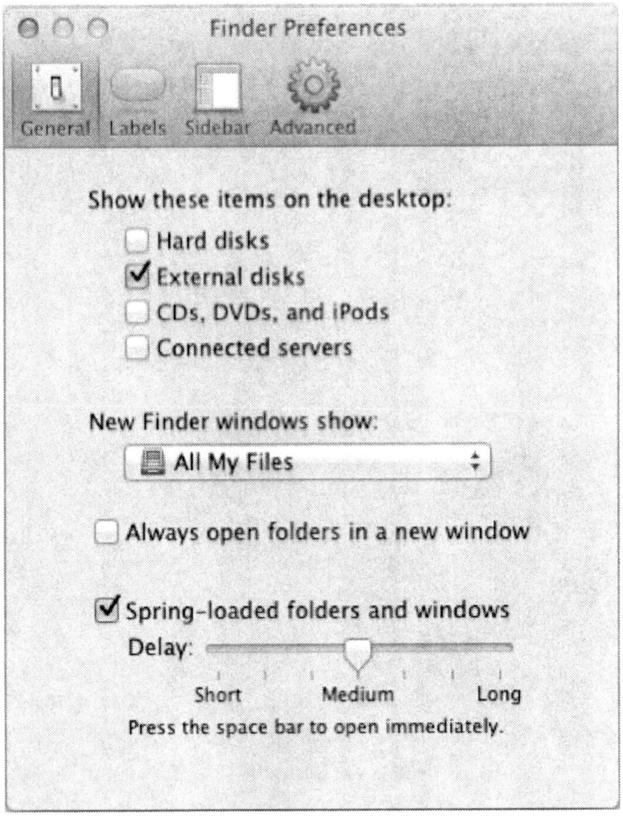

Figure 1–4. *The General Preferences tab, showing the new All My Files option*

Sidebar Preferences

These options have changed quite a bit since Snow Leopard. As you know, Sidebar refers to the items that appear on the left sidebar in Finder windows (more on Finder windows later in this chapter). Unlike previous versions of Mac OS X, Lion offers 18 options across three categories: Favorites, Shared, and Devices. See Figure 1–5.

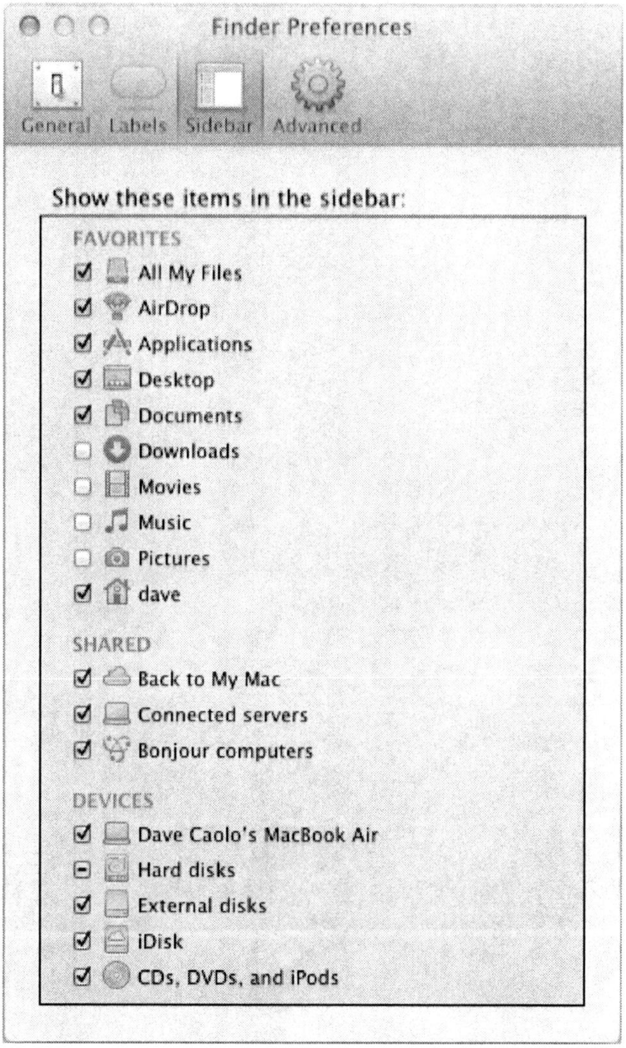

Figure 1–5. *The Finder window sidebar preference options*

New Favorites options include All My Files and AirDrop (which will be discussed in Chapter 2). All My Files offers a sorted list of nearly every document on your Mac. Previously, Finder offered an All Documents smart folder that dumped its contents into an unsorted "everything bucket." Lion arranges the contents of the All My Files folder quite neatly.

The other Favorites options are as follows:

- Applications
- Desktop
- Documents
- Downloads
- Movies
- Music
- Pictures
- Your Home Folder

From that list, Downloads, Movies, Music, and Pictures are new as one-click options. Previous versions of Mac OS X would let you drag these folders into a Finder window sidebar (Lion does as well), but this is the first time they've been offered as one-click options by the Finder preferences.

The Shared category offers Back to my Mac, Connected servers, and Bonjour computers, just as Snow Leopard did. Finally, the Devices category offers your machine, Hard disks, External disks, and, iDisk and removable media (CDs, DVDs, and iPods), just as Snow Leopard did.

The difference is the arrangement. Snow Leopard offered four categories (Devices, Shared, Places, and Search For). The Searched For category is completely missing, and its options—Today, Yesterday, Past Week, All Images, All Movies, and All Documents— are gone, having been replaced by the all-encompassing All My Files.

Finally, the Advanced preferences are the same as they were in Snow Leopard.

Finder Windows

The Finder windows in Lion feature several changes when compared to older versions of the Mac operating system. Most significantly, the sidebar (on the left side) and the toolbar (the top of each window) offer new options and functions. Here's a rundown of what's new in Lion's Finder windows.

The Sidebar

Right away you'll notice the absence of color among the sidebar icons. Apple has indeed gone with gray icons on a field of gray with Lion. See Figure 1–6.

Figure 1–6. *Default Finder window sidebar in Mac OS X Lion*

The sidebar icons are divided into three sections: Favorites, Shared, and Devices (just as you saw in the preferences). This arrangement is similar to that of Mac OS X Snow Leopard, with a few notable additions.

The first is All My Files. Click it to reveal a sorted list of nearly every file that's on your Mac. This "everything bucket" sorts your documents into several categories, such as Images, PDF Documents, Music, Movies, Presentations, Spreadsheets, and Documents. Of course, your Mac's listings may differ, depending on what you have.

> **NOTE:** There's a hidden tribute to Apple's advertising past in the All My Files icon. Here's how to find it. First, right-click or Command-click the sidebar icon and then select Get Info. A new window appears. Click the icon in the upper-left corner and then select Copy from the Edit menu (or hit Command-C). Finally, open Preview and select New from the File menu to view the icon's source file. You'll find that snippets of the "Here's To The Crazy Ones" poem that appeared in early "Think Different" TV ads are written on the "pages" in the drawer.

The next addition is a major new feature of Mac OS X Lion: AirDrop. In short, AirDrop lets you share files with other Lion users on your network. AirDrop and All My Files are explained in detail in Chapter 2.

The Toolbar

At the top of each Finder window is the toolbar, where you'll find handy tools for quickly finding documents and directories you need. Lion adds a new button for altering a folder's arrangement of its contents. Click it to see a list of options, similar to Figure 1–7. Again, this new feature is explained in detail in Chapter 2.

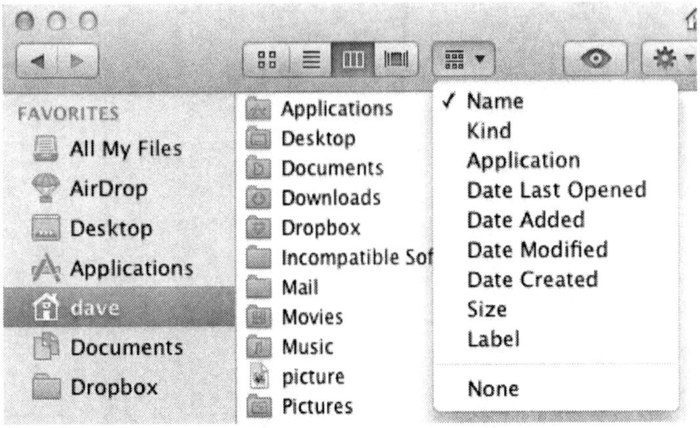

Figure 1–7. *Item arrangement button and options in a Finder window*

Quick Look

Quick Look is a feature of Mac OS X first introduced with version 10.5, or Leopard. It provides a one-tap preview of a file. To use it, simply click a file once to select it in Finder and tap your keyboard's spacebar. A window appears with a preview of your file, be it a text document, an image, an audio file, or so on.

The benefit is time saved. Because you can examine a file without opening the parent application (quickly examine a text document without launching Microsoft Word, for example), Quick Look lets you quickly examine reference material and then get back to what you were doing.

Mac OS X 10.7 Lion offers several significant enhancements to Quick Look, including a choice of applications and persistent audio tracks. Here's what's new with Quick Look under Lion.

Appearance

Quick Look has been updated in both its appearance and its functioning. The most striking change to its look is the white background. Previously, Quick Look presented previews on a field of black.

Also, the buttons for interacting with the file have moved from the bottom of the Quick Look window to the top. See Figure 1–8.

Figure 1–8. *Updated Quick Look window replaces the black background color with white and offers new parent application options via the button in the right corner.*

Function

In several ways, Quick Look is much more functional under Lion. The biggest change is the number of parent software options. In the upper-right corner of most Quick Look windows, you'll find a button labeled Open With [Name of default app], which will open the previewed item in an application. Here's how it works:

1. Click the button to open the file with the default application. For example, the button might say Open With Preview while browsing a PDF. Click the button to open that PDF in Apple's Preview.

2. Right-click the button to see a list of compatible applications. Click any application in the list to use it to open the previewed file. For example, if I right-click the button while previewing that same PDF, I could open it with Evernote, Pages, or Skitch. (Your options may vary.)

Another welcome change is that the Quick Look preview persists when you navigate away from Finder. For example, use Quick Look to open an audio file. The window will pop up, and your audio file will begin to play. Then, open another application, like Safari or Mail. Your audio file will continue to play in the background. Previously, the audio file would have stopped playing after you navigated away from Finder.

Also, you can resize the Quick Look window from any spot, not just the lower-right corner. This is consistent with Finder behavior in Mac OS X Lion.

Useful New Features of Quick Look

In the next section, I'll explain some cool tricks that Quick Look can manage with four popular file types: images, audio files, PDFs, and movies.

Adding a Photo to iPhoto

As with Leopard and Snow Leopard, you can use the following steps to add an image directly to iPhoto from a Quick Look window:

1. While browsing a file in Quick Look, right-click the button in the upper-right corner.

2. From the drop-down menu that appears, select Add to iPhoto.

3. iPhoto will launch to import the photo. (iPhoto's main window will not appear.)

From there, you can close the Quick Look window and quit iPhoto.

Unfortunately, the next time you browse that file with Quick Look, you won't find any indication that it's previously been sent to iPhoto. Under Snow Leopard, the iPhoto icon displayed a check mark on previously imported images.

Audio Files

Audio files can be expanded to full-screen via Quick Look under Lion, which is new since Snow Leopard. While in full screen, you'll see the album art and timer.

PDFs

PDFs previewed with Quick Look now offer thumbnails of all pages. You can scroll through the thumbnails and click to jump directly to any one.

Movies

As with the other types of files, movies viewed with Quick Look can go full-screen by clicking the arrows in the upper-right corner or can be opened in a supported application by clicking the labeled button.

Window Resizing and the Scroll Bar Overlay

Lion offers to significant changes that aren't unique to Finder, but this is as good a place as any to introduce them. Specifically, window resizing and scroll bar behavior are much different than they've ever been in the Mac OS. Note that I'm describing the default settings here. Some changes can be made to alter this behavior.

For the first time, you can resize a window from any corner or edge. Previously, you'd "grab" the lower-right corner of a window with the cursor, click and hold with your trackpad or mouse, and drag to resize the window.

Mac OS X 10.7 Lion lets you grab a window from any corner or edge. Simply hover the cursor over the window's border until it changes from the familiar cursor arrow into a smaller, two-headed arrow. At that point, you can drag to resize that window.

This works with nearly every app; there's no need for special optimization or updating from developers to make apps compliant.

Scroll bar behavior has also changed. Specifically, the ever-present scroll bar has been replaced with one that appears only when needed (on apps updated to support this feature and when browsed with compatible mice) and then fades away after scrolling is complete. Figure 1–9 shows how it works.

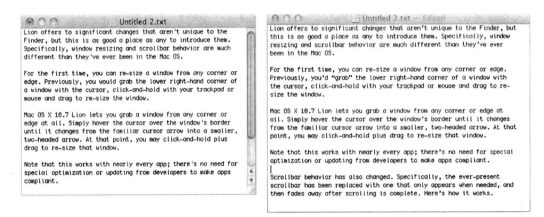

Figure 1–9. *Old scroll bar behavior on the left (Snow Leopard) vs. default scroll bar behavior in Lion (on the right)*

On the left you see a TextEdit document in Snow Leopard. Note the scroll bar on the right side.

On the right is the same document in Lion. You'll notice that the scroll bar seems to be missing. It's there, but it has not yet been "called into service." To produce it, I must either swipe my laptop's trackpad, swipe the scroll wheel of a mouse or the surface of Apple's Magic Mouse, or swipe the surface of a Magic Trackpad. When I do so, a thin, gray scroll bar will appear. At that point, I can move the cursor over to it, click and hold to grab it, and then drag it up and down (or simply continue to swipe the previously named devices).

Another huge change in Lion's scrolling behavior is scroll direction. By default, Lion adopts a "natural" scrolling direction, similar to that of the iOS used by iPads, iPhones, and iPod touches. Here's how it works.

Imagine that you have a TextEdit document open that's full of text and that you have a mouse with a scroll wheel. Start at the top of the document, place your finger on the mouse's scroll wheel, and move it from south to north. That is, start with your finger curled under and then straighten it out as you move across the scroll wheel.

As you do that, you'll move toward the *bottom* of your document, or "down."

Likewise, move your finger from north to south on the mouse's scroll wheel (that is, start with your finger straight and curl it in toward your hand as it moves across the scroll wheel) to move toward the top of your document, or "up."

This is the exact opposite of how scrolling has always worked in Mac OS X. It will take some getting used to for many. Fortunately, the "old dogs who dislike new tricks" (like yours truly) can disable this behavior and restore "proper" scrolling by opening System Preferences, clicking Trackpad and then Scroll & Zoom, and, finally, deselecting Scroll direction: natural. See Figure 1–10.

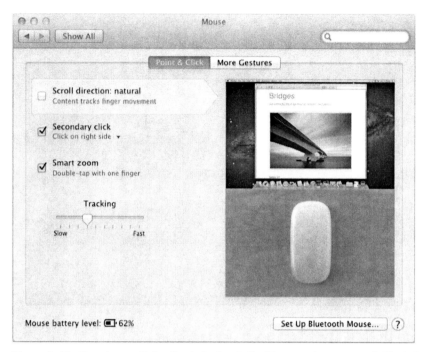

Figure 1–10. *Changing scroll direction behavior via the Mouse preference pane in Lion's System Preferences app*

Multi-Touch Support

Lion takes a huge step toward expanding support for Multi-Touch functions. Those with a laptop or a Magic Trackpad will find all-new ways to interact with and navigate through the Mac OS and several of their favorite apps with swipes, drags, and other gestures.

It's important to note that Apple's Magic Mouse supports fewer gestures than a trackpad (either the one built into your laptop or the Magic Trackpad). I've described which gestures each device supports in the following sections, starting with the trackpad.

The Trackpad and Multi-Touch Gestures

You'll find all of the trackpad Multi-Touch options in the System Preference applications. Just click Trackpad and start exploring.

Trackpad Multi-Touch options are sorted into three categories: Point & Click, Scroll & Zoom, and finally More Gestures. Here's a look at what you'll find in each.

Point & Click

You now have the following options:

- *Tap to Click*: Tap with one finger to register a left-click.

- *Secondary Click*: You have three options for registering a right-click or Control-click: Click or tap with two fingers, click in the bottom-right corner, or click in the bottom-left corner.

- *Look up*: This one is pretty neat. While using a compatible application, select a word of text and double-tap with three fingers to bring up its dictionary definition.

Scroll & Zoom

Here you'll find four options:

- *Scroll direction*: *natural*: This setting alters your Mac's scroll direction.

- *Zoom in or out*: Reverse-pinch with two fingers to zoom in on a photo, and pinch to zoom back out. A reverse-pinch is performed by placing your thumb and index finger close together and spreading them apart; a pinch is the exact opposite.

- *Smart zoom*: Here's a function borrowed directly from iOS. To zoom in on a specific area of a file like a Pages document or a web page, simply place your cursor on the section you'd like to examine and then double-tap with two fingers. That section will expand to fill your screen. Double-tap again to zoom back out to the previous view.

- *Rotate*: Place a thumb and forefinger on the trackpad and slowly twist your hand while keeping them in place to rotate a photo.

More Gestures

The following are six gesture options that you'll want to play with and show off:

- *Swipe between pages*: This option lets you move between pages of a multipage document like Pages or your browsing history in Safari. You have three options for triggering this gesture: scroll left or right with two fingers, swipe left or right with three fingers, and finally swipe with two or three fingers.

- *Swipe between full-screen apps*: Full-screen apps are a marquee feature of Lion. With a click, you can let a single app commandeer your entire screen. Once you have more than one app running full screen, move between them by swiping left or right with either three or four fingers.

- *Mission Control*: This fantastic new feature (explained in detail in Chapter 5) represents a more mature version of Snow Leopard's Spaces. You'll use it by swiping up on your trackpad with either three or four fingers.

- *App Expose*: Get an at-a-glance overview of all the open windows that belong to a given app by swiping down with either three or four fingers.

- *Launchpad*: Browse an iOS-like presentation of installed application icons by pinching with three fingers. (For a detailed description of Launchpad, see Chapter 5.)

- *Show Desktop*: Finally, dismiss all open windows and get to your Mac's desktop by spreading your thumb and three fingers on your trackpad.

The Magic Mouse and Multi-Touch Gestures

The Magic Mouse is Apple's wireless computer mouse that features a touch surface. First introduced in 2009, the Magic Mouse replaced the scroll wheel–based Mighty Mouse. The following sections describe the gestures supported by the Magic Mouse in Lion.

> **NOTE:** To access the Magic Mouse gesture features, open System Preferences and then click Mouse. There you'll find six options across two categories.

Point & Click

The following options are now available:

- *Scroll direction*: *natural*: As described earlier in this chapter, this setting alters your Mac's scroll direction.

- *Secondary click*: Opt to use the right or left side of your Magic Mouse to produce a secondary click.

- *Smart Zoom*: Zoom in on a given area of a document, iOS-style. You have only one option here, which is to double-tap with one finger.

More Gestures

Here are some additional options now available:

- *Swipe between pages*: Move from page to page in large documents or in Safari by scrolling either left or right with one finger, swiping left or right with two fingers, or swiping with either one or two fingers.

- *Swipe between full-screen apps*: Move from one full-screen app to another by swiping left or right with two fingers on your Magic Mouse.

- *Mission Control*: Double-tap with two fingers to bring up the Mission Control interface, which is described in detail in Chapter 6.

Summary

In this chapter, you learned how to purchase Lion from Apple's Mac App Store and how to determine whether your Mac is ready for the upgrade. You also saw how to use Lion's new login screen and Finder-specific features such as the preferences, sidebar, and toolbar Finder window options, as well as features such as enhanced Quick Look, the new scroll bar overlay, and Multi-Touch gestures. Here are a few points from this chapter to wrap things up:

- For the first time, Apple is not distributing Mac OS X on disc or DVD. You must purchase it as a download from the Mac App Store.

- Lion's new login screen is tidier than previous incarnations but offers less information.

- Icons for Launchpad, the Mac App Store, and FaceTime have been added to the Dock by default.

- The Finder window sidebar options have been reorganized and expanded.

- Finder window sidebar icons are gray and no longer colorful.

- Quick Look has been enhanced with new functionality, such as a choice of parent application, a thumbnail view when viewing lengthy PDFs, and persistent audio previews that remain even when you navigate away from Finder.

Multi-Touch gestures have been significantly enhanced, though the Magic Mouse supports fewer gestures than trackpads.

Chapter 2

File Management and Sharing

One of the more confusing aspects of using any personal computer is managing the thousands of files that can accumulate over a very short span of years. If you're like me and keep all of your documents, photos, music, videos, and other random bits of information on your Mac, pretty soon you'll find it becomes difficult to navigate around all of that data.

Apple has made some great improvements to file management in Mac OS X 10.7 Lion, and that's what I'll be describing in this chapter. There are new views available in Finder that make browsing and organizing your files much more like playing with an iPhone or iPad, flicking through lists of file icons.

AirDrop is a new and intuitive way of sharing files between your Mac and other Lion users on the same wireless network as you. Sometimes, you may not want anyone to have access to your files. I'll talk about the improved FileVault 2 encryption feature that locks your data away from others.

Have you ever wondered what you'd do if your Mac was lost or stolen, exposing all of your personal files to the world? The new Find My Mac feature in Lion can tell you where your missing Mac is, let you lock it remotely or change the password to keep prying eyes from seeing your files, or even wipe the computer remotely. Similar to the way Find My iPhone and Find My iMac work, Find My Mac brings a new level of security to Mac owners.

Since sharing is a nice thing to do, I'll also fill you in on screen sharing. Lion brings this old feature up-to-date with improved control of screen sharing and different login options.

Once you've spent time and effort creating documents, you also want to make sure that those documents are safe in case of a computer hardware failure. Time Machine has been an easy way for many Mac owners to back up and restore all of the valuable documents on their computers; now Time Machine even works when your computer isn't connected to your external hard disk drive.

The Finder Sidebar

The Finder window is your window into the files that are stored on your Mac. It's been this way since the first Macs rolled off the assembly line back in 1984, and today's Finder window is a highly refined reflection of the advances in user interface design that have been made at Apple.

To display a Finder window, you can do one of four things:

■ Click the Finder icon on the far left side of the Dock.

■ Select **File ➤ New Finder Window** from the menu bar.

■ Choose Open in Finder or More in Finder when viewing applications, documents, or downloads in folders or stacks in the Dock.

■ Double-click the icon of a hard disk, removable media (CD, DVD, or USB flash drive), or connected server icon on the Mac desktop.

In Figure 2–1, you see a typical Finder window with a set of icons in it.

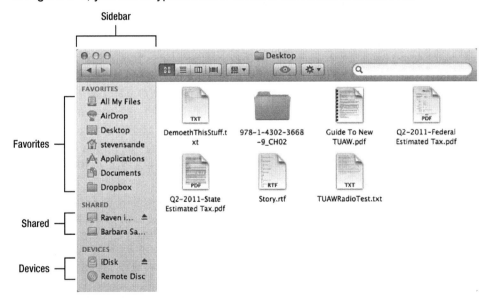

Figure 2–1. *A typical Finder window under Mac OS X 10.7 Lion, showing the new categorizations that appear in the Finder sidebar*

The sidebar—that grayish area on the left side of the Finder window—is different than it appeared in earlier versions of Mac OS X. One of the differences is that the icons in the list are not quite as colorful as they were in the past. Now they're all a dark gray color that is easy on the eyes.

The sidebar in Mac OS X 10.6 Snow Leopard was divided into four categories—Devices, Shared, Places, and Search For. Devices listed any physical internal or external drives plugged into your Mac (including USB flash drives and SD memory cards) as well as your Apple iDisk if you were a MobileMe subscriber, Shared displayed any other computer workstations or servers on the same network as you, Places displayed a list of common locations on your Mac (Desktop, Pictures, Applications, Documents, and so on), and Search For was a tool used to look for all files that had been created within a certain time period (Today, Yesterday, Past Week) or of a specific type (All Images, All Movies, All Documents).

The Favorites Category

Lion's sidebar is much simpler. The Favorites category consists of the following:

- *All My Files:* A list of all the files you have created or updated on the Mac.

- *AirDrop:* This is used to send files to other Mac OS X users on your same Wi-Fi network (and discussed in detail later in this chapter).

- *Desktop:* This is a listing of all files and folders currently on the desktop of your Mac user profile.

- *Home:* This is the folder marked "stevensande," one of the authors of this book, in Figure 2–1. Your Home contains folders for the desktop, movies, pictures, downloads, applications, documents, and music belonging to the currently logged in user of the Mac. There are also folders named sites and public in the Home directory. Sites is where you can save web site files to be hosted by your computer, while Public is a shared folder available to anyone else on your network.

- *Applications:* Clicking this icon displays all the applications installed for shared use on the Mac as well as those installed for the current user.

- *Documents:* By default, many Mac applications try to save document files such as spreadsheets, letters, presentations, and drawings into this folder, which is accessible by clicking the Documents icon.

- *Dropbox:* This is an example of a third-party application that installs its own icon in the favorites list for instant access from any Finder window, so if you're not a Dropbox user, you won't see this icon. Dropbox (www.dropbox.com) is a "cloud-based" storage solution that syncs files between all Macs and PCs that you might use.

The Shared Category

Next, there's a Shared category. All other Macs or PCs that are currently turned on, not in sleep mode, and connected to the network are listed in this area. Each Mac icon is a miniature of the model of Mac that is connected to the network. Here, the top icon (Raven i...) is for an iMac, while the lower one (Barbara Sa...) is my wife's MacBook Pro.

Clicking these icons provides a Finder view of the folders that are currently shared on the other computer. To see all the folders on the other computer, you need to sign in as a user with full rights for that machine; otherwise, you are connected as a guest user and can view and access only the other Mac's public folder.

The Devices Category

Finally, there's a Devices category. Devices lists all external disk drives, CDs, DVDs, USB flash drives, and SD cards. It's also where remote disks appear—for example, this book was written while Apple's MobileMe service was still around and provided an online "disk drive" called iDisk. You can see the iDisk icon in Figure 2–1. At the time of publication, Apple's iCloud service had just been announced, and it does not appear that a virtual online drive is part of the service. Instead, any iCloud-equipped app can save content "to the cloud" where it is available immediately on all other Macs and iOS devices belonging to a user.

Macs that shipped without internal optical drives (Superdrives) have another device listed—the Remote Disc. This feature was introduced with the MacBook Air, and with Remote Drive you can put a software installation disc into the Superdrive on another Mac and then install software onto your computer over the network. Remote Disc is an extremely slow way to install software; it's usually a much better idea to install apps using the Mac App Store or an external optical drive.

I'll make one final comment about the sidebar. You may have noticed a tiny black icon to the right of Raven i... under Shared and iDisk under the Devices category. That icon, called the Eject button, means that those devices are currently logged in using a secure password. Click the Eject button to "eject" those devices so that nobody without your password can access the information stored on them. The Eject button disappears, indicating that you currently have an unsecured connection to the devices and that you must enter your password before you can gain full access to your information.

Hiding Sidebar Categories

Remember that the Finder sidebar can vary in appearance and in the number of icons shown. There's a very useful feature built into the sidebar categories that is invisible most of the time—the ability to hide or show those icons.

This is indispensible in offices or schools where there are a lot of devices on the same network. If any of those devices are set up for file sharing—and they usually are—then you might see dozens of Macs and PCs listed under the Shared category. To make navigation of the sidebar less confusing, you can hide all of the icons in a category when you don't need to see them.

Hiding a sidebar category is easy—just hover your cursor over the word Favorite, Shared, or Devices, and the word Hide appears on the right side of the sidebar. Click Hide, and the icons in that category disappear, and the word changes to Show. To make the icons reappear in the sidebar category, click Show.

File and Folder Icon Views in the Finder

Now that the icons in the sidebar make more sense, I'll move on to the icons in the top of every Finder window (Figure 2–2). Some of these should be familiar to you from previous versions of Mac OS X, but I'll give you a quick refresher just in case you're new to the Mac.

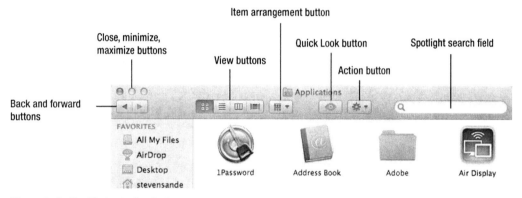

Figure 2–2. *The Finder toolbar buttons*

The "traffic light" of red, yellow, and green icons in the upper left of a Finder window is used to close, minimize, or maximize the window. Minimizing places the Finder window in a small icon in the lower-right side of the Dock, while maximizing increases the window the maximum possible size required to display all the icons. If I'm looking at the Documents category in the sidebar, for example, and I have only a few items in my Documents folder, then the window may shrink to the point that it displays all of the sidebar icons. If that same folder contains more icons than can be seen without scrolling the window, then the window's height could expand to the height of my screen.

The left- and right-pointing triangles at the top-left side of the Finder window act in a similar manner to the back and forward buttons on a web browser. If you have navigated through a series of nested folders to find a document and want to figure out how you got to that document, you can click the back (left-pointing) button to back through the series of folders. To return to the document, click the forward (right-pointing) button to retrace your steps through the folders.

You can also find your path to any folder shown in a Finder window by either Control-clicking or using a two-finger click gesture (with a Magic Trackpad or laptop trackpad) on the current folder name shown at the top center of the window.

The next icons in Figure 2–2 are the view buttons. As you can see, there are four of them—view by Icon, view by List, view by Column, or view in Cover Flow. Figure 2–3 shows the Applications folder displayed in each view.

Figure 2–3. *Finder windows arranged as view by Icon (upper left), view by List (upper right), view by Columns (lower left), and view in Cover Flow (lower right)*

The next button on the Finder window toolbar is the item arrangement button, which is a new feature of Mac OS X 10.7 Lion. Some Lion testers have mentioned that the item arrangement button does not appear by default after upgrading to the new operating system, in which case you may want to add it. To include the button or customize any other features of the Finder window toolbar, Control-click or two-finger click the toolbar. This displays a drop-down menu containing the item Customize Toolbar. Selecting this menu item lets you drag and drop other buttons onto the Finder window toolbar that aren't visible by default.

In any of the views shown earlier, you can further organize the files and folders in a window by choosing one of the ways to group items. In Figure 2–4, the applications in my Applications folder are being viewed in Cover Flow but are also arranged by application category—Graphics & Design, Photography, Reference, and so on.

Figure 2–4. *Using the item arrangement button to display the Applications folder by application category*

The item arrangement button also arranges your items by name, kind, date last opened, date added, file size, and by label. The latter are color labels that can be applied by Control-clicking or two-finger clicking a file and selecting a color from the labels shown.

When you're viewing a favorite by icons and using the item arrangement button to further classify your files, the icons are listed in one "line" of the display. Flicking them to the left or right provides a way to view all the icons in the list.

The next button that looks like an eye should be familiar to Snow Leopard users— clicking it displays either a document in QuickLook or, if applied to a folder of pictures, an instant slideshow.

Next is the action button. Click any file icon, and the action button displays a pop-up menu of available actions that can be performed. Actions can be added to the action button menu during the installation of applications, so don't be surprised if you see menu items that are specific to a certain application on your Mac. One of the new features in Lion is an action that takes the selected file and attaches it to a new, blank e-mail.

At the far-right side of the Finder window toolbar is the Spotlight search field. Spotlight is the powerful search engine built into Mac OS X and was detailed in Chapter 1.

Does there seem to be something missing from the Finder windows in Lion? Sure enough, there are two major changes. First, there are no visible scroll bars in Finder windows most of the time. The only time they'll appear is when you're in a list or column view and need to scroll up or down, and then you'll see them only when you use the flick gesture (two fingers up or down on a trackpad, Magic Trackpad, or Magic Mouse) to scroll vertically. Likewise, if there's a lot of information listed in a Finder view and you need to scroll left or right, the scroll bars appear only when you flick left or right. The only exception to this is that if you're using a mouse manufactured by a company other than Apple, the scroll bars are permanently visible in Finder windows.

That's a *huge* change from all the previous versions of the Mac operating system, in which scroll bars were available in every window and you scrolled by moving a scroller up, down, left, or right. Why this change to almost invisible scroll bars by default? It appears that Apple is trying to make the Mac operating system more like iOS, the operating system that drives every iPad, iPhone, and iPod touch.

AirDrop

Mac file sharing has never been all that easy or intuitive. In the past, sharing files with another co-worker or somebody in your home meant you either had to use the public "drop box" feature of File Sharing and then dig around and try to find the files or had to give the other person an account on your Mac and let them have full access to your folders. Now Apple's AirDrop makes sharing files with others as easy as dragging and dropping files on an icon.

To use AirDrop, both the sending and receiving Macs must be running Mac OS X 10.7 Lion. Although most Macs able to run Lion contain Wi-Fi cards that are AirDrop-compatible, some third-party and older Apple Wi-Fi cards do not work with this feature. To transfer a file to someone else within range of your Wi-Fi network, click the AirDrop icon under the Favorites category in the Finder sidebar. A window similar to Figure 2–5 appears, with icons containing that computer's login picture displayed for every Mac that currently has an AirDrop window open in Finder. For more information on how to determine if your Mac can run AirDrop, check this Apple knowledge base article: http://support.apple.com/kb/HT4783.

Figure 2–5. *The AirDrop window, showing both the sending Mac (below) and the receiving Mac running Lion (above) as picture icons*

In Figure 2–5, you see both the Mac that files are being sent from (called Steven Sande's MacBook Air) and another machine named Steven's iMac. To send files to Steven's iMac, I select them, drag them to the Steven's iMac icon, and drop them on the icon.

Just in case I accidentally dragged and dropped some files onto the iMac's icon, AirDrop verifies that I really do want to send the file or files (Figure 2–6).

Figure 2–6. *AirDrop verifies that you do intend to send a file to another Mac user on your Wi-Fi network.*

To send the files, click the highlighted Send button, and a small speech balloon appears over the top of the receiving Mac's icon (Figure 2–7).

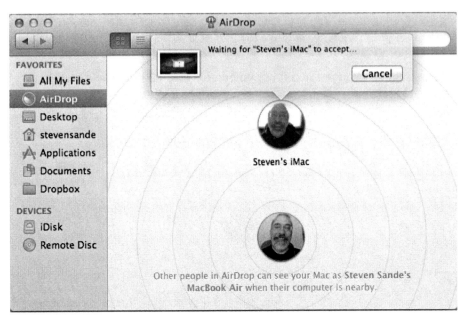

Figure 2–7. *The recipient has received a message saying that a file is being sent to them, and the sender is waiting for a reply.*

On the receiving end, a different message appears (Figure 2–8).

Figure 2–8. *What the AirDrop recipient sees and must respond to*

The recipient faces three choices: Save the file, in which case it is sent to their Downloads folder; Save and Open, in which case the file is also opened in a compatible application; or Decline, which means the recipient doesn't want the other person to send them a file.

If I decline the file, the sending party gets a note informing them of my decision (Figure 2–9).

Figure 2–9. *What the sender sees when a recipient has declined a file transfer*

Remember, both the sender and the recipient need to have the AirDrop window open in order for this to work, so the best way to start the process may be to use a FaceTime session or iChat message to let the recipient know you're sending a file and to tell them to open AirDrop.

What makes AirDrop so useful is that there is no setup involved other than informing the recipient that you're sending a file. If your Mac is running Lion and has a compatible Wi-Fi card, AirDrop can transfer files to any other Lion-equipped Mac. There's no need to enable file sharing, set up accounts, or remember passwords, and almost anyone can figure out how to send files with AirDrop with just a few words of instruction. Once you're done transferring files, close the Finder window so your Mac is no longer visible to others on the network.

FileVault 2 and File Encryption

You've probably heard about situations like this on the news—a laptop computer containing personal information like Social Security numbers or credit card data is stolen or lost, and thousands of innocent victims are suddenly in jeopardy of having their identities stolen.

Apple's FileVault file encryption has been available for the last several versions of the Mac operating system, providing a folder on a Mac that can be locked with a password.

Unless someone has that password, the contents of the folder are completely encrypted, that is, written in a virtually unbreakable code.

When you enable FileVault 2, the entire disk is encrypted, and other security features are turned on as well—a password is required to log in, after waking the Mac from sleep, and after leaving a screen saver. Only users who were enabled in FileVault 2 are able to log in, with other users requiring an administrator to log in first.

FileVault 2 is enabled on the Security & Privacy page of System Preferences (see Chapter 11 for more details about System Preferences in Lion). An administrator must click the lock icon at the bottom of the page and enter the password in order for FileVault to be turned on or off (Figure 2–10).

Figure 2–10. *To enable FileVault 2, an administrator must unlock the FileVault preference pane and then click the Turn On FileVault button.*

Click the Turn On FileVault button. FileVault creates and displays a 24-character recovery key (Figure 2–11). This is a "back door" in case you forget your password for FileVault. For this reason, it is important to write down or print the recovery key and keep it in a safe place.

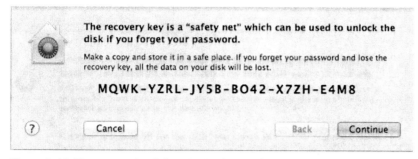

Figure 2–11. *The recovery key is important to have tucked away somewhere, whether you write it down on a piece of paper or have Apple store the key for you.*

Once you've written down the recovery key, click the Continue button. On the next page, Apple offers to store the recovery key for you (Figure 2–12). Apple encrypts the key using answers to three questions you provide. These questions are very detailed personal questions to which only you will most likely know the answers. Once you've entered the answers, your Mac needs to be restarted and begins encrypting the disk drive in the background.

Apple can store the recovery key for you.

If you need the key and cannot find your copy, you can contact Apple to retrieve it. To protect your privacy, Apple encrypts the key using the answers to three questions you provide*.

○ Store the recovery key with Apple
○ Do not store the recovery key with Apple

*Apple can only decrypt the recovery key using exact answers. If you cannot provide these answers, then Apple will be unable to access the key. Answer attempts may be restricted. Apple is not responsible for failing to provide the recovery key. Fees may apply, subject to support eligibility.

| Cancel | Back | Continue |

Figure 2–12. *Apple can store your FileVault recovery key for you, but you'll need to provide exact answers for three very personal questions.*

During the encryption process, you may find that your Mac runs a little sluggishly as it encodes every piece of data on the disk drive. Once initial encryption has taken place, there is no noticeable slowdown as new data is written to the drive. When you open a file, FileVault actually decrypts the encrypted data and makes it visible to you.

If you need to change the recovery key at any time, visit the Security & Privacy page in System Preferences, click the lock icon and enter an administrative password, and then click the Change button. Lion creates a new 24-character recovery code, and upon clicking the Continue button, it once again asks whether you want to store your recovery key with Apple. If so, you get to provide the answer to three personal questions again.

FileVault can be turned off later if you so desire. To do so, make sure you have no confidential or proprietary information left on your Mac, and then go back to the Security

& Privacy page of System Preferences. Click the lock icon at the bottom of the page and enter an administrative password, and then click the Turn Off FileVault button.

As with encryption, full-disk decryption can take some time to accomplish, but you can continue to work on your Mac while decryption is taking place.

Find My Mac

Apple sells a lot of laptops. In fact, sales of the MacBook, MacBook Air, and MacBook Pro lines account for well over half of total Mac sales. There's one big security issue with mobile Macs, however—the possibility of losing your MacBook or having it stolen is greater than that of a desktop device like an iMac.

With Lion, you'll now have a way to find a lost or stolen MacBook, lock it so that another person can't see your data, or even wipe all the data off of the computer. This service, known as Find My Mac, is akin to Apple's Find My iPhone and Find My iPad applications and in fact uses the same iOS apps to report the location of your Mac.

Find My Mac won't be available until the fall of 2011 when Apple's new iCloud service is rolled out, but here are instructions on how to set up and use this free feature when it arrives. To begin with, you'll need a free iCloud account. According to Apple, existing MobileMe accounts will be transformed into iCloud accounts, and there is also a mechanism available for creating a new iCloud account.

When iCloud becomes available, you set up features using the Mail, Contacts, & Calendars page in System Preferences. Clicking the iCloud button displays a list of the services that can be synced between your Mac and other devices through iCloud, including Mail & Notes, Contacts, Calendars, Bookmarks, PhotoStream, Back to My Mac, and Find My Mac (Figure 2–13).

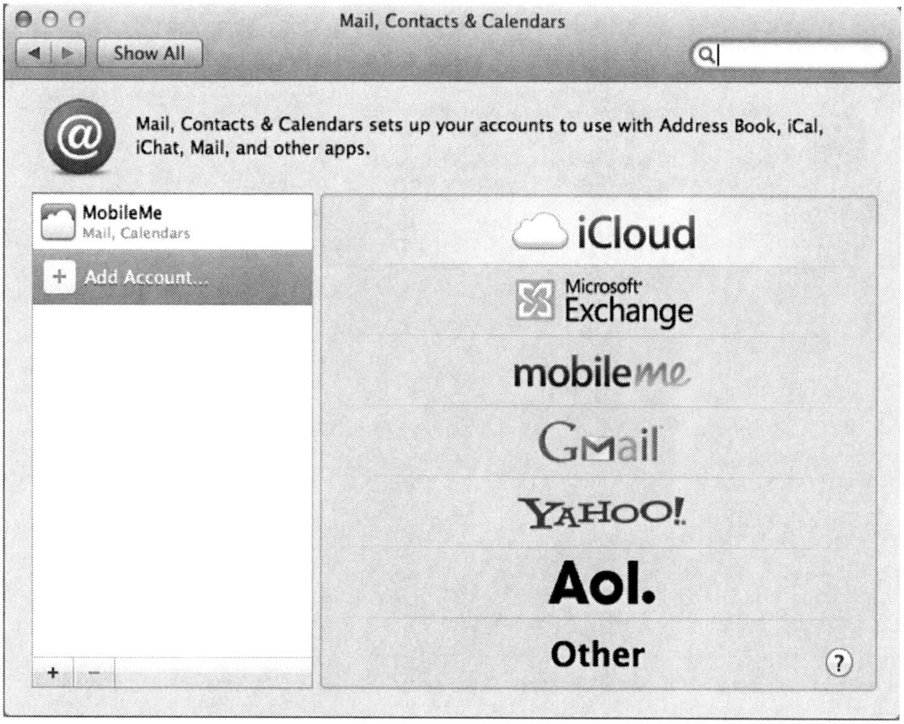

Figure 2–13. *Adding iCloud (available in the fall of 2011) to Lion enables synchronization of Contacts, Calendars, and other apps, including Find My Mac.*

To enable the Find My Mac feature, make sure that the box next to Find My Mac is checked as it is in Figure 2–14. That's all you need to do on the Mac end.

Should your Mac be stolen or lost, you'll need to use the Find My iPhone/Find My iPad/Find My Mac apps or iCloud web site (the latter two items were not available at publication time) to determine where your Mac is and secure it.

In this example, the Find My iPhone app on an iPhone 4 is launched and logged into using an iCloud Apple ID. Once logged in, the app shows the approximate location of a MacBook Air running Lion on a Google map (Figure 2–15). Tapping the name of the computer displays an Info screen, from which a number of actions can be initiated.

Figure 2–14. *Checking the Find My Mac box in the list of iCloud services enables this handy computer recovery system.*

Figure 2–15. *The Find My iPhone app on an iPhone 4 has located a "lost" MacBook Air and displays the location on a map (left). Tapping the computer name displays three actions (right) you can take to help recover your Mac or safeguard your data.*

The first thing you might want to try is playing a sound and sending a message to the person who currently has your computer up and connected to a network. Tap the Play Sound or Send Message button, and an edit field is displayed into which a message can be typed (Figure 2–16, left). If you prefer, the sound (a loud alert tone) can be turned off. Press the Send button, and seconds later the Mac sounds the alert and displays the message.

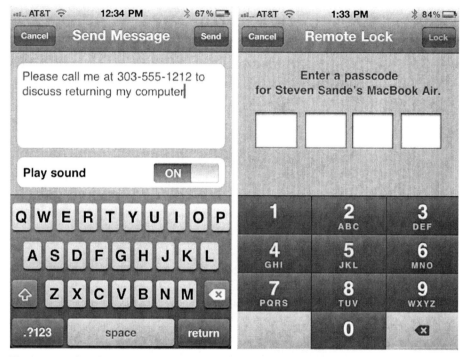

Figure 2–16. *Sending a message and playing a sound can alert passersby to a lost Mac (left), while Remote Lock (right) keeps your computer from being used except for web browsing in Safari.*

If repeated entreaties to the person who has your Mac fail to have any effect, you can take steps to keep them from using it. Remote Lock is another button available in the Find My iPhone/iPad/Mac applications. After clicking or tapping this button, enter a four-digit passcode to be the "combination" for unlocking your Mac. You'll be asked to enter the passcode again in the Find My... app, and then you have the opportunity to enter a message to be shown on the Mac after it has been locked.

Clicking or tapping the Lock button displays a warning that a locked Mac cannot be located or wiped. That's important to know, since that means you won't be able to track the Mac's location after it is locked. When you lock the lost or stolen Mac, it reboots immediately and then displays a screen telling the user to enter the system lock PIN code to unlock it.

The finder of your Mac can still use the device to help return it to you. The screen displays a Restart to Safari button when locked, which can be used to connect to a network only for web browsing. By doing this, Find My Mac is able to ascertain the physical location of your computer.

When your Mac is returned, getting it unlocked is simple—just enter the four-digit passcode that you used to lock it. Once you've done that, the Mac reboots again normally.

What about wiping your Mac remotely? This is a good thing to do if your Mac contains private or proprietary information and it's critical that the data remain secret. Tapping or clicking Remote Wipe erases the information on your Mac. That means you'll need to have a backup handy to restore the Mac if it is returned, but it ensures that your data remains unseen by others.

Remote Wipe even works if the Mac is currently offline. The next time it connects to a network, Lion begins to erase the information on the drive. You'll receive a confirmation e-mail at the address you listed for your Apple ID, telling you that the wipe has been initiated.

One word of warning to readers: if you do have information about where your lost or stolen Mac is, do not try to recover it directly by yourself. Instead, contact law enforcement officials and let them recover your property.

Screen Sharing

For IT support employees in small companies or parents in a family, being able to share the screen of another Mac on your network can be a godsend. Screen sharing is sometimes used just to see the screen on another Mac but is most often used to actually control a remote Mac as if you were sitting in front of it. Screen sharing has been available in Mac OS X for a few years, but Lion provides some enhancements to make it more useful.

To let someone share your screen, launch System Preferences and click the Sharing button. On the left side of the screen is a list of services that may be shared on your Mac, and checking the Screen Sharing box turns the service on.

You can choose to give all users access to your Mac's screen or create a list of approved users. In Lion, it's now possible to add a user's Apple ID to the list of authorized users. Those users log into your Mac for screen or file sharing with their Apple ID—you no longer need to create a user account for them. You must enter a user name and password to share your screen, and that user name can also be an Apple ID (Figure 2–17).

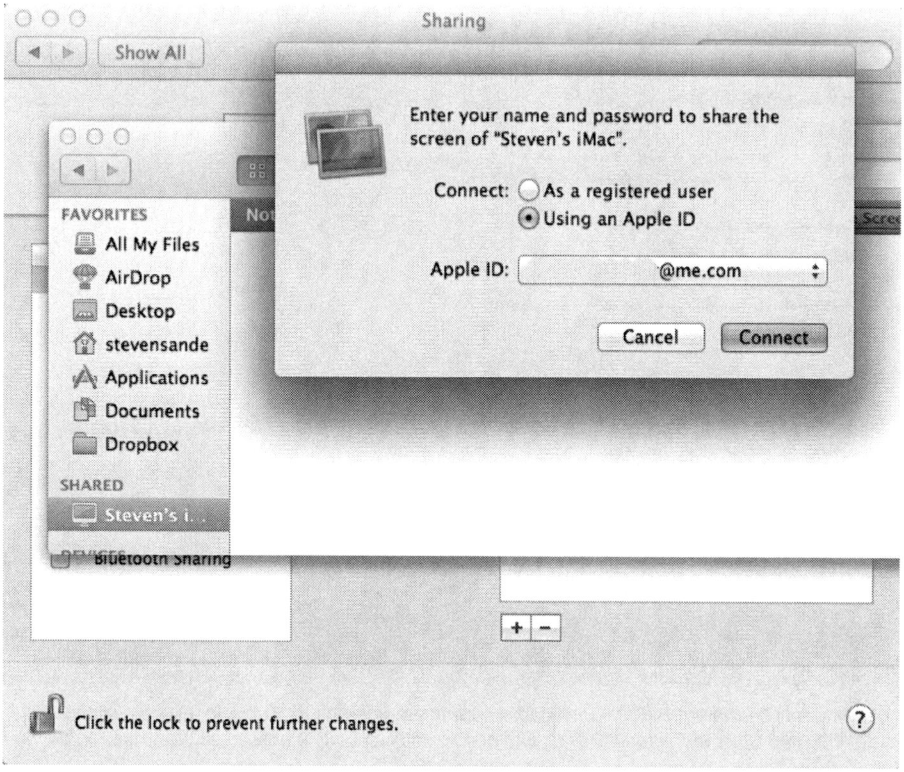

Figure 2–17. *Either a registered user name on a Mac or Mac server or an Apple ID is necessary to enable Lion's screen sharing.*

For the first time, screen sharing in OS X is now on a per-user basis. What does that mean? Well, imagine if you share your Mac with your kids and wife and one of the kids is currently logged into her account on your Mac. From another Mac, it's possible to log into a virtual screen sharing session (Figure 2–18) for viewing your desktop, your files, and your programs, all without your daughter knowing that you're working on the same Mac at the same time. Like many other built-in apps in Lion, screen sharing is now a full-screen app. When you're controlling another Mac, a click of the full-screen icon (double-ended arrow) in the upper-right corner of the screen-sharing toolbar in Figure 2–19 allows the app to take over the full screen. If you're controlling another computer with a similarly sized display, you'll feel like you're sitting at the keyboard of the other Mac. To disable full-screen mode or view the menu bar on your Mac, take your cursor to the top of the screen. The menu bar appears, and you have a choice to either quit screen sharing or disable full-screen mode.

Figure 2–18. *Connecting to a virtual display allows access to a user's desktop and files without interruption to another user who is actually seated at the Mac.*

Figure 2–19. *The new screen-sharing toolbar is used to switch to full-screen mode, toggle between scaled and real-size views, take screen shots of the remote Mac, and enable copy and paste actions between the remote and local Macs.*

There's a new Observe Only mode, which should be wonderful for parents who want to keep an eye on their children's computer usage. In Observe Only mode, you can watch what's going on with the remote computer without controlling the mouse or trackpad.

Finally, the new screen-sharing toolbar provides easy access to features with a click. To toggle between a scaled view of the other Mac screen and a real-size view, there's a resolution button (Figure 2–19, far left). To take a screenshot of the remote Mac, click the camera button. There are also buttons providing access to the clipboard of the other Mac for copying content on your Mac and pasting it to the other, or vice-versa.

Time Machine

Keeping your documents and apps backed up is the job of Time Machine, which has been part of Mac OS X since version 10.5 (Leopard). Time Machine is very easy to set up and run: attach an external disk drive to your Mac, acknowledge that you want to use it for Time Machine backups, and Mac OS X takes care of the rest, constantly backing up files behind the scenes so you don't have to think about it. Through the Time Machine settings in System Preferences (covered in more detail in Chapter 11), it's possible to exclude certain items—such as applications and system files—from Backup to conserve space on your backup drive.

Time Machine works great when your backup drive is attached to your Mac, but what about when you're using a MacBook on the road and you don't have the drive with you? In previous versions of Mac OS X, no backups were performed during that time. If you accidentally deleted a file, you were out of luck.

Time Machine now creates local snapshots of data. These are spare copies of files that you create, modify, or delete, and they're kept right on the Mac. If you delete a file while you're away from that Time Capsule or backup drive, no problem — there's a local copy on your Mac for you to restore using Time Machine.

When you return home and connect your Mac to the backup drive, those local snapshots are combined with the previous Time Machine backups so that all of your work, home and away, is viewable from Time Machine as one continuous series of backups.

If you're not familiar with the Time Machine user interface, Figure 2–20 demonstrates what I'm talking about.

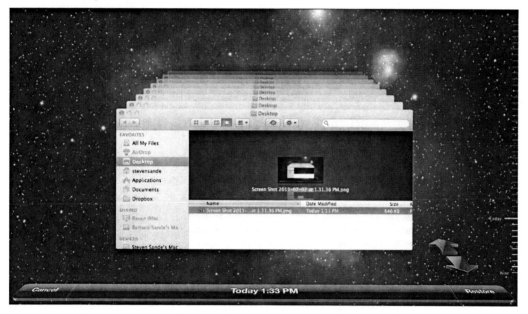

Figure 2–20. *Clicking the Time Machine icon in the Dock displays this animated image showing "snapshots" of the contents of your Mac backward in time.*

To scroll back or forward in time to see files created or deleted in the past, click the arrows on the lower-right side of the screen. Clicking the up arrow sends you back to a snapshot of your Mac earlier in time, while clicking the down arrow brings you closer to the current time and date.

Time Machine's power lies not only in how easy it is to back up files but in the simplicity of restoring them if accidentally deleted. Select a deleted file or folder by clicking its icon "in the past" and then click the Restore button — that's all it takes. The file reappears in the folder it was deleted from, ready for you to continue working on it.

Earlier in this chapter, I talked about FileVault 2. Time Machine now provides a way to keep your backups secure. By encrypting an external drive with FileVault 2, your Time Machine backups are protected by encryption as well.

Summary

Whether you're managing your cache of files on your Mac, sharing your screen or your files with others, or making sure your data is secure, Mac OS X 10.7 Lion makes your user experience easier and more enjoyable. Here are some key points to remember from this chapter:

- New Finder views and the item arrangement button, combined with MultiTouch gestures discussed elsewhere in this book, make organizing and browsing files much more like working on an iPhone or iPad.

- AirDrop is a new Lion feature that makes sharing files with other Macs on the same wireless network as easy as dragging and dropping file icons onto a graphical representation of another Mac.

- Protect your files from snooping by encrypting your disk with FileVault 2.

- Find My Mac lets you locate a lost or stolen Mac and then alert others through audible and visible notification. With the Find My Mac, Find My iPhone, and Find My iPad apps, the Mac can be locked with a special passcode or even erased, all from a safe remote location.

- Lion's screen-sharing options now include the ability to log into a virtual screen session while another user is working on the Mac.

- Time Machine now makes local snapshots of documents you create, delete, or change while you're away from a backup drive.

Chapter 3

The Mac App Store

When Apple introduced the original App Store for the iPhone, it revolutionized the way people looked for and obtained software. Virtually overnight the iPhone App Store was a stratospheric hit. Now Apple has brought the App Store to the Mac (called the Mac App Store). This chapter covers everything you need to know about the Mac App Store, from getting an account to searching for apps to reinstalling apps on other computers you own. Let's get started.

What Is the Mac App Store?

The Mac App Store is the easiest way to find and download software for your Mac. It's also the future of app delivery. If you've walked around an Apple Store lately, you'll have noticed that Apple has virtually eliminated all software from its shelves. That's because Apple believe that people can find and obtain software much more easily by doing everything from their computer. Of course, an added benefit is environmental; people buying their apps through the Mac App Store means app developers won't have to make, print, and ship retail boxes containing little more than a CD or just an activation code.

Launching the Mac App Store

You can see the icon for the Mac App Store in Figure 3–1. It's a blue and white circle with the letter *A* for "apps" made out of a ruler, a pencil, and a brush. By default the Mac App Store can be found in Lion's Dock at the bottom of the screen. You can also find it in your Applications folder as well as in the Launchpad (see Chapter 5). To launch the Mac App Store, double-click its icon.

Figure 3–1. *The Mac App Store icon*

After you click the icon, the Mac App Store will appear (Figure 3–2). Let's take a quick look at the layout of the store. I'll go into detail about all its sections later in the chapter.

Figure 3–2. *The Mac App Store*

- *Navigation bar*: At the very top of the Mac App Store window is the Navigation bar. This bar lets you switch between parts of the store including Featured, Top Charts, Categories, Purchased, and Updates.

- *Navigation buttons*: These arrows work like the forward and backward buttons in a web browser. They let you navigate through the pages in the store you've visited.

- *Search field*: Start typing in a search term, and you'll see a drop-down menu filled with suggested results. Press Return on your keyboard to be taken to the search results page. The search field can be accessed no matter what section of the Mac App Store you are in.

- *Banners*: Banners are basically just billboards advertising specific apps of groups of apps. Developers can't buy billboard space. Apple just highlights apps here that it thinks users will be interested in.

- *Quick Links*: In this box on the right, you'll find access to your Mac App Store account, code redemption, and support. You'll also find a drop-down categories menu, which allows you to go to a specific category of apps.

Setting Up and Signing into a Mac App Store Account

Before you can buy or download an app from the Mac App Store, you first need to set up an account. If you're thinking, "Gosh! I have to create another account?" relax. If you already have an iTunes account, current MobileMe account, or new iCloud account, you can simply log in with your Apple ID. To do so, click the Sign In button in the Quick Links box. A dialog box will appear (Figure 3–3) asking you for your Apple ID and password. Enter it and then click Sign In.

Sign in to download from the App Store.

If you have an Apple ID, sign in with it here. If you have used the iTunes Store or MobileMe, for example, you have an Apple ID. If you don't have an Apple ID, click Create Apple ID.

Apple ID   Password   Forgot?

[Create Apple ID]   [Cancel]   [Sign In]

Figure 3–3. *The sign-in dialog box*

If you don't have an Apple ID already, click the Create Apple ID button in Figure 3–3, and you'll be guided through the steps to create one. These steps are short and quick and include agreeing to Apple's terms and conditions, entering your e-mail address and the password you want to use for your Apple ID, and then entering your credit card details, including billing address. Once that is all done, you'll have your Apple ID and password all set up and ready to use!

Managing Your Account

Apple lets you easily manage your Mac App Store account. To do so, click Account in the Quick Links box. You'll be asked to reenter your Apple ID password in the dialog box shown in Figure 3–3. Once you do that, you'll be taken to an account management screen where you can edit your Apple ID e-mail address and password or change your billing details.

Now that all the tedious stuff is out of the way, let's start exploring the store!

Exploring the Mac App Store

As I've mentioned, at the top of the Mac App Store you'll see a navigation bar with five icons (Figure 3–4). Clicking each icon brings you to a different section of the store. Let's take a look at all of these sections individually.

Figure 3–4. *The Mac App Store navigation bar*

Featured

The Featured section is the section you'll automatically be taken to when you launch the Mac App Store. This is essentially the home page for the store. You can see what it looks like in Figure 3–2. The Featured section of the Mac App Store is populated with apps grouped into subsections. Usually you'll see three subsections: New and Noteworthy, What's Hot, and Staff Favorites. Also, along the right side of the store, below the Quick Links box, you'll see the Top 10 charts: Top Paid, Top Free, and Top Grossing.

In the subsections and Top 10 lists, apps are displayed by their icons. You can click any banner or spotlighted app to be taken to that app's information page. You can also buy or download an app right from the front page without reading more about it. I'll talk more about buying apps later in this chapter.

Top Charts

The second button in the navigation bar takes you to the Top Charts section of the Mac App Store, as shown in Figure 3–5.

Figure 3–5. *The Top Charts section in the Mac App Store*

Here you'll find a list of the top downloaded apps in the Mac App Store. The Top Charts section takes into account apps from all categories and, as you can image, will change frequently. The Top Charts section is important because it is probably the single best way to figure out what's worth buying. It's the wisdom of the masses. If an app isn't really good, it probably won't show up in the Top Charts lists.

The Top Charts screen is composed of three sections labeled Top Paid, Top Free, and Top Grossing.

- *Top Paid:* Lists the top 12 paid apps people have purchased in the Mac App Store.

- *Top Free:* Lists the top 12 free apps people have downloaded in the Mac App Store.

- *Top Grossing:* Lists the top 12 biggest moneymakers in the Mac App Store. Top Grossing ensures that costlier apps get eye-time with customers and aren't pushed out of the way by all the 99-cent games.

In any of the Top Charts sections, you can click the See All link to see a complete list of apps organized by their popularity. Also, on the right side of the Top Charts screen you'll see a list of Top Charts Categories. Clicking any of these categories allows you to see a list of top apps that match only those categories (finance apps, for example).

Categories

The third button in the navigation bar takes you to the Categories section of the Mac App Store, as shown in Figure 3–6.

Figure 3–6. *Categories on the Mac App Store*

This section of the Mac App Store divides apps into 21 categories. Categories is a great feature when you know you want a certain type of app but are not sure exactly what app that is. Tap any category to be taken to that category's screen.

On the individual category screens, you'll see some of the most popular apps in that category, as well as charts listing the Top Free, Top Paid, and Top Grossing apps for that category. The goal of the Categories section of the Mac App Store is all about making apps easier for you to find.

Purchased

The fourth button in the navigation bar takes you to the Purchased section of the Mac App Store, as shown in Figure 3–7.

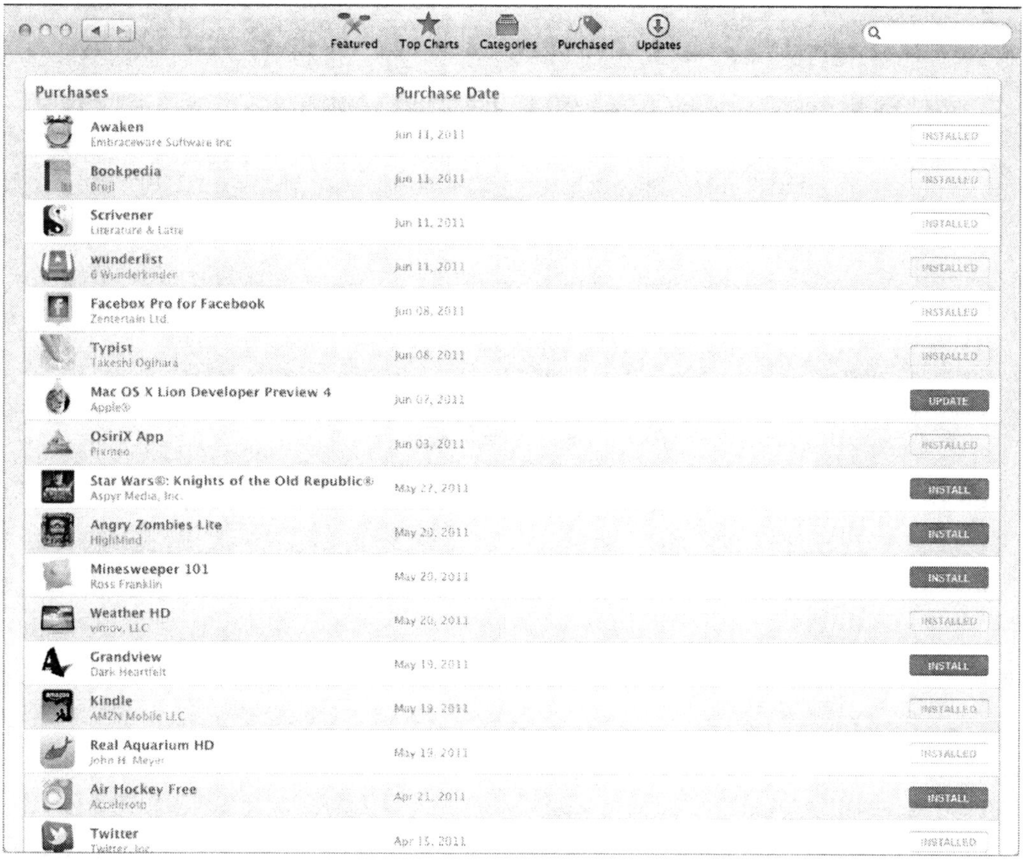

Figure 3–7. *List of your purchases in the Mac App Store*

This is actually my favorite screen. I love it so much because it shows me every single Mac app I've ever bought through the Mac App Store. It's also a permanent backup of every app I've ever purchased. Let me explain that a little more.

It used to be that when you bought a software application in a store, it often came on a CD or DVD and had an associated serial number with it. If you ever deleted the app from your computer and wanted to reinstall it, you would need to find the original CD it came on and also track down the serial number for the software (which was often not written on the CD). Needless to say, it was easy to lose one or both of those.

Since the Mac App Store is linked to your Apple ID, it tracks every piece of software you buy through it. If you get a new Mac, you don't have to hunt for CDs and serial numbers to install your apps; just log into the Mac App Store on the new Mac and go to the

Purchased section of the Mac App Store. There you'll see the list shown in Figure 3–7, and you can simply click the Install button for every app you've bought and want to install on your new Mac. No CDs to track down, serial numbers to find, or apps to back up. Beautiful, huh?

The Purchased section of the Mac App Store will list all your purchased apps (free apps are considered "purchases") and the date you originally purchased them. Next to each app you'll see a button. It will read Installed, Update, or Install (Figure 3–8).

Figure 3–8. *Possible buttons on the Purchased screen*

- *Update*: When you see this button, it means there is a software update for the app. Click it to download the latest version. Apple also has a dedicated Update section, which I'll discuss next.

- *Installed*: This button cannot be clicked. It means that the app is currently installed on the Mac you are using.

- *Install*: Clicking this button will install the previously purchased app on the Mac you are using.

Updates

The fifth button in the navigation bar takes you to the Updates section of the Mac App Store, as shown in Figure 3–9.

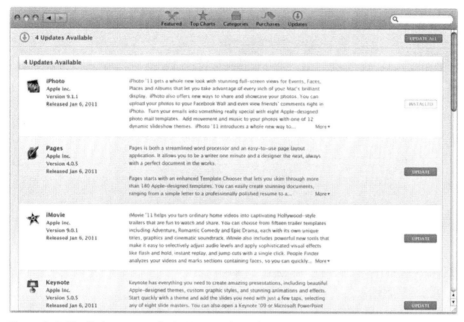

Figure 3–9. *The Updates screen in the Mac App Store (image courtesy of Apple)*

While the Purchased screen will show whether you have any updates to your apps, the Updates screen will automatically notify you when you do. Whenever there is an update for one of your apps, the Mac App Store icon (Figure 3–1) will show a read notification badge with a white number in it. That number will tell you how many of your apps have updates waiting.

When you see that badge, launch the Mac App Store and click the Updates button. There you'll see a list of all apps with waiting updates and also a description of what the update delivers to the app. You can download the updates to your apps one at a time by clicking the Update button next to the app, or you can download all the updates at once by clicking the Update All button at the top of the screen.

Anatomy of an App Listing

Now that you know how to navigate and find apps in the Mac App Store, let's look at an individual app's listing. Each app has its own page where you can find a wealth of information about it, including pictures and user reviews.

To get to an app's listing page, simply click the app's name or icon on any Mac App Store screen to be taken to its information page (see Figure 3–10). You'll see only parts of the listing page at a time since you have to scroll through it, but Figure 3–10 shows you what the entire listing page for an app looks like for clarity's sake.

Figure 3–10. *An app's information listing*

The listing page is basically divided into three parts: the top, the preview images, and the bottom. At the top of the page you'll find the app icon and name, as well as a description about the app and notes on any updates.

In the center of the listing page you'll see a series of pictures. These pictures are screen shots of the app; they show you what the app looks like. Below the current screen shot you'll see a series of thumbnails. Each thumbnail represents a picture. Click them to view the full screen shot.

Next to the screen shots you'll also see an Information box. This box is very important because it tells you the version number, size, and language of the app, but it also tells you the app's system requirements. You always want to make sure to check this information box before you buy an app to make sure your Mac has enough processing power, memory, and the required OS to run the app.

The bottom of the listing page is where you'll find customer ratings and reviews. Keep in mind ratings and reviews aren't always reliable. A developer can easily have a bunch of his friends rate his app five stars. It doesn't happen all the time, but it does happen. As we mentioned previously, the best way to tell whether an app is really good is if it appears in a Top Charts list.

Buying and Downloading Apps

There are two kinds of apps in the Mac App Store: paid and free. Depending on which the app is, you'll see either a blue Free button or a blue button with a price in it at the top of an app's info page. To download the app, click the blue button. If it's a free app, the blue button will turn into a green Install App button. If it's a paid app, the blue button will turn into a green Buy App button (see Figure 3–11).

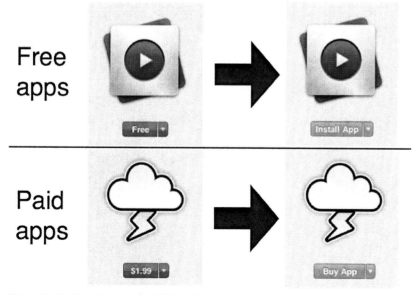

Figure 3–11. *Free becomes Install App; $1.99 becomes Buy App.*

Click the Install App or Buy App, and a confirmation dialog box will appear asking you to enter your iTunes account password. Enter it and click Sign In. Once you have done so, the app's icon will jump from the app's listing page into your Launchpad. The app's icon will be blurred out on the Launchpad, and a progress bar will appear while it downloads to your computer (Figure 3–12). Once it is done downloading, you'll be able to click the app to launch it.

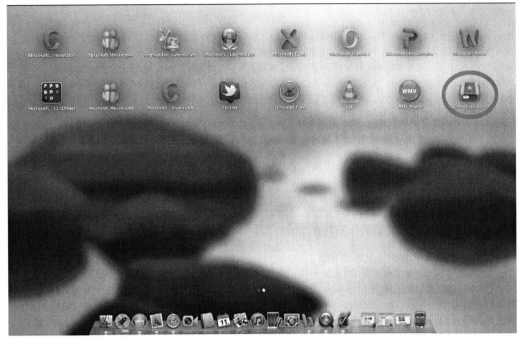

Figure 3–12. *After you buy an app, you are returned to your Launchpad where the app proceeds to download. The download (circled) is signified by the progress bar.*

NOTE: Notice the little arrow by the purchase buttons in Figure 3–11? Click it to be presented with a drop-down menu that allows you to copy the link, which will copy the link to your clipboard so you can paste a Mac App Store link to your Twitter or Facebook feeds; or click Tell a Friend to be presented with an e-mail field that allows you to send someone an e-mail telling them about the selected app.

Redeeming a Code

You can redeem gift certificates and codes in the Mac App Store. On the Featured screen in the Quick Links box, you'll see a Redeem link (Figure 3–2). Click the Redeem link, enter your gift card number or other Mac App Store into the text box, and click Redeem. If you entered a code from a gift card, your Mac App Store account will update, and you will be able to spend those funds directly in the Mac App Store. If your entered an app code from a developer, the specific app the code was good for will begin downloading. Remember to type carefully, or else you might get a "code not valid" error. If you see an error, go back and carefully type in the code again.

Using the Mac App Store to Open a File You Don't Have an App For

Sometimes we'll have a file on our computer but won't have the right app to open it. It used to be that we would have to go searching the Web to find out what app could open our mystery file, but now with the Mac App Store, you are always only a few clicks away from finding the appropriate app.

When you have a file but not an app to open it with, follow these steps:

1. Select the file.

2. Right-click the file, choose "Open with" from the contextual menu, and then choose App Store... from the submenu (Figure 3–13).

3. The Mac App Store will open and show you all the apps that are available to open the file you selected. Pretty cool, huh?

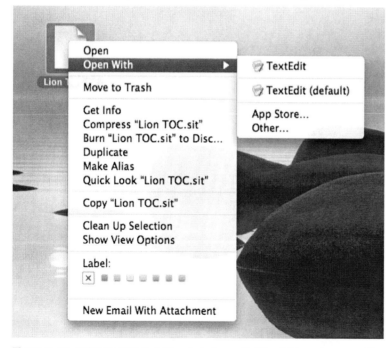

Figure 3–13. *Using the Mac App Store to help you find the right app to open a file*

Summary

The Mac App Store is one of the coolest things about Mac OS X Lion. It's your gateway to hundreds or thousands of apps that constantly turn your Mac into an amazing machine possible of new things. Here are some tips to take away with you:

- Many apps on the App Store are free or very cheap, but don't overlook the more expensive ones! Many times they are worth the money.

- Use the Mac App Store to check for updates to your apps. All updates will always be free.

- Any app purchased on the Mac App Store app can be redownloaded for free on any other Macs you own.

- Mac App Store categories like Top 10 frequently change. Check back often for new apps!

- All newly downloaded apps are automatically added to your Applications folder and your Launchpad!

Chapter 4

Managing Your Data: Auto Save, Resume, and Versions

Computers were supposed to make our lives easier. In many ways, that's been the case; people work more quickly and efficiently than ever before. Others, however, have lost hours of hard work (if not days worth) to freezes, crashes, or other hardware or software failures. "You should have saved" has become a familiar yet unwelcome chorus for many.

At the same time, office workers and other professionals juggle several revisions of a single document while hunting through a series of folders and files for the correct version to share.

In this chapter, you'll learn how Apple intends to eliminate these hassles with three features new to Mac OS X Lion: Resume, Auto Save, and Versions. I'll explain what (if anything) you must do to set them up, what you can expect from each, and finally all of the options available. Let's start with Resume.

Resume

Resume is a terrific time-saver and works on both an application level and systemwide. There's nothing to set up or configure. All you have to do, in fact, is wave those hard drive hunting expeditions goodbye. Here's how to use Resume.

Resume with Applications

First, let's look at using Resume with individual applications. In short, it offers a "pick-up-where-you-left-off" method of handling software and documents. When you quit a piece of software, such as Microsoft Word or Apple's Pages, Resume "notices" everything about it right then, including the documents you're working on, where the cursor is, how the windows are arranged, what text is selected, and so on. The next time you open that piece of software, everything is put back exactly as you left it.

For example, when I'm browsing the Internet with Apple's Safari web browser, Resume notices the pages and tabs I have open as I quit the application. The next time I launch Safari, it will reload those pages and tabs for me. Likewise, a word processing document created with Microsoft Word or Apple's Pages will be presented to me exactly as I left it the last time I quit Word or Pages, including its location on my screen, cursor placement, and so on (provided that I didn't first close the document before quitting Word or Pages).

Finally, an application that uses palettes that I've arranged just so will replace everything as I had it the next time it's opened. In this way, Resume is a real time-saver. I no longer have to hunt for that Word or Pages document, rearrange my palettes, or reload a series of tabs or pages in Safari.

> **TIP:** Concerned about Safari revealing your browsing history at launch? Press Option-Command-Q when quitting, and it'll load your default home page the next time it's launched, regardless of the pages that are open as you quit.

Systemwide Resume

Resume also performs its magic when you shut down your Mac. The difference is that it notices everything that's happening, not just with a single application. Here's what to expect from Resume when restarting your Mac running Lion.

- *All previously open applications will reopen*: As you turn off your Mac, Lion notices which pieces of software you're using. For example, if you're composing an e-mail message with Apple's Mail and referencing the Web with Safari, Lion will reopen both applications at restart, just as they were at shutdown.

- *Application location will be restored*: If you're like me, you arrange application windows "just so" while you work. Resume notices that arrangement at shutdown and puts everything back where it was once your Mac is running again. In the previous example, Resume remembers that Mail was in front of Safari. Likewise, Finder windows, preference panes, and so on, that were open at shutdown will reappear in their previous locations.

- *Each application's state will be restored*: Not only does Resume remember which applications were running and how they were arranged on your screen, it remembers what you were doing with them. For example, in our e-mail scenario, Resume will put the cursor back where it was within that e-mail message.

▧ *Making software updates easier*: Installing software updates requires that software to be closed. Now, you can simply quit the application, install the update, and then reopen it, picking up where you left off.

> **NOTE:** Applications that you've elected to open via the Login Items system preference will launch when your Mac is restarted, even if they aren't running at the time of shutdown.

The best part is that there's nothing to set up, maintain, or configure. Resume is a functioning aspect of Mac OS X Lion from the moment you turn on your Mac.

Of course, you can opt out of a systemwide Resume at any time. To get a "fresh start" and find only a clear desktop the next time your Mac boots up, follow these steps:

1. First, select Restart... (or Shutdown...) from the Apple menu.

2. A new window appears (see Figure 4–1). Deselect "Reopen windows when logging back in."

3. Click Restart.

Figure 4–1. *The Fresh Start dialog box. Deselect the check box, and your Mac will boot to a clean desktop.*

Your Mac will reboot with a clear desktop, no matter what was running when you gave the command to restart.

Note that this "fresh start" mode is temporary. In other words, you must manually deselect the "Reopen windows when logging back in" button each time you want your Mac to present a clear desktop at startup. Otherwise, Resume will function normally.

That's great, but Resume's real power is in how it cooperates with Auto Save.

Auto Save

With a handy new feature called Auto Save, Apple wants to eliminate our decades-old habit of clicking the Save button. It's a huge feature, because Auto Save could prevent that heart-stopping moment when you realize that your hard work has been lost. It works quietly in the background, and as with Resume, there's nothing you must do to set it up or turn it on. Here's what to expect from Auto Save.

As you're working, Auto Save will save changes made to your document on the following schedule:

- Once every five minutes

- When you've stopped working for a period of time (stopped typing, for example)

- When you manually perform a save by clicking the Save button, selecting Save from the application's File menu or pressing Command-S (⌘-S) on your keyboard.

Each time, Auto Save adds changes to the document itself, so you needn't worry about cluttering your Mac with a new copy every five minutes. Here's how Auto Save and Resume work together.

> **NOTE:** You must be using a Lion-compatible application that supports Auto Save for it to work. As of this writing, Apple's iWork suite of productivity apps, including Pages (word processing), Numbers (spreadsheet), and Keynote (slide presentations) are compatible, as well as TextEdit, the simple text editor that comes with every Mac. Expect developers outside of Apple to add Auto Save functionality to their software soon.

In a way, there's no "unsaved" state with Auto Save in Lion. In fact, it's possible to maintain a document without ever selecting Save (provided that the parent software is compatible with Auto Save). Here's what I mean.

Imagine that I've created a document in TextEdit, the simple text editor that's included on every Mac. After typing several paragraphs, I quit the application without first closing the document.

The next time I launch TextEdit, my document will be intact. From there I can add more paragraphs, quit, and relaunch, only to find my document as I left it.

When I do try to close the document, either by pressing Command-W or by clicking the red close button in the document's upper-left corner, a dialog box appears asking me to save the document to a permanent location and give it a name. (See Figure 4–2.)

Note that Resume allows each application to maintain several documents without permanent save destinations in this manner. For example, I created several documents in Apple's TextEdit and Preview applications that remained intact each time I relaunched their respective parent applications, as long as I did not attempt to close those documents. Although this is handy, it is not how I recommend maintaining your work. Instead, designate a permanent save location by selecting Save from an application's File menu or hitting Command-S on your keyboard.

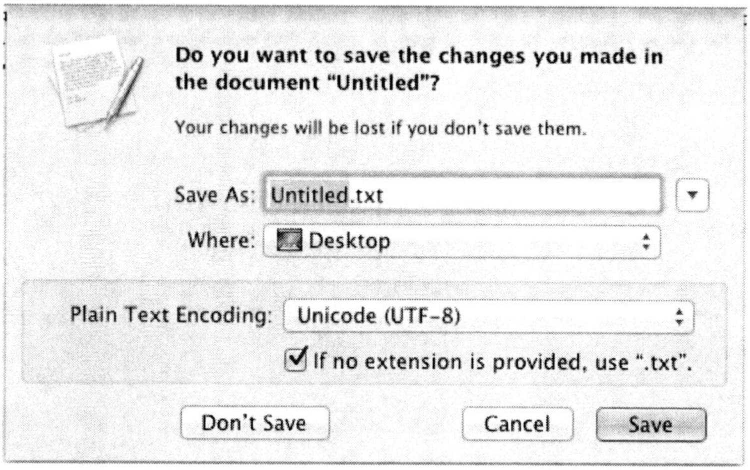

Figure 4–2. *Dialog box requesting a permanent save location for a TextEdit document*

Of course, Auto Save isn't limited to text editors. The Safari web browser remembers the pages and tabs you had open the last time it was closed and reloads them when launched. Applications with palettes that you've arranged in a particular way will reopen with their placement intact. Just remember that an application must be compatible with Lion's Auto Save feature. How can you identify a compatible application? Here's one method.

At the top of most applications' main window, you'll find three buttons in the upper-left corner: one red, one yellow, and one green (called the close button, minimize button, and zoom button, respectively). Their purpose is to close a document, minimize it into the Dock, or resize it, respectively.

Prior to Mac OS X Lion, the red button acquired a black dot when the document in its window had unsaved changes. Once you've saved your changes, the black dot disappeared. This is also true of files created with applications under Lion that do not support Auto Save.

Conversely, the red button never acquires the black dot in applications that support Auto Save, regardless of how much has been changed since the last manual save. You'll see an illustration of the difference in Figure 4–3, using TextEdit (left) and Microsoft Word 2011 (right), which did not support Auto Save at the time of this writing.

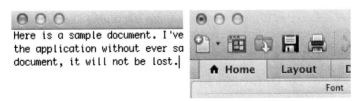

Figure 4–3. *TextEdit (left), which supports Auto Save, does not have a black dot in the red close button, despite the document's unsaved changes. Conversely, Microsoft Word 2011 on the right (which did not support Auto Save as of this book's writing) does indicate unsaved changes with the black dot.*

Auto Save and the Menu Bar

Although the red button indicator is gone, an Auto Save–savvy application's menu bar still offers clues as to a document's state. Here's what to look out for.

- *No permanent save location*: A document that hasn't been manually saved by you (for example, you haven't selected Save from the File menu, pressed Command-S, clicked a Save button, and so on) will simply display that application's default title for new documents and will not display a document icon. For example, Figure 4–4 shows an unsaved TextEdit document simply called "Untitled," because that's the default name for new documents made with TextEdit.

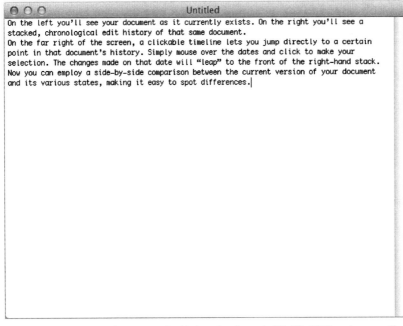

Figure 4–4. *This TextEdit document's title bar simply reads "Untitled." There's no application icon or other text. It has not been assigned a permanent save location.*

■   *Previously saved with no new edits*: A document that's been saved to
your Mac's hard drive and has no unsaved changes will bear the title
you gave it and a document icon, as illustrated in Figure 4–5.

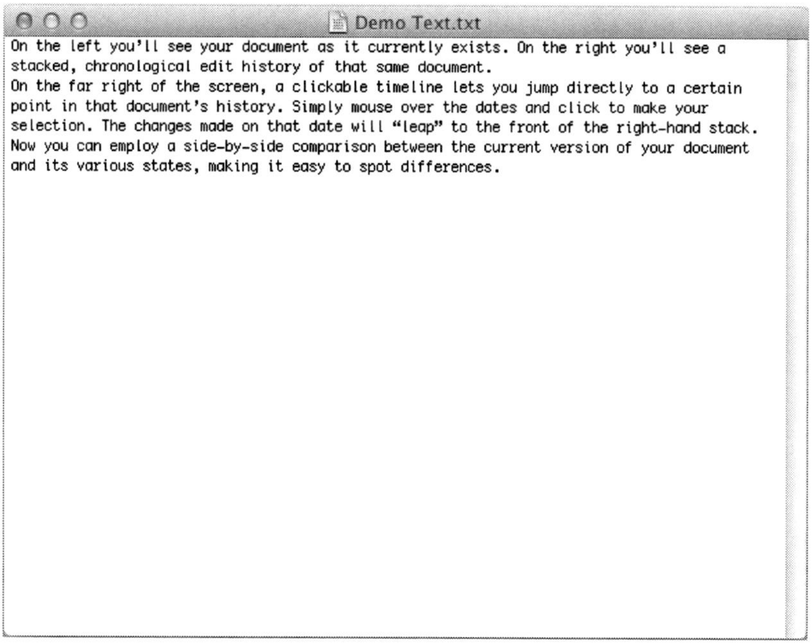

On the left you'll see your document as it currently exists. On the right you'll see a
stacked, chronological edit history of that same document.
On the far right of the screen, a clickable timeline lets you jump directly to a certain
point in that document's history. Simply mouse over the dates and click to make your
selection. The changes made on that date will "leap" to the front of the right-hand stack.
Now you can employ a side-by-side comparison between the current version of your document
and its various states, making it easy to spot differences.

Figure 4–5. *The menu bar of this TextEdit document bears the custom title, "Demo Text," as well as a document icon on the left of the title.*

■   *Previously saved with new edits*: A document that's been saved to
your Mac's hard drive and has unsaved changes bears its title plus
"Edited," as illustrated in Figure 4–6.

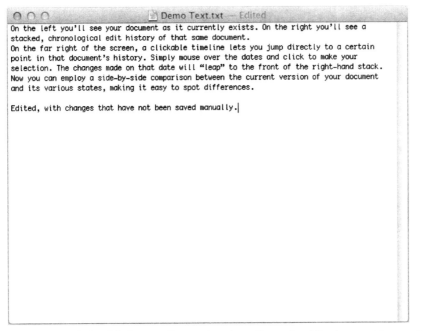

On the left you'll see your document as it currently exists. On the right you'll see a stacked, chronological edit history of that same document.
On the far right of the screen, a clickable timeline lets you jump directly to a certain point in that document's history. Simply mouse over the dates and click to make your selection. The changes made on that date will "leap" to the front of the right-hand stack. Now you can employ a side-by-side comparison between the current version of your document and its various states, making it easy to spot differences.

Edited, with changes that have not been saved manually.

Figure 4–6. *This TextEdit document's menu bar shows the custom title, document icon, and "Edited," indicating that it has been saved to a permanent location and has unsaved changes.*

- *Locked*: Finally, a document that's been locked features a padlock icon in the menu bar, as illustrated in Figure 4–7. Locking a document will be explained later in this chapter.

At this point, you may be wondering, where do the autosaved versions of my documents go? How do find them, and how can I use them effectively? The good news is that Apple has made this both automatic and simple. Here's what you need to know.

Working with Autosaved Versions

Documents created with Auto Save–ready applications display a new drop-down menu in the center of the menu bar, offering immediate access to your document's edit history (see Figure 4–7). Clicking it reveals four options, including Lock, Duplicate, and Browse All Versions. The fourth menu item will say either Revert to Last Saved Version or Revert to Last Opened Version, depending on the document's state (more on that later in this chapter). Each menu item performs a particular task. Here's how they work.

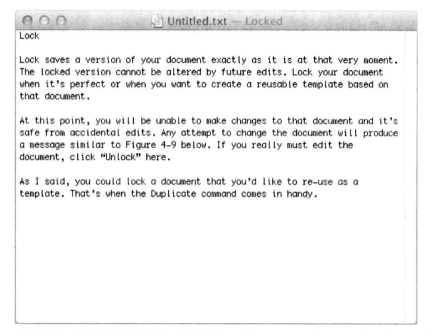

Figure 4–7. *This Text Edit document is locked, and the menu bar shows a locked document icon as well as the word "Locked."*

Lock

Lock saves a version of your document exactly as it is at that very moment. The locked version cannot be altered by future edits. Lock your document when it's perfect or when you want to create a reusable template based on that document. When a document is locked:

- The document's icon in the menu bar will acquire a small padlock icon.

- The document's desktop icon will acquire a padlock icon.

At this point, you will be unable to make changes to that document, and it's safe from accidental edits. Any attempt to change the document will produce a message similar to Figure 4–8. If you really must edit the document, click Unlock here.

> **NOTE:** I'll describe Duplicate in the next section.

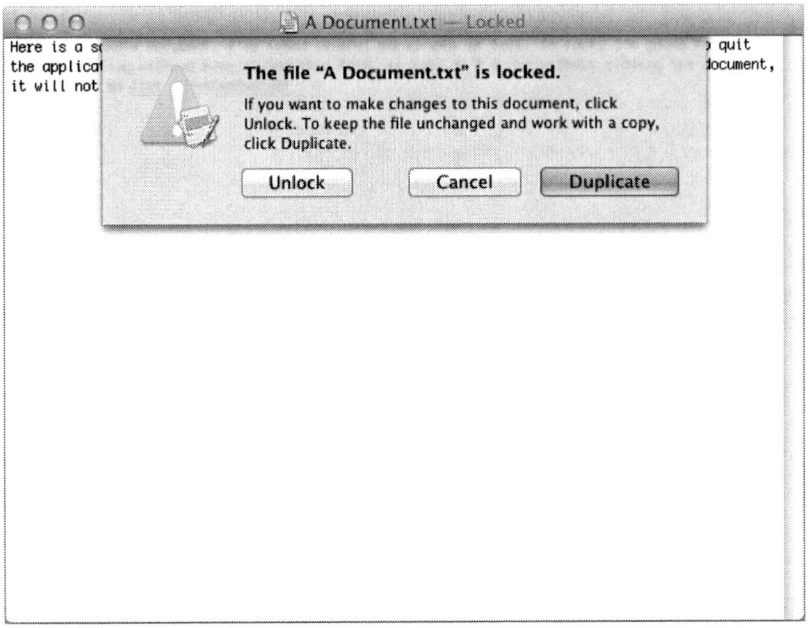

Figure 4–8. *A locked TextEdit document showing the locked dialog box. Choose Unlock to edit, Cancel to leave it as it is, or Duplicate to make an editable copy, leaving the original intact.*

Another way to make changes to a locked document is as follows:

1. Open the document.

2. Click the menu bar to reveal the drop-down menu.

3. Select Unlock.

As I said, you could lock a document that you'd like to reuse as a template. That's when the Duplicate command comes in handy.

Duplicate

Selecting Duplicate from the drop-down menu makes an exact copy of a given file, right then and there. It will appear on your screen right next to the original.

Note that you can duplicate both locked and unlocked documents. If you duplicate a locked file, the copy will be unlocked and ready to accept edits, while the original file stays locked and unchanged. Also, you needn't unlock a file to duplicate it.

Lastly, the Resume and Auto Save features treat files created via duplication as they do any other.

Revert to Last Opened vs. Revert to Last Saved Version

What appears as the third option in the drop-down menu depends on a document's state. There are two possibilities: Revert to Last Opened and Revert to Last Saved Version. In this section, I'll explain the difference between the two, how and when they appear, and how you use each. Let's begin with Revert to Last Opened.

This option returns your document to exactly how it was the first time you opened it, which is extremely handy. Imagine that you've sat down to work on a Keynote presentation, only to realize that you've fouled it up in a big way. No problem! Simply select Revert to Last Opened from the menu bar, and presto! You're back to where you were when you last opened that document.

The important phase here is "last opened." That is to say, Revert to Last Opened restores your document to how it existed *at the start of the current work session* only, not its initial creation or any earlier point in its version history. To go further back in your document's version history, see "Versions," later in this chapter.

Selecting Revert to Last Saved Version will revert your document to how it existed the last time you manually saved changes *during a given work session*, via the File menu or by hitting Command-S. Let's use that Keynote presentation as an example again.

After creating several slides, you save your progress as described earlier (File > Save or Command-S). Next, you make more changes that you're not happy with. So, select Revert to Last Saved Version to restore the presentation to how it looked the last time you executed a manual save.

When is Revert to Last Opened available vs. Revert to Last Saved Version? Good question. The deciding factor is when you manually save a document. If you open an existing document, that is to say, a document that you previously saved to a permanent location, and make changes without manually saving (selecting File and then Save or pressing Command-S), Revert to Last Opened will be available. As long as you don't perform a manual save, Revert to Last Opened will be available.

On the other hand, when you open that document, make changes, perform a manual save, and then make *additional changes*, Revert to Last Saved Version becomes available. In other words, you must perform a manual save within a given work session for Revert to Last Saved to become available.

Browse All Versions

This last option is actually the introduction to the next section. Selecting Browse All Versions offers just that: a chronological review of a document's entire edit history, all the way back to day one. With a click, you can scan every version of your document ever saved, restore previous edits to your current document, and more. It's managed through a new application called Versions. Here's how it works.

Versions

Nearly any document you create on your Mac will go through several changes. Wouldn't it be great to be able to browse a chronological history of those changes, retrieving anything you might want and inserting it into the current version? Versions lets you do just that. First, let's explore how Versions creates its document history.

Each time you open a document, Lion creates a new version based on its state at that time and tucks it away. Likewise, it saves one additional "snapshot" for every hour that you spend working on it. Finally, you can create an additional snapshot whenever you like by selecting Save a Version from the File menu.

Your Mac stores document versions neatly and efficiently. Instead of copying your document in its entirety, Versions saves only what's changed since the last save. This saves space on Mac's drive.

How many versions of a file are saved? Lion uses the following schedule:

- Hourly versions are saved for a day.

- Daily versions are saved for a month.

- Weekly versions are saved for all previous months.

To view a document's version history, select Browse All Versions from the menu bar drop-down menu described earlier.

Your Mac's desktop will instantly disappear and be replaced with what Apple calls the "star field." This will be familiar to anyone who's used Time Machine, Apple's backup software. See Figure 4–9.

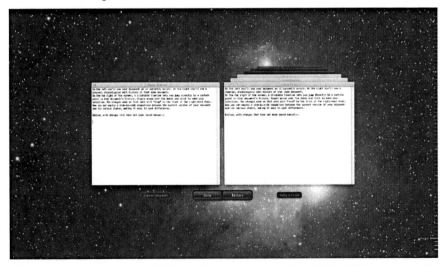

Figure 4–9. *The Versions "star field" showing the current version of a TextEdit document on the left and that document's version history on the right.*

On the left you'll see your document as it currently exists, labeled "Current Document." On the right you'll see a stacked, chronological edit history of that same document. Each is labeled with the time and date it was last modified. To move through the stack, click the version that's behind the current version. You'll notice the date in the label change as you do so.

On the far right of the screen, a clickable timeline lets you jump directly to a certain version of that document's history. To use the timeline, mouse over the various points along its length. Each represents an existing version of that document. You'll see each point's date as you move your mouse up and down.

When you make your selection via the stack or the timeline, that version will leap to the front of the pile. Now you can employ a side-by-side comparison between the current version of your document and its various states, making it easy to spot differences.

As for restoration, you have two options. First, you can copy from an old version and paste it into the current version. For example, if a paragraph you wrote six versions ago is superior to what you're currently using, simply navigate to the appropriate version as described earlier, select the paragraph, and copy (Command-C). Next, click the proper location in the current version and paste. The old paragraph will be restored.

Likewise, you can copy a photograph. For example, if you're working on a poster in Apple's Pages and want to reuse an image you deleted from the current version, simply select it from the historical version as described earlier, copy, place your cursor into the current version, and paste. It's that simple.

Optionally, you can revert to a previous version entirely. Here's how:

1. Navigate to the old version that you'll use to replace the current version, either by using the timeline or by clicking through the stack of various versions.

2. Once you've found the one you're after, click the Restore button. The star field will disappear, replaced by the desktop, and you'll see the old version fly on top of the current one, replacing it entirely.

It's also possible to delete any of the old versions. Simply find the version you no longer need in the history and click the arrow in its title bar. Choose Delete This Version, and it's gone.

Finally, Mac OS X Lion is smart enough to share only the most recent version. If you send a document to a friend or colleague via e-mail, iChat, and so on, they'll receive the most recent version only. The history of revisions never leaves your Mac.

Summary

In this chapter, you learned how Lion's Resume feature restores your applications and system to their previous states when reopened. You discovered the benefits of the Auto Save feature and how to work with a document's edit history with the powerful Versions feature. To wind things up, here are a few quick points from this chapter:

- When you relaunch an application, it appears just as you left it.

- When you restart your Mac, all windows, running applications, and so on, will reappear as they were when it was last running.

- You can temporarily avoid a systemwide Resume by deselecting "Re-open windows when logging back in" from the dialog box that appears when you restart or shut down your Mac.

- Auto Save frees you from having to manually save your progress in documents.

- You can easily restore a document to its launch state if current editing efforts go awry.

- It's easy to duplicate a document.

- Perfect documents can be locked as they are or turned into reusable templates for future projects.

- The new Versions feature automatically creates a chronological, searchable edit history of your documents.

- You can copy and paste from an old version into the current one.

- You can also restore an old version of a document at once.

- A new, Time Machine–like interface makes it easy to browse a document's version history.

- Versions offers side-by-side comparisons of current and previous versions of a document.

- It's possible to delete unwanted older edits.

Privacy is assured because Lion will send only the most recent version of a document to contacts with whom you want to share your document.

Chapter 5

Controlling Your Mac: Launchpad

Many Apple customers refer to the company's products as "easy to use" and "revolutionary." Apple has earned that reputation through years of hard work and applied research focused on how people use its hardware and software. Apple's products evolve.

An example of that evolution can be found in Launchpad. This feature was clearly borrowed from iOS, which powers the iPad, iPhone, and iPod touch. Launchpad lets Mac users open, launch, delete, and organize their applications like never before.

In this chapter, I'll explain how to use Launchpad in detail. I'll also touch on adding applications with and without the Mac App Store, deleting applications, and reinstalling Mac App Store purchases with little fuss (and even less cost). Let's begin with Launchpad.

Launchpad is one of the marquee features of Mac OS X Lion and offers a new way to organize, browse, and launch your applications. Apple calls it "a full-screen home for all your apps," and that's certainly what it is. To use it, you'll first have to open it to see the interface shown in Figure 5–1.

Opening Launchpad

Application Icons

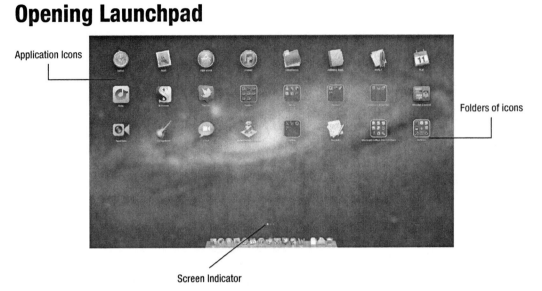

Folders of icons

Screen Indicator

Figure 5–1. *Launchpad interface showing application icons, folders, and screen indicators*

You can open Launchpad in several ways.

The easiest way is to use a Multi-Touch gesture (discussed in detail in Chapter 1). To do so, you'll need a trackpad (either built into your laptop or Apple's Magic Trackpad accessory). Interestingly, Apple's Magic Mouse does not offer a gesture for opening Launchpad (as of this writing). To open Launchpad with a gesture, place three fingers and a thumb on the trackpad, slightly spread apart. Then move them all together in a single motion, as if you were picking up something small, like a paperclip or a pencil. In my experience, a confident, quick gathering of your fingers is most effective. Moving too slowly often doesn't work. If you perform the gesture correctly, your desktop and any open windowns will fade into the background as Launchpad becomes the frontmost application. You'll see your available applications' icons over a blurry rendition of your desktop background. Any open application windows are not visible while Launchpad is active.

You can also open Launchpad by clicking its icon on the Dock. The icon looks like a black rocket on a silver circle. Lion places Launchpad in the Dock by default.

You can assign Launchpad to a *hot corner*. Every time you place your cursor in the designated corner, Launchpad will open. Use the following steps to assign Launchpad to a hot corner via System Settings:

1. Open System Settings.

2. Click Desktop & Screen Saver.

3. Click the Screensaver tab, and then click the Hot Corners... button in the lower-left corner.

4. When a new sheet appears (Figure 5–2), select Launchpad from the drop-down menu of your choice.

From now on, Launchpad will open whenever you put your cursor into that corner of the screen.

Lastly, you can use Spotlight by hitting Command-F on your keyboard, typing **Launchpad**, and then hitting Return.

You can dismiss Launchpad in one of the following ways:

■ Perform the launch gesture in reverse by placing three fingers and a thumb together on your trackpad and then spreading them apart.

■ Click anywhere other than on an application icon.

■ Press the Escape key on your keyboard.

No matter how you dismiss Launchpad, you'll see the icon display disappear as you're returned to your desktop and to any documents you had open.

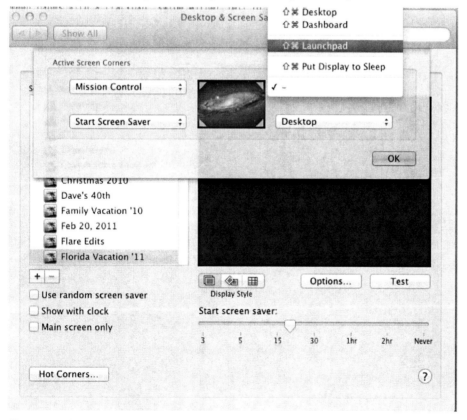

Figure 5–2. *Creating a hot corner to open Launchpad*

Navigating Launchpad

Once you have Launchpad open, you can browse your available applications, launch any of them with a click, arrange and organize applications, and delete those you no longer need. To get started, I'll discuss navigating your way around.

Launchpad displays your app icons on *pages*, with a maximum of 40 per page, provided there aren't any folders (more on folders later in this chapter). A series of white dots at the bottom of the screen indicates how many screens of icons you have. For example, in Figure 5–3, three dots indicate I have three pages of icons. Also, the brightest, or whitest, icon indicates the current page. The bright dot on the left in Figure 5–2 means I'm on the first page of icons.

Figure 5–3. *Three dots at the bottom of the Launchpad interface identify how many screens of applications I have as well as the current screen.*

Of course, you'll want to navigate from page to page. You can do that in three ways:

- You can navigate using a Multi-Touch gesture. To move between pages with a trackpad, swipe either left or right with two fingers. You'll see one page of icons slide away as the next page takes its place. Also, Apple's touch-based Magic Mouse will let you swipe between screens with two fingers.

- If you have a mouse with a scroll wheel, like Apple's Mighty Mouse, scroll the wheel to either the left or the right (other manufacturers' mice may differ; check their respective web sites for information) to move from page to page.

- Use the left and right arrow keys on your keyboard.

Launching an Application

Launching an application from within Launchpad is simple. Just position the cursor over it and click. Launchpad will disappear as the app opens.

Organizing Launchpad

Here's where Launchpad offers a huge benefit over the traditional Applications folder found in Finder. Nice organization options let you put frequently used applications on the first page and seldom used ones toward the end, while folders let you group applications with something in common. Here's how to organize your apps with Launchpad.

Rearrange Your Icons

First, it's simple to rearrange the icons. To start, simply click and hold on any icon. You'll see that it becomes darker in color. Then drag it to your desired location. You'll notice that the other icons "scoot" out of the way to make room. Once you've found the perfect spot, just let go, and it will fall into place.

If you want to move an icon to a different page, drag it all the way to the edge of the current page and wait just a second or two. Launchpad will then jump to the next page. You can repeat this as many times as necessary until you find the proper page. Again, once you're satisfied, simply drop the application's icon into place.

> **NOTE:** There's no limit to the number of pages you can create in Launchpad, so go nuts!

Folders in Launchpad

Folders add another layer of organization. Much like the iPhone, iPad, and iPod touch, Launchpad lets you gather several icons into a single folder. It's super handy to collect related applications into one spot. Here's how to create a "work" folder that contains Microsoft Word, Pages, Keynote, and Mail.

1. Drag any one of those applications' icons over the top of one of the others (Word on top of Pages, for example). A rounded rectangle with a white border appears beneath Pages. Then the folder "opens" as the rest of the icons fade away, revealing its contents (in this case, Pages).

2. Drop Word into the folder.

3. To change the folder's name, double-click its title and enter your own. (Of course, you're free to accept the suggested name.)

4. Click anywhere outside the folder to close it.

Repeat this process with the remaining applications. Note that a folder can be repositioned on a screen or even dragged to another screen as described previously. Finally, you can remove an application from any folder simply by dragging it outside of the folder.

Adding New Applications

Adding new applications to Launchpad takes almost no effort on your part. There are two methods: either using the Mac App Store or installing them directly from a web site, CD, or DVD.

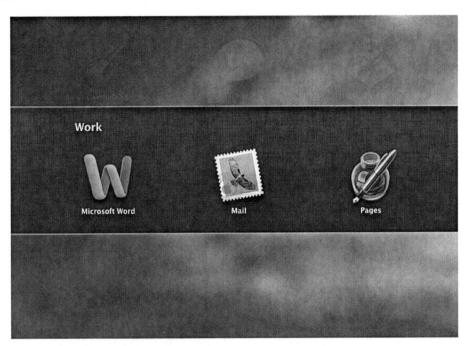

Figure 5–4. *Creating a folder in Launchpad*

The Mac App Store

First, any application purchased from Apple's Mac App Store will appear in Launchpad automatically. Second, software acquired from without the store (such as from a developer's web site) will appear in Launchpad once it's placed in your Mac's Applications folder.

When you purchase an application, you'll see its icon momentarily "jump" out of the store's window. Next, Launchpad will automatically open, and your new app's icon will appear among the others. A status bar will appear on the icon itself as it downloads. Once the download is complete, the status bar will read "Installing." When the app is finally ready to use, the status bar disappears completely.

It's also possible to move applications from Launchpad into the Dock. With Launchpad open, simply drag and drop any icon from a Launchpad page into the Dock.

Without the Mac App Store

It's possible to add applications to Launchpad without purchasing them from the Mac App Store. Specifically, applications purchased from a web site or installed from a CD or DVD will appear in Launchpad when you drag them into your Mac's Applications folder. Most installers will place applications in this folder by default, but if not, simply open a Finder window, click the Applications icon on the left, and drop your application inside.

Deleting Applications

If you thought organizing and launching apps was easy, you're going to love Launchpad's process for deleting unwanted apps. Again, this is an example of Apple borrowing heavily from iOS.

To delete an unwanted application, follow these steps:

1. Open Launchpad.

2. Click and hold the target application's icon for a couple of seconds. The icons will enter "jiggle mode," quivering in place.

3. When the white X appears in a small, black circle in the icon's upper-left corner, click it. A dialog box will appear, confirming your action (Figure 5–5). Click Delete.

Figure 5–5. *A dialog box confirms your request to delete an application from Launchpad.*

That's it! The icon will fade from view as it's deleted from your Mac. When deleting applications in this fashion, keep the following considerations in mind:

- Once they're gone, they're gone. Launchpad's delete function does not put an application in the trash; it nixes it for good. Be sure that's what you want to do before you hit that Delete button.

- Not all applications are available for deletion by this method. Specifically, applications that are bundled with Mac OS X Lion (such as Photo Booth and Address Book) and not available for download cannot be deleted from Launchpad.

- If you accidentally delete an application you purchased from the Mac App Store, you can redownload it at no charge.

> **NOTE:** Even if you keep your Dock hidden, it will appear when you open Launchpad. Also, Launchpad will "follow" the Dock when you use more than one display. That is to say, it will open on whichever display has the Dock.

What Launchpad Doesn't Do

Although Launchpad is great for organizing and launching your Mac's applications, there are several tasks it doesn't perform. For one, you can't store shortcuts to documents, folders, or web pages. For example, there's no way to put a shortcut to your Documents folder or link to a favorite web site in Launchpad. Aliases don't work, either.

Additionally, you cannot drag an application into the trash via Launchpad, and some applications cannot be deleted via jiggle mode (such as those purchased outside the Mac App Store and those that are installed on your Mac by default, such as Photo Booth).

Finally, no contextual menus are available. That is to say, you can't right-click or Control-click an app's icon to bring up options such as Show Package Contents, Get Info, or Make Alias.

Summary

In this chapter, you learned how to use Launchpad to launch, sort, and organize your applications, as well as group similar apps by folders. You also learned to how to add new applications and delete unwanted ones. Finally, you learned what Launchpad cannot do. Here are some highlights from this chapter:

- Launchpad is an all-new way to launch applications on the Mac.
- Launchpad borrows heavily from iOS on iPads, iPhones, and iPod touches.
- You can rearrange icons in Launchpad by dragging them around.
- Folders allow you to group like apps together.
- Many applications are deleted via jiggle mode, just like in iOS.
- Launchpad won't let you do some things, such as make an alias or store folders or documents.

Chapter 6

Using Mission Control, Spaces, Exposé, and Dashboard

It's not a NASA initiative, despite the name's interstellar overtones. Mission Control represents the evolution of three technologies introduced in earlier versions of Mac OS X: Spaces, Exposé, and the Dashboard. These technologies have been combined into a single interface that tidies our busy desktops and offers an at-a-glance overview of all open projects. That's Mission Control.

In this chapter, I'll explain how Spaces and Exposé have been combined, and I'll point out how the Dashboard and Dashboard widgets have been integrated into Mission Control. In the context of the evolution of these technologies, I'll offer a full overview of how Mission Control looks, how it works, what it offers, and how it can become part of your daily workflow.

Finally, I'll explain the available preferences. Let's get started!

Launching Mission Control

There are several ways to launch Mission Control, most of which I'll cover when explaining its preferences later in this chapter. For now, I'll describe the four most common methods: by using a Multi-Touch gesture, by clicking the app's icon, by using an Apple keyboard, or via a hot corner. Here's how to use each method.

Gesture

As described earlier in this book, Mac OS X Lion offers significant support for Multi-Touch gestures. Those with a trackpad (either on a laptop or with Apple's Magic Trackpad accessory) or Magic Mouse can use a gesture to launch Mission Control.

When using a trackpad, swipe up (away from yourself) with three fingers. Alternatively, you can opt to use four fingers in the System Settings app, as described in Chapter 1.

While using an Apple Magic Mouse, double-tap the mouse's surface. Note that Lion doesn't offer alternative gestures for launching Mission Control with a Magic Mouse like it does with a trackpad. It's double-tap or nothing.

> **NOTE:** The Magic Mouse settings appear in the System Preferences application only if your Mac is paired with a Magic Mouse. Otherwise, you'll simply see a prompt to set one up. The same is true for desktop systems not paired with a Magic Trackpad.

The Application

You can also launch Mission Control by double-clicking its icon (Figure 6–1). You'll find it in the Applications folder. For quick access, drag the icon to the Dock.

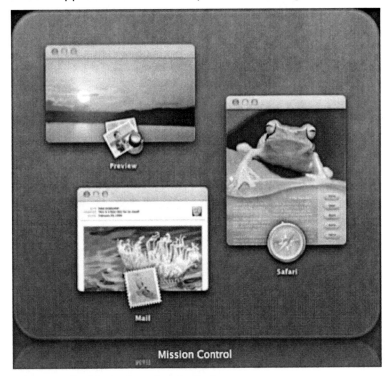

Figure 6–1. *The Mission Control application icon*

Dashboard Key

Current Apple keyboards have a Dashboard key (F3 on both the wired and Bluetooth keyboards, as of this writing). Pressing it will launch Mission Control.

Hot Corner

Finally, you can assign Mission Control to a hot corner. Moving your cursor into that corner will launch Mission Control. Here's how to set that up:

1. Open System Preferences.

2. Click Mission Control (or Desktop and Screen Savers), and then click Hot Corners in the lower-left corner.

3. A new sheet appears. Select Mission Control from one of the drop-down menus, and then click OK.

From now on, you can launch Mission Control by moving your cursor into that corner of your display, as shown in Figure 6–2.

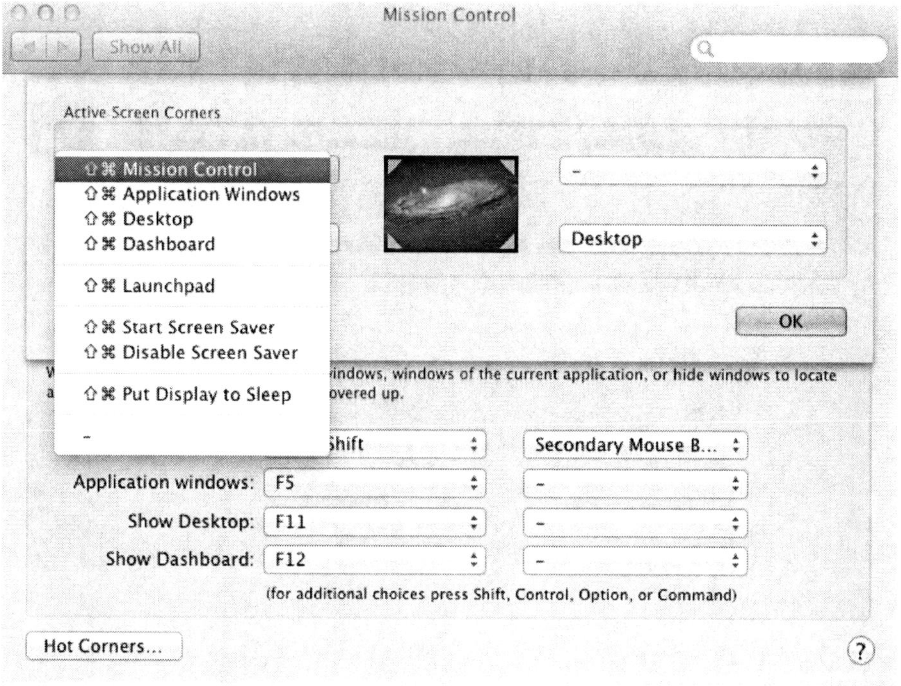

Figure 6–2. *Creating a hot corner to launch Mission Control*

Now that you know how to launch Mission Control, I'll describe how it looks and behaves, starting with the integration of Spaces.

> **NOTE:** To experience a bit of slow-motion eye candy, launch Mission Control via your favorite method while holding down the Shift key on your keyboard.

Mission Control and Spaces

Spaces was introduced to Mac OS X with Leopard and lets you create unique workspaces, or "virtual desktops." You could assign an application to a given desktop, keeping it out of sight until needed. That way, you could move from desktop to desktop—and therefore, application to application—while keeping things tidy. The goal was to benefit those who work in several applications simultaneously and struggle with "piles" of windows.

Today, Spaces, and the notion of multiple desktops (I'll call the individual workspaces *desktops* in this book), is one aspect of Mission Control.

How It Looks

Figure 6–3 shows what Mission Control looks like.

Desktop Thumbnails

Exposé Area

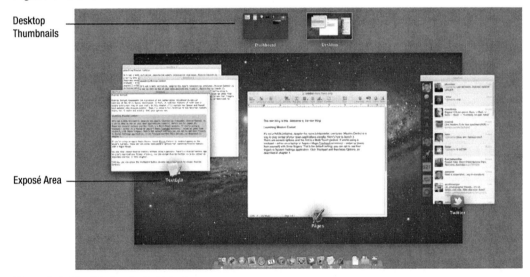

Figure 6–3. *The Mission Control interface*

When Mission Control is launched, your desktop appears to recede into your display. You'll find two main features against a backdrop of gray linen. In the top one-third of the screen is a row of thumbnail desktops. This is the implementation of Spaces within Mission Control. All of your available desktops appear in a tidy, vertical row. See Figure 6–4.

Figure 6–4. *Spaces—or the horizontal row of desktop thumbnails—as presented by Mission Control*

Beneath that, an Exposé-like overview of the current desktop's open windows fills the rest of the screen. I'll discuss this feature later in this chapter.

By default, two desktops appear in that top row. On the left is the Dashboard, or the widget interface introduced with an earlier version of Mac OS X. On the right is the current desktop. Each desktop is labeled, as in, for example, Dashboard, Desktop 1, Desktop 2, and so on. The current desktop is highlighted with a silver border.

Navigating Between Desktops

There are two ways to navigate between desktops. One will push you out of Mission Control, while the other won't. Here's the difference.

You can move from desktop to desktop while staying in Mission Control by using a gesture or your keyboard. To use a gesture, use four fingers to swipe left or right on your trackpad. If you're using a Magic Mouse, swipe with two fingers.

Alternatively, you can use your keyboard. Hold down the Control key and press the left and right arrows. Using either method, you'll see the silver highlight move between the desktop thumbnails in the top row, and the Exposé area in the lower half of the screen will show the open windows in each desktop. This is useful when you want a quick reference.

To move to another desktop and exit Mission Control simultaneously, simply click any desktop thumbnail in the top row. The Mission Control interface will fade away, and you'll jump to that desktop and all of its contained applications and windows.

Why choose one over the other? Stay in Mission Control to find a certain app or file; jump out once you have it and are ready to get back to work.

To fully take advantage of the organization that Mission Control offers, you'll want to add applications to a desktop, create new desktops, and delete desktops you're no longer using. Here's how to do each of those things.

Adding a New Desktop

You can easily add a new desktop while in Mission Control. There are two methods. Here is the first:

1. Move your cursor to the upper-right corner of the Mission Control interface. A new desktop will partially appear with a + symbol near its edge (see Figure 6–5).

2. Confirm the addition by clicking that desktop. It slides into line with the other thumbnails and receives a title (Desktop 2, for example).

Figure 6–5. *A new desktop thumbnail emerges from the upper-right corner. Click the + symbol to create the new desktop.*

The other method allows you to create a new desktop and add an application to it in one fell swoop. Here's how.

1.   In the Mission Control interface, drag an application's window from the Exposé area in middle of the screen to the upper-right window. A new desktop will partially appear, as described in the previous procedure.

2.   Drop the window onto the new desktop. The application will be assigned to that desktop, and it will slide into line with the others. See Figure 6–6.

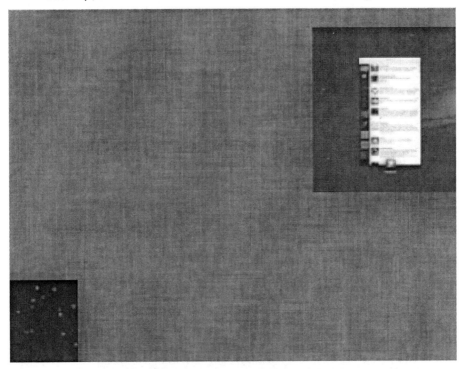

Figure 6–6. *Drag and drop a document from the Exposé area and onto a new desktop thumbnail to create a new desktop and populate it with that application's open windows simultaneously.*

Adding and Subtracting Applications

As described in the previous section, it's easy to add applications to a given desktop. Simply launch Mission Control and then drag the target application's windows onto the desired desktop. Fortunately, it's just as easy to relocate an application. Here's how:

1. Launch Mission Control.

2. Select the desktop with the application you'd like to move.

3. Grab that application's windows and then drag them onto a different available desktop (or create a new one as described earlier in this chapter).

Closing Desktops

There may be a time when you want to close a given desktop, such as when you're using only one or two applications that can happily coexist in the same workspace.

To close a desktop, simply mouse over its thumbnail image and allow the cursor to rest for a second or two. A white X on a field of black will appear on that desktop's upper-left corner. Click it to close that desktop. If that desktop contained applications, all of its windows will be assigned to Desktop 1. Conversely, you can mouse over a desktop while holding down the Option key to bring up the X instantly.

Mission Control and Exposé

Now let's look at Exposé. This feature offers an overview of all of your open windows, neatly grouped by application. Here's how to use the Exposé-like feature of Mission Control.

How It Looks

With Mission Control running, you'll see the Exposé area beneath the desktop thumbnails. In fact, the Exposé area occupies most of the Mission Control interface (as shown earlier in Figure 6–3).

Mission Control groups all of your open windows by their parent applications into neat "stacks." An icon represents each application that's in use.

For example, Microsoft Word documents will be stacked together. The bottom of that stack will bear a Word icon. Likewise, Pages documents will display a Pages icon.

Navigating Between Applications

To move from one application to another, simply click its stack. You'll exit Mission Control and jump to that application.

You can also view the contents of a given stack while in Mission Control. This is useful if you have several documents open at once and need to find a certain one fast. Here's how:

1. Place your cursor over a stack.

2. Swipe up with two fingers on your trackpad or Magic Mouse. (If you don't have a device with a Multi-Touch surface, place your cursor above the stack and press the spacebar on your keyboard.)

The documents fan out, offering a good look at each.

The Dashboard

Apple has moved the Dashboard feature to Mission Control (see Figure 6–7). It functions exactly as it did before, with the exception of launching options. As you saw earlier, the Dashboard is the leftmost desktop space in Mission Control by default. You have an option to turn that off or assign it to a hot key.

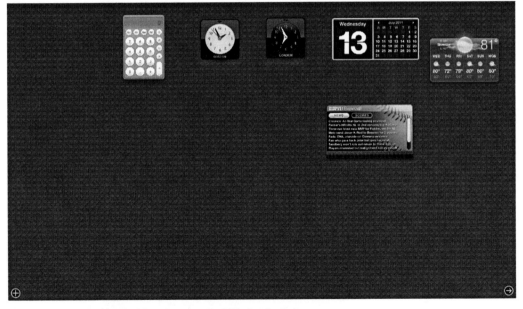

Figure 6–7. *The familiar Dashboard, now part of Mission Control*

A Few Things to Remember

While that covers the main features of Mission Control, there are a few smaller things to keep in mind regarding multiple displays and desktop images.

Mission Control and Multiple Displays

Many people work with a second display connected to their Mac. In those cases, each display gets its own Mission Control interface and collection of desktops. For example, when I connect an external display to my MacBook Air and launch Mission Control, the applications running on the laptop's display appear as desktops on its screen, while those running on the external machine appear on the external screen.

Also, note that it is not possible to move applications between desktops that are on different displays via Mission Control. In other words, if I'm running Safari on my MacBook Air and want to drag it onto a desktop on my external display, that won't work.

Mission Control and Desktop Images

Desktop images, or wallpapers, are unique to individual virtual desktops. That is to say, you can assign a unique desktop image to each virtual desktop, and they will remain consistent and appear in the desktop thumbnail images. For example, if the desktop you have labeled as Desktop 1 has wallpaper featuring a moonlit sky, that same moonlit sky will appear in that desktop's thumbnail image. Likewise, if you're using an image of the kids at the beach for Desktop 2, that shot will also appear in the desktop thumbnail for Desktop 2.

Mission Control Preferences

A number of useful preference options offer nice control over how Mission Control behaves. Here's an overview of what's available.

You'll find the Mission Control preferences by opening System Preferences and then clicking Mission Control from among the Personal options in the top row. The preference pane appears as in Figure 6–8.

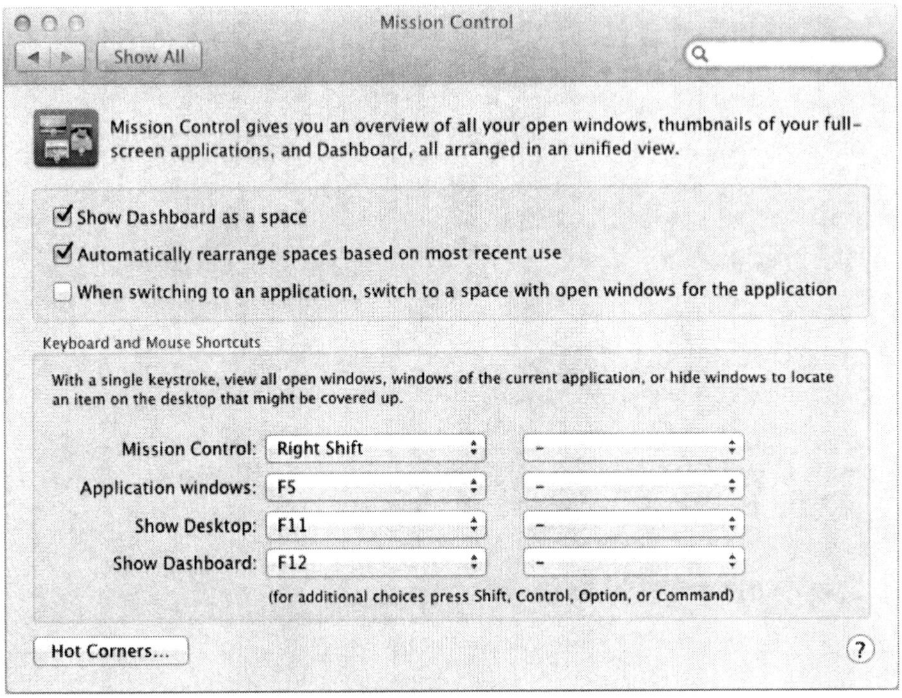

Figure 6–8. *The Mission Control preference pane*

There are several options to choose from. The first three are check boxes:

■ *Show Dashboard as a Space*: When selected, the Dashboard appears as the leftmost desktop thumbnail, as described earlier. When deselected, you must use the Dashboard application to open the Dashboard.

■ *Automatically rearrange spaces based on most recent use*: By default, Mission Control will keep your desktop thumbnails sorted by creation order. With this option selected, they'll be sorted by most recently used.

■ *When switching to an application, switch to a space with open windows for the application*: This affects the behavior of moving between applications that are in different desktop spaces without using Mission Control. For example, if you're working in Desktop 1 on a Word document and switch to Mail in another desktop space (by clicking its icon in the Dock or by hitting Command-Tab), you'll move to that space. Deselect this option, and you'll stay in the current desktop space.

The other preference settings refer to keyboard and mouse shortcuts. This is where you'll find additional options for launching Mission Control, and there are many.

Basically, you can assign the following functions to a myriad of shortcuts:

- Launch Mission Control

- Display all application windows

- Show the desktop (hide all application windows)

- Show the Dashboard

Next to each option is a pair of drop-down menus, with one on the left and one on the right. Those on the left offer keyboard shortcuts. Click any one of them to see a huge list of options that can be assigned to each function.

The options on the right offer mousing options. For most users, this will be restricted to the secondary click (or right-click).

As you can see while browsing these options, you have a huge number of customization options. Surely you'll find a setup that works for you.

Summary

In this chapter, you learned that Mission Control brings three previously released features of Mac OS X—Spaces, Exposé, and Dashboard—into a single interface. You can create new desktops and drag items between them. Also, gestures provide quick access to all of your desktops and apps. Here are a few points to remember:

- Mission Control can be launched with a gesture, a hot corner, or a customizable keystroke.

- The Mission Control preferences offer additional options for launching and managing Mission Control's behavior.

- You can click a desktop to jump right to it or use keystrokes to review what's in each desktop.

- Unwanted desktops can be closed with a Control-click.

- Mission Control's Exposé feature organizes your open windows into tidy stacks.

- Stacked windows identify their parent application by displaying its icon.

- You can fan out all of the documents within an Exposé stack to find the one you're looking for.

- Desktop images remain unique to each desktop space.

Each display maintains its own Mission Control interface and collections.

Chapter 7

Mail

For many Mac users, e-mail and Web browsing are the two main reasons they use their personal computers. While Web browsing is predominantly accomplished through Safari, the aptly named Mail app is the Mac user's e-mail client of choice. With Mac OS X Lion, Apple has taken the Mail app to a new level of usability and speed.

Using the full-screen app capabilities of Lion, Mail is now able to organize your mail and focus your attention on the work at hand. If you're a fan of Mail on the iPad, you're sure to love the way that the mailbox list can now be hidden to let you see more of your e-mails. Your message list is different as well—a small preview displays a few lines of the e-mail and contact photos for e-mails from senders in your address book.

There's a new Favorites bar above the messages, providing access to mail folders with a single click. Message headers now display only the sender's e-mail address, the subject, and when the message was received, giving your e-mails more room on small screens (think of an 11.6" MacBook Air).

Do you get flustered with long e-mail conversations that are all but unreadable by the time an e-mail has been bounced back and forth a few times? If you do, you're going to love Mail's new Conversations feature. With Conversations, Mail groups your related messages and numbers each message in order, making short work of figuring out the order and logic of e-mailed conversations.

Searching through hundreds or thousands of saved e-mails is now easier than ever thanks to search tokens, another new feature of Mail. As I'll discuss in a few pages, search tokens can be combined to narrow searches to find exactly what you need. Attachments can be searched by name, by content, or by whether a message contains an attachment.

My personal favorite new tool in Mail is the addition of inline controls that appear just above messages that you're reading. With a click, you can reply to, forward, or delete a message. Those controls disappear when you don't need them, so they don't take up any space or detract from the readability of messages.

If you want to clean out your inbox but keep messages for future reference, archiving e-mail now takes a single click. While those e-mails are now in a special archive file, they're still searchable using a special search token.

Mac users who get their mail, calendar, and address book information from a Microsoft Exchange 2010 server are finally able to use Mail to connect to Exchange, rather than having to use Microsoft Entourage or Outlook for Mac. Exchange users are also able to set their vacation messages from Mail now.

In this chapter, I'll take you through all of these new features, plus a few others that may surprise you.

Mail Setup and Conversion

Many of the readers of this book are upgrading Macs from earlier versions of Mac OS X to Lion. Fortunately for you, setting up Mail under the new operating system requires just a single click to have your e-mail accounts migrated to the newer software.

If you're new to the Mac or to using the Mail app, you'll find that setting up your e-mail accounts to work with Mail is fairly straightforward. As an example, follow along as I set up MobileMe and Gmail accounts in Mail.

Just like earlier versions of Mail, clicking the "postage stamp" icon in the Dock launches the app. Once Mail is up and running, your existing accounts installed under a previous version of Mac OS X are converted to a new format and all of the mailboxes appear in the app.

What if you want to add new accounts to Mail? You'll find that the process is considerably easier than before. In this example, I'm going to add a Google Mail account to Mail. With Mail launched, select **File ➤ Add Account**. A dialog similar to that in Figure 7–1 appears.

Figure 7–1. *To add an account, enter your name, the e-mail address you want to add, and the password for that account; then click Create.*

Enter the name of the person to be listed as the sender of e-mails (usually your name), the e-mail address, and the password for the e-mail account. Click the Create button, and a second dialog appears on the screen (Figure 7–2).

With most major e-mail providers, including Gmail (Google Mail), Yahoo! Mail, AOL, MobileMe, and Exchange servers, the e-mail application recognizes the type of server and automatically configures the account for you, as shown in Figure 7–2. If the e-mail provider also has a chat or calendar service, checking the boxes marked Calendars and iChat sets up accounts for iCal and iChat that are linked to the e-mail account. As before, clicking the Create button has an immediate effect. In this case, it causes the account to be added to Mail, and if you requested, accounts are added to iCal and iChat as well.

Like many Mac users, you may have web mail accounts set up with various providers. Safari now recognizes when you're logging into a web mail page and offers to set up the account in Mail. In Figure 7–3, I've entered Safari and logged into a Yahoo! Rocketmail account. The dialog shown in the figure appears at the top of the browser window.

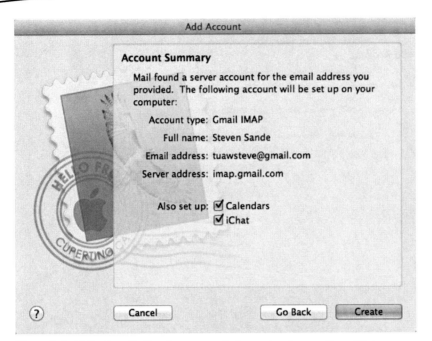

Figure 7–2. *Mail automatically sets up accounts for most major e-mail providers.*

Figure 7–3. *When logging in to a web mail page in Safari, a dialog similar to this appears. Click the Add Account button to begin the setup process.*

To begin adding the account to Mail (and iCal and iChat if desired), I click the Add Account button. To clarify the services I want to use with the Rocketmail account, Safari now displays a second dialog (Figure 7–4).

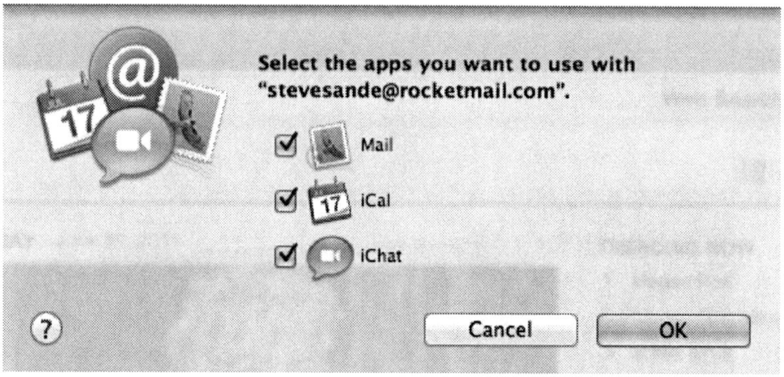

Figure 7–4. *Select only the Lion apps that you want to synchronize with the service you're setting up. In this figure, Mail, iCal, and iChat are being linked to Yahoo! services.*

If I want to use Mail to send and receive Rocketmail, iCal to display Yahoo! Calendars, and set up iChat to use Yahoo! Chat, I keep the three boxes checked and then click OK. The account is set up with the proper applications, and Mail is ready to roll.

Mail User Interface

Just about every Mac and monitor made by Apple over the past several years has come with a wide-screen display. That means it matches the dimensions of a wide-screen HDTV, with an aspect ratio (the ratio of width to height of the screen) of 16:9.

Mail has been redesigned in Lion to take advantage of all that wide-screen goodness. In Figure 7–5, the Mail app is expanded to take advantage of the full screen on an 11.6" MacBook Air. On the left, the inbox is displayed as a list of messages showing the sender's name or e-mail address, the subject of the e-mail, and the first two lines of the message. On the right is the e-mail message itself, and it fills all of the available space from the bottom of the screen up to the toolbar. For messages with attached images or documents, it's a wonderful way to see all of the content immediately.

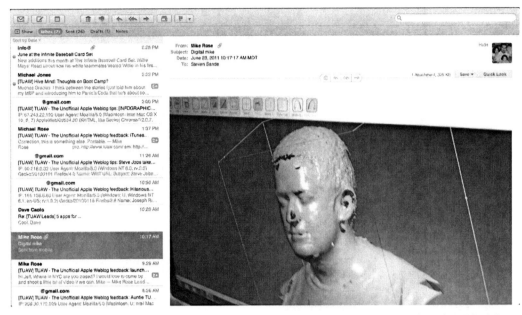

Figure 7–5. *The new user interface of Mail works well in wide-screen format, and the app is designed for full-screen use in Lion.*

This two-column format is perfect if you have only one e-mail address. But what if you have several accounts, all with separate mailboxes? Just above the list of messages you'll see the Favorites bar. This is where you can place links for mailboxes, notes, and other items, and I'll discuss it in further detail later in this chapter. By default, the Favorites bar includes a Show/Hide toggle at the far left. If you don't see a list of mailboxes, click the Show button in the Favorites bar, and a third column appears (Figure 7–6).

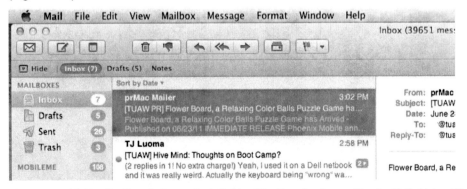

Figure 7–6. *Clicking the Show button on the left side of the Favorites bar enables the Mail sidebar. When the sidebar is visible, the Show button turns into a Hide button as shown here.*

As with the Finder terminology introduced in Chapter 2, this gray area is known as the Mail sidebar. When the sidebar is visible, as in Figure 7–6, the Show/Hide toggle button displays the word *Hide* and does exactly that to the sidebar.

Above the Favorites bar and below the menu bar is the toolbar, familiar to anyone who has used Mail in the past. However, the icons have changed, and there are several that may be strange to you. That's a good reason to look at the toolbar first.

The Mail Toolbar

The first time you launch Mail on your freshly upgraded or new Mac, you'll see the default set of toolbar icons (Figure 7–7).

Figure 7–7. *The default Mail toolbar icons*

If you forget what these icons are used for, you have two choices. The first is to change your toolbar settings so that the icons are labeled with text. To do this, right-click or two-finger click the toolbar. A small drop-down menu appears, with one of the options being Icon and Text; selecting that item displays the icon function underneath the icon. The second way is to use your cursor to hover over the icon. This displays a light yellow text tip box that describes the function of the icon.

These are the icons from left to right:

- *Get Mail*: Attempts to receive and send mail from all accounts.

- *New Message*: Creates a blank message.

- *Note*: Pops up a small yellow lined notepad into which you enter reminders or short documents.

- *Delete*: Deletes the currently highlighted message from the mailbox.

- *Junk*: Marks as spam or junk mail.

- *Reply*: Displays a reply e-mail addressed to the "reply-to" address containing the original e-mail message or any text that had been highlighted prior to clicking the icon.

- *Reply All*: Same as Reply, but addressed to all recipients of the original e-mail message.

- *Forward*: Displays an e-mail with a blank "To" address, containing the original e-mail message or text highlighted prior to clicking the icon.

- *Show Related Messages*: A new icon in Mail for Lion, clicking Show Related Messages displays any replies and forwarded messages that are related to the currently highlighted message.

■ *Flag*: Would you like to flag certain messages as a reminder to take action on them? The flag icon provides a rainbow of colored flags to choose from. After applying flags, all messages tagged with a particular color are immediately visible under Reminders in the Mail sidebar.

Customizing the Toolbar

If you're not going to use one or more of the toolbar icons or if you'd like to add a capability that isn't displayed with the existing icons, you're in luck. Right-clicking or two-finger clicking the toolbar displays the drop-down menu mentioned earlier (Figure 7–8).

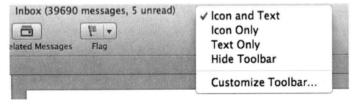

Figure 7–8. *Right-clicking (or using a two-finger click on a trackpad) displays this menu for customizing the Mail toolbar.*

I discussed the ability to add or remove the icon labels on the previous page, but hiding the toolbar altogether is also possible. This is helpful in cases where you may want to maximize the amount of screen space available for messages when using a Mac with a size-limited display. To display the toolbar after you've hidden it, select **View ➤ Show toolbar**.

Selecting Customize Toolbar from the drop-down menu displays the palette of icons shown in Figure 7–9.

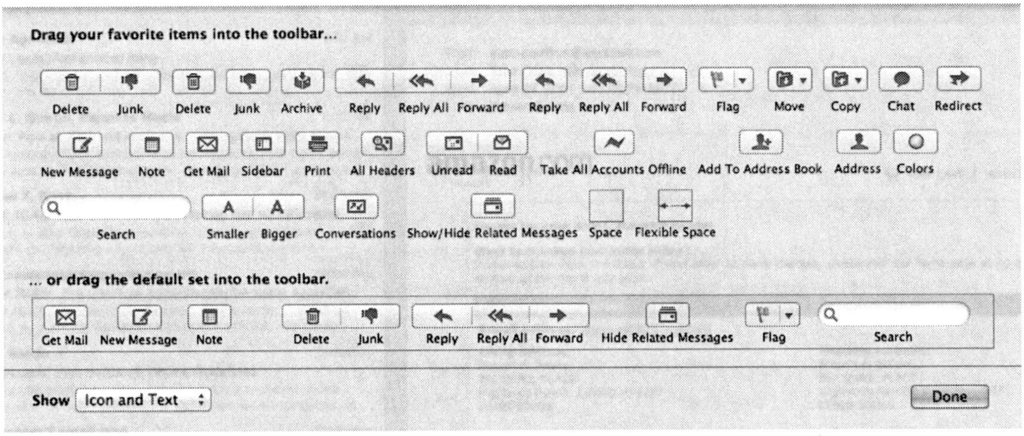

Figure 7–9. *By customizing the Mail toolbar with icons that reflect the most common actions performed, you can become more efficient in your use of the Mail app.*

To add any of these icons to the toolbar, just drag them from this palette to the appropriate location on the toolbar.

On the previous page, I described the purpose of a number of the common icons. Here's what some of these other icons do for you:

- *Archive*: Selecting a message by clicking it and then clicking this icon places the message into an Archive mailbox where it is held until you want to take further action. Depending on the type of account you're using, the Archive mailbox may be local (on your computer) or on a mail server.

- *Move*: Do you use folders to organize your Mail messages? The Move button provides a quick way to move a selected message into a specific folder by clicking the icon and selecting the target folder.

- *Copy*: To make a copy of a selected message and then move it to a folder, click the Copy icon and choose a target folder. The message stays in the Inbox folder and is copied to the target folder as well.

- *Chat*: By default, Mail is set up to display "buddy availability." If you receive a Mail message from a friend and there's a small green circle displayed, that means your friend is currently online in iChat. Clicking the Chat icon launches iChat and creates a chat session with your friend.

- *Redirect*: Have you ever received a message that was intended for delivery to someone else? Selecting the message and clicking Redirect displays a copy of the message. Add a new recipient address and any message you want to pass along, and then send the message on its way. Redirect is a great way to report spam mail to IT departments.

- *Sidebar*: There's another way to make the Mail sidebar appear and disappear. Add the sidebar icon to your toolbar, and then click it to toggle visibility of the Mail sidebar.

- *Print*: Even in this electronic age, it's sometimes necessary to print an e-mail message. If the Print icon is added to the toolbar, a selected message is printed with a single click.

- *All Headers*: This icon forces Mail to display all header information in an e-mail. Although most people never need to see this information, it's useful to IT departments for determining the source of anonymous or spam messages.

- *Unread*: The Unread icon is useful for displaying only the messages, in an Inbox folder, that have not been read. With a click, all read messages are hidden, which is a wonderful way to focus on incoming mail.

■ *Read*: The Read icon does the opposite of the Unread icon by displaying only the messages that have been previously read.

■ *Take All Accounts Offline*: On occasion, it's useful to be able to stop Mail from its ceaseless chattering with mail servers. To do so, you need to take all of your e-mail accounts offline, and this icon does so with a click.

■ *Add to Address Book*: If you want to add the sender of an e-mail to your address book with a click, the Add To Address Book icon performs just that task.

■ *Address*: A very helpful icon, Address displays a mini address book (Figure 7–10) so you can find an e-mail address without having to launch the Mac Address Book app. Address books that are stored on your Mac, in iCloud, or on a local Directory Services server on your network are shown, and individual addresses or groups may be added to a message by clicking the To, Cc, or Bcc button.

Figure 7–10. *The Address button displays a mini address book for quickly finding e-mail addresses and adding them to outgoing messages.*

■ *Colors*: This icon has nothing to do with those flags I discussed a couple of pages ago. Instead, Colors displays a standard Mac color picker.

■ *Search*: The search capabilities of Mail have improved markedly in Lion, and the search field is your gateway to finding messages. If you're customizing your toolbar and want to add back a missing search field, drag and drop it from the palette to the toolbar.

■ *Smaller/Bigger*: Having problems reading a message in small font size? Adding Smaller/Bigger to the toolbar gives you an instant way to increase the font size (or decrease it if it's too big) of a selected message.

- *Conversations*: I'll talk about Conversations, another new feature of Lion Mail, shortly. This icon is used to toggle the conversation view of any message thread.

- *Space/Flexible Space*: The last two icons to be discussed in this section are there to add spaces between other icons that you've dragged and dropped to the toolbar.

The Message Toolbar

While I'm on the topic of toolbars, I think it's a good time to discuss another useful set of tools that exist in the Message toolbar. This toolbar appears when you create a new blank message, reply to a message, or forward a message and is at the top of the blank message by default. As with the regular Mail toolbar, the Message toolbar can be hidden if you find that it gets in the way of writing, sending, or reading e-mail. You can also hide or show text labels for the icons and customize the Message toolbar to meet your needs.

Like the Mail toolbar, the Message toolbar contains a default set of icons (Figure 7–11).

Figure 7–11. *The Message toolbar is at the top of this blank message. Just below is the Format toolbar, which I'll discuss shortly.*

From left to right, the Message toolbar contains the following icons:

- *Send*: When you're finished writing a new message, composing a reply, or adding text and other content to a forwarded message, clicking the Send icon sends the message to the proper mail server for the account being used.

- *Attach*: Sending documents in Mail messages is done in one of two ways. First, clicking the Attach icon displays a standard Mac Finder window (see Chapter 2) that is used to choose a file to attach to the document. The second way is to drag and drop a file icon onto your blank message.

- *Format*: This icon toggles the visibility of the Format toolbar, which is used to format the text in a Mail message. I'll have more details about the Format toolbar in a minute.

■ *Photo Browser*: Photos are a type of file, so you could think about using the Attach icon to pick an image file and attach it to a message. The Photo Browser gives you a way to actually see those images, much in the way that they are stored in iPhoto. Clicking this button provides access to the standard Mac Photo Browser (Figure 7–12).

Figure 7–12. *The Photo Browser is used to look through iPhoto images by event, face, or place, and it is keyword-searchable as well.*

■ *Show Stationery*: As with previous versions, Lion Mail provides a selection of virtual stationery for sending unique and colorful e-mails to friends and relatives (Figure 7–13). With a click of the Show Stationery icon, a gallery of stationery included in Mail is displayed.

Figure 7–13. *Selecting stationery in Mail applies a bright and professionally designed look to your messages.*

Clicking any one of the stationery thumbnail images applies that stationery to the current message, and images are selected from your iPhoto library to replace the placeholder images in the stationery template.

As with the Mail toolbar, the Message toolbar is customizable. A right-click or two-finger click displays a drop-down menu that is identical to the one shown earlier on the Mail toolbar. Selecting Customize Toolbar shows you a palette of icons to drag and drop to the Message toolbar. All of them, with the exception of the following four, have been discussed previously:

- *Append*: On occasion, you may want to include information from an existing e-mail in a new message. This happens automatically when you click Reply, Reply All, or Forward but not when a new message is created. Click Append, and the text of any highlighted message is added to a new unaddressed message.

- *Lists*: Messages often contain lists of items. To format a list automatically as a numbered or bulleted list, select it and click the Lists icon.

- *Link*: When typing a hyperlink into a message (an Internet address or a "mailto" link), click the Link icon to add the underlying address to turn the hyperlink into a clickable link. Note that Mail does this automatically when you send a message containing a typed Internet address.

- *Rich Text/Plain Text*: Plain text is readable by all e-mail recipients, because it contains no special fonts, text styles, and formatting. A small percentage of e-mail recipients cannot read rich text, which does contain special fonts, styles, and formatting. Mail defaults to rich text, but if you need to send e-mail messages in plain text, clicking this icon removes any special formatting.

The Format Toolbar

The Format toolbar (Figure 7–14), which appears just above the To address field and below the Message toolbar in a Mail message, is used to change the font, font size, color, emphasis, alignment, bullets or numbering, and indentation of text.

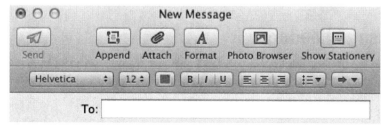

Figure 7–14. *The Format toolbar is enabled by clicking the Format icon in the Message toolbar and is used to format the text in the body of your message.*

When writing a message in Mail, the Format toolbar is useful in making changes to the format of selected text. The Format toolbar contains the following icons:

- ▨ *Font*: Clicking the font icon displays a scrolling list of all the fonts currently installed on your Mac.

- ▨ *Font Size*: Whether you want to write your e-mail in 9-point (1/6th of an inch tall) Helvetica or 288-point (4 inches tall) Copperplate, there are many font sizes available for you.

- ▨ *Color*: Sometimes it's important to call a reader's attention to a certain phrase in an e-mail, and color is a good way to do that. Clicking the color swatch (indicated by a black square) displays a grid of 144 tiny colored squares to choose from. Clicking any one of the squares changes the color of the text.

- ▨ *Bold/Italic/Underline*: Another way to emphasize text is to put it in **bold** or *italics* or underline it.

- ▨ *Left/Center/Right Justification*: This book is left justified, as are most English-language documents. There are situations where you may want to center text, most likely for a header at the top of an e-mail. You might also want to right-justify text in certain cases. The left, center, and right justification icons rejustify text with a click.

- ▨ *Lists*: This button is used to insert bulleted or numbered lists in the body of your e-mail.

- ▨ *Indent/Outdent*: This list has been indented slightly from the left margin, and the indent button does the same to your message text. When you've typed an indented paragraph and need to start at the left margin again, click Outdent.

Reading Mail Messages

So far in this chapter, I've introduced you to many of the new tools that are at your command in Lion Mail. Now I'll talk about three new features designed to make reading e-mails much easier: redesigned message headers, Conversations, and hidden quoted text.

Redesigned Message Headers

When new messages appear in your mailboxes, you are notified audibly, and the Mail icon in the Dock displays a small red counter with the number of unread messages. Looking at the list of messages in a mailbox, those unread messages are indicated by a small blue dot on the left side of the message.

By default, your messages appear on the right side of the Mail window with only three lines of information: the name and e-mail address of the sender, the subject of the message, and the date and time the message was received (Figure 7–15, top). The idea here is to give you the important information you need without cluttering up the top of the message.

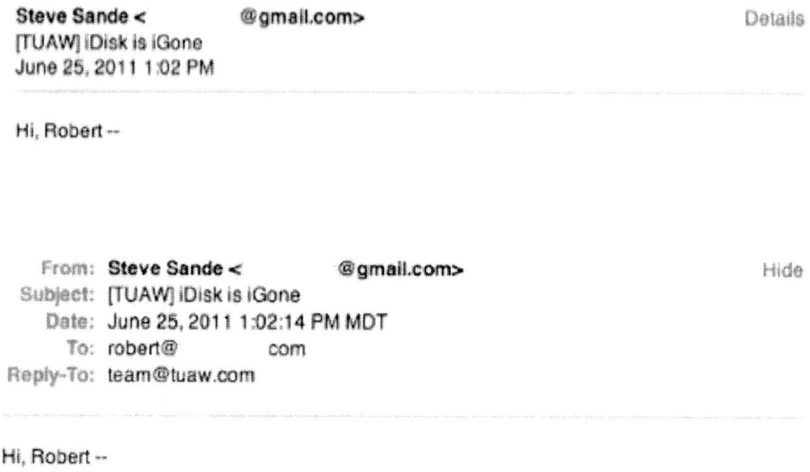

Steve Sande <   @gmail.com>   Details
[TUAW] iDisk is iGone
June 25, 2011 1:02 PM

Hi, Robert --

     From: **Steve Sande <**   @gmail.com>   Hide
    Subject: [TUAW] iDisk is iGone
      Date: June 25, 2011 1:02:14 PM MDT
        To: robert@   com
Reply-To: team@tuaw.com

Hi, Robert --

Figure 7–15. *A message header with details hidden (top) and displayed (bottom)*

There's a light blue link marked Details on the right side of the message. Clicking that link displays more information in the message header (Figure 7–15, bottom), including the person or group it was sent to and the reply-to address (where replies will be sent). As mentioned earlier in this chapter, adding the All Headers button to the Mailbox toolbar and clicking it shows even more information.

Conversations

When I'm working on a project, I often have e-mail "conversations" with my co-workers. Someone starts by sending an e-mail, and I click Reply All and send my views on the topic. Others do the same, and pretty soon we have a long e-mail message containing everyone's replies. It's a mess and quite difficult to work backward through the chain of e-mails.

Lion Mail has a new feature called Conversations to help organize these related messages. With Conversations, those related messages are automatically grouped together in your inbox (Figure 7–16). Each message is numbered so that you know exactly which e-mail was first and which replies followed.

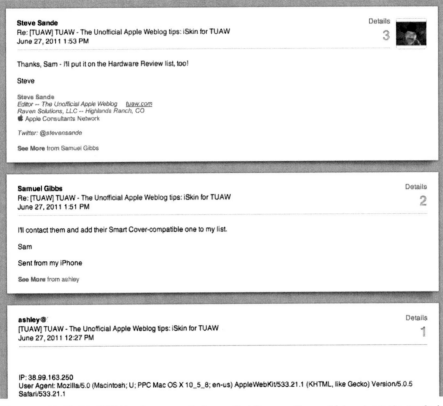

Figure 7–16. *Mail in OS X Lion has a new feature called Conversations, which reduces the confusing tangle of messages and replies in long threads of e-mails.*

There's another clue that Conversations is at work organizing those threads of messages. In the list view of e-mail messages for a specific mailbox, a small number appears with an arrow pointing to the message body at right (Figure 7–17). This number denotes the number of related messages that are in the conversation.

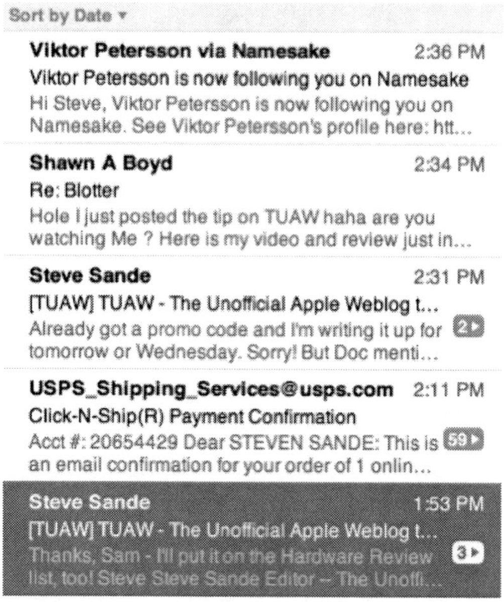

Figure 7–17. *The numbers on the right side of the bottom three messages shown in this image indicate the number of related messages that have been grouped into a conversation.*

If for some reason you do not like the way that Conversations organizes related messages, disabling the feature is a simple matter of deselecting **View ➤ Organize by Conversation**.

Hidden Quoted Text

One way that Lion Mail makes conversations easy to read is that it automatically hides quoted text that appears repeatedly in replies so that only the new parts of the e-mail discussion are visible. What if you don't want to scroll down through all the individual messages in a thread and would actually like to view all of the replies in one message?

In Conversations, there will always be a blue link that says "See More from [sender's name]" (Figure 7–18).

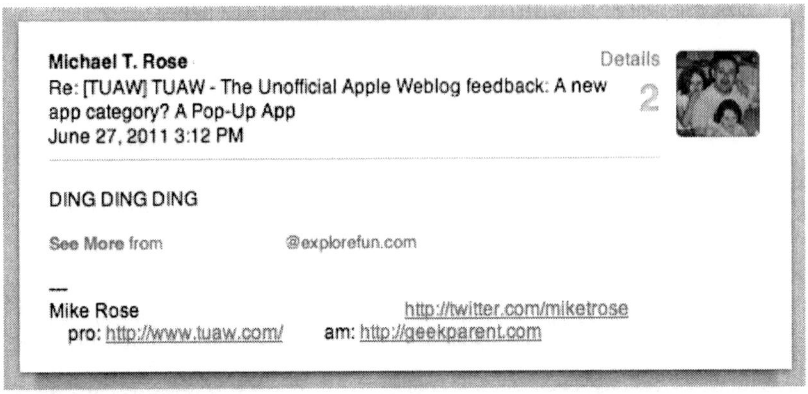

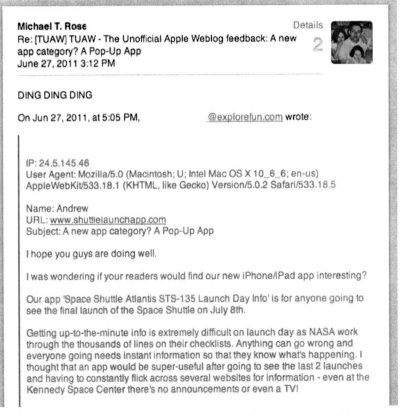

Figure 7–18. *For the Conversations feature, clicking the "See More from" link displays the original quoted text in the series of e-mails.*

When that link is clicked, the original quoted text, no matter how many levels deep the Conversation goes, is displayed (Figure 7–19).

Figure 7–19. *The original quoted text is now visible in this part of a conversation.*

If you no longer want to view the quoted text in the conversation, just click another e-mail message and come back to this message later. The quoted text is gone, replaced by the familiar "See More from" link.

Searching Mailboxes

Some of us have a hard time getting rid of e-mail messages.

If you look closely at Figure 7–6, you'll notice that one of my e-mail accounts has more than 39,000 messages in it. I keep a lot of e-mail that I receive and respond to because I often refer to old messages for stories that I write for The Unofficial Apple Weblog. One of my complaints about Mail in the past is that it did a fairly poor job of helping me search through those thousands of messages to find a specific one.

With Mac OS X Lion, Apple added a much more powerful search engine to Mail. In this portion of the chapter, I'll explain search suggestions, search tokens, and how Mail now searches attached files.

Search Suggestions

All searches of Mail messages begin in the same place: the Search field in the Mail toolbar. It has the same magnifying glass icon that you may be familiar with from using the Mac OS X search tool, Spotlight.

To begin searching for a specific name or word, start typing into the Search field. As you type, suggestions dynamically appear in a drop-down list. The suggestions are classified into different groups such as "Search messages," People, Subjects, Status, and Dates.

In Figure 7–20, I'm searching for messages containing the last name of one of the authors of this book: Grothaus. The more letters of Mike's name I type into the Search field, the more focused the search becomes. When I'm done typing his name, a list of suggestions is neatly displayed below the Search field, such as messages containing the letters *grothaus*, Mike's full name, different subjects containing Mike's last name, and files attached to messages. One of these suggestions may be just what you're looking for; to use the suggestion, just select it from the drop-down menu.

Several other things happen after you type something into the Search field. First, if you do not select an item from the drop-down menu, the number of items that match your search is displayed just below the Search field. Next, the mailbox that you are currently searching is highlighted in blue in the Favorites bar. By default, the Inbox folder is searched, but you can also select All to look at all mailboxes including Drafts and Sent messages.

For searches that might be used frequently, there's also a Save button that appears on the far right side of the Favorites bar. The function of this button is to save the search as a smart mailbox for future reference so that any incoming e-mail that satisfies the search criteria is automatically displayed in that mailbox.

Figure 7–20. *Search suggestions are displayed in a drop-down menu below the Search field.*

Search Tokens

Search tokens are a new feature of Lion Mail that narrow search results with a single click. Whenever you search for a person, a phrase, or a specific subject, the search can be displayed as a clickable token in the Search field (Figure 7–21).

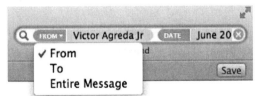

Figure 7–21. *Search tokens appear in the Search field when you type in a person's name, a phrase, or some specific label and then select that item from the drop-down menu.*

To turn a search phrase into a search token, select that item from the drop-down menu that appears. For names, clicking the left side of the token displays a small drop-down menu that provides a way to narrow the search down to messages from or to a specific person or who are referenced somewhere in a message. The drop-down menus vary from token to token, so if you see a small downward-pointing arrow on a token, be sure to click it to see what search options are provided.

The power of search tokens is that they can be combined to create very focused searches of the mailbox. In Figure 7–21, for example, I was searching for all e-mails from a particular person that were sent in June 2011. If I wanted to widen my search, I could change the date token to 2011. To make the search more restrictive, I could add a third token to add a subject label of "podcast."

While performing research for this book, I was able to find a number of different token types:

- ▨ Name: Drop-down menu displays From, To, Entire Message
- ▨ Date
- ▨ Attachment
- ▨ Subject: Drop-down menu displays Subject, Entire Message

For those readers who also use iOS devices (iPhone, iPod touch, iPad), search tokens are coming your way in the iOS 5 Mail app in the autumn of 2011.

Search Attachments

As you saw in the previous section about search tokens, it's now possible to display only messages that have files attached. One other new feature is the ability to search attachments by file name and by content.

In the example shown in Figure 7–22, a search has been performed with the attachment search token for any message with an attachment that contains the word *Cardinals*.

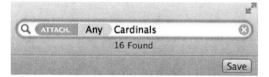

Figure 7–22. *A sample search using a search token for messages with attachments that contain the word* Cardinals

The result of this search consisted of 16 messages with an attached Microsoft Excel spreadsheet that contained the name of the St. Louis Cardinals, so Mail is now able to search the content of a number of different file formats. As noted previously, additional search tokens could be used to focus the search even more, such as to the present year or from a specific person.

Additional Lion Mail Features

There are several more new features in Lion Mail that you should know about. Data detectors have been available for some time, allowing Mail users to click a physical address or phone number to add it to Address Book or to click a date and time in the body of a message to add an appointment to iCal. Now Apple has added several new twists to data detectors to make them even more useful.

Mail also adds a way to view web pages without leaving the Mail app and provides support for Microsoft Exchange 2010.

The Power of Data Detectors

When you receive an e-mail message containing several different types of data, such as a date or time, an address, or a hypertext link, in the body of the text, Mail highlights that data with a gray box with a small arrow signifying the presence of a drop-down menu (Figure 7–23).

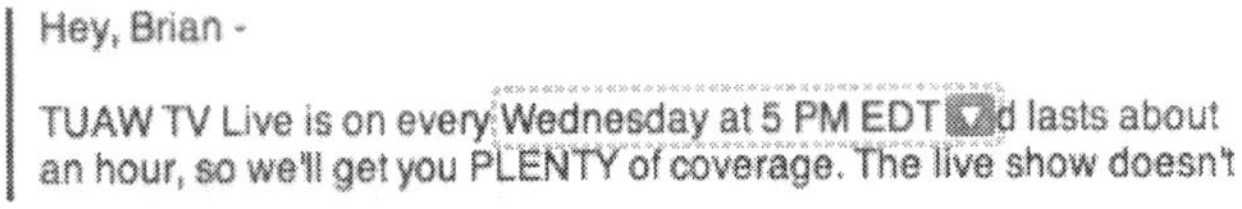

Hey, Brian -

TUAW TV Live is on every Wednesday at 5 PM EDT and lasts about an hour, so we'll get you PLENTY of coverage. The live show doesn't

Figure 7–23. *Data detectors, as shown in this image, are nothing new in the Mail application. What you can do with data detectors is completely different.*

Now in Mail, clicking the drop-down arrow for this date and time data detector displays a Quick Look (see Chapter 1) of your calendar for the day (Figure 7–24).

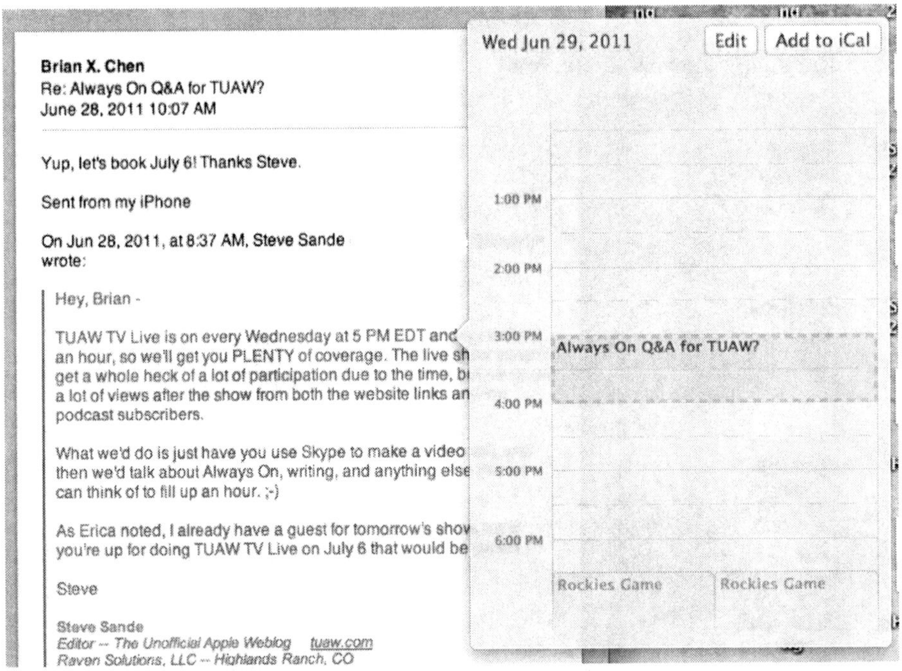

Figure 7–24. *The data detector for Mail displays a mini-calendar showing the date and time of the appointment in the text of the message*

That calendar is indicative of what is actually in iCal for that date and time. Mail is even smart enough to make the change from Eastern Daylight Time to Mountain Daylight Time. To add this appointment to iCal, there's an Add to iCal button in the upper-right corner of the Quick Look of the calendar.

If the information was somehow interpreted incorrectly by the data detector, clicking the Edit button brings up the standard iCal edit dialog, where you can change the length of the appointment, the start time, the end time, the calendar the appointment belongs on, and the desired alerts.

Viewing Hyperlinks in Mail

Another data detector has been added to Mail. Previously, clicking an Internet address launched your default web browser and opened the link. Now all hyperlinks in Mail messages appear as data detector links as well, featuring the gray box and drop-down disclosure triangle. Clicking the disclosure triangle opens a Quick Look representation of the web site at the Internet address (Figure 7–25).

Figure 7–25. *Clicking the disclosure triangle for the hyperlink data detector brings up a Quick Look of the web page.*

This feature is helpful because you no longer need to open a web browser to see where an embedded hyperlink in a Mail message is pointing. If you decide that it would be advantageous to view the original page, click the Open with Safari button, and the link is transferred to Apple's web browser.

Exchange 2010 Support

Up to this point, Mail, iCal, and Address Book have not supported the latest version of the Microsoft Exchange 2010 enterprise mail server. As a result, Mac users on networks using Microsoft Exchange 2010 have been required to install and use Microsoft Office 2011, which includes the Outlook for Mac messaging client.

Mail under Mac OS X Lion works well with Microsoft Exchange 2010, as do iCal and Address Book. One feature that Mac users have been missing for quite a long time is the ability to set their vacation out-of-office messages from Mail. With Lion, that's finally possible.

Summary

One of the most widely used applications on any Mac is Mail, and with the introduction of Mac OS X Lion, the app gains new ease-of-use and powerful features. Some of the major points to remember from this chapter are as follows:

- The process of setting up Mail accounts is now more automated than before, and you'll now be asked whether you want to set up web mail accounts in Mail when you visit those accounts using Apple's Safari web browser.

- The Mail user interface has changed, with new additions to the Mail toolbar, a new Favorites toolbar, and customizable Message and Format toolbars.

- Message headers now show minimal information by default but can be expanded to show additional information about the sender, the recipients, and to whom replies will be sent.

- Conversations is a new view that simplifies reading "back and forth" e-mail threads by hiding repeated text strings and putting all responses into a separate pane in the message.

- Searching e-mail messages is faster and more focused with the new search tokens and the ability to search inside attachments.

Adding appointments to iCal and viewing web sites noted in e-mail messages is now easier with the help of more powerful data detectors and an in-app Quick Look function.

Chapter 8

Organizing Your Life with Address Book and iCal

Let's face it, today we have a lot of information to keep track of. We have work contacts, family, and friends we need to communicate with, bills we need to pay, and gatherings we need to arrange. Keeping track of all we need to do and how to contact the people involved can be a real mess. Luckily, Apple has two excellent apps built into Lion that help us keep track of the people we know and the events we need to attend. In this chapter, we'll look at Address Book and iCal and learn how each app can make your life easier.

> **NOTE:** In this chapter, you'll learn how to create new contacts and events in Address Book and iCal. To learn how to easily set up syncing with your existing contacts and calendars in Gmail or Yahoo! Mail, see Chapter 7.

Address Book

Address Book is quite simply an app that is an electronic version of old physical address books. In it you can keep track of your contacts, arrange them into groups, and even get quick access to maps of where they live. To launch the Address Book app, just click its icon (Figure 8–1) in the Dock or on the Launchpad or double-click its icon in the Applications folder.

Figure 8–1. *The Address Book icon looks like a book with a big @ symbol on it.*

When you launch Address Book, an address book appears on your screen as shown in Figure 8–2. Note that the address book in the figure is already filled with both groups and contacts. If you haven't added any contacts to your address book, its pages will be blank.

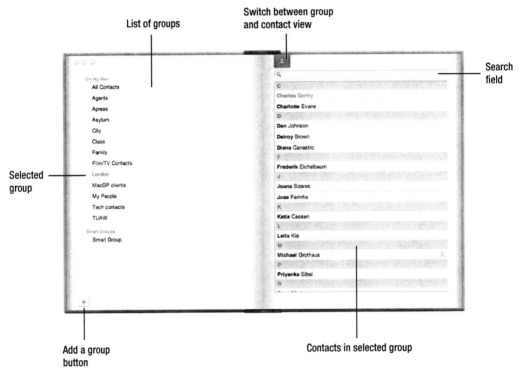

Figure 8–2. *A full address book*

As you can see in Figure 8–2, the address book has many components. Here is a breakdown of what they do:

- *List of groups*: This is the left-side page of the address book. On this page you can see both regular and smart groups. Both will be covered later in this chapter.

- *Selected group*: A selected group appears in blue. All the contacts in a selected group appear on the right-side page.

- *Add a group button*: This + button allows you to add a regular group.

- *Contacts in a selected group*: All the contacts in a selected group appear on the right-side page.

- *Search field*: Enter text here to search your address book.

- *Switch between group and contact view*: Clicking this red ribbon allows you to enter the group so that you can see individual contact cards.

In Figure 8–3 you'll see what the address book looks like when you are inside a group and viewing an individual's contact information. To enter a group, simply double-click the group's name or select the group by clicking it once and then click the red ribbon near the "binding" of the address book.

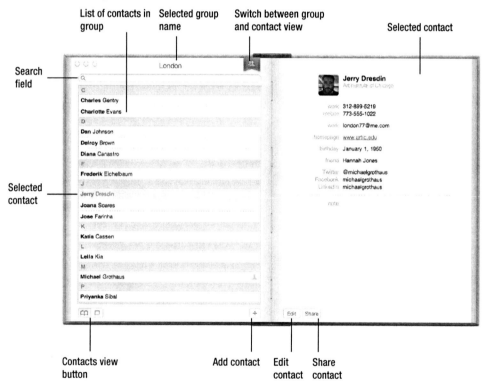

Figure 8–3. Viewing an individual's contact information

Once you have selected the group you want to see the contents of, the address book page will flip over and the address book will display all the contacts of the group on the left and the selected contact on the right. Here are the other elements of the address book when viewing the contents of a group:

- *Selected group name*: This tells you the name of the group you are in.

- *List of contacts in group*: This displays all the contacts in a group.

- *Search field*: Enter text to search through the group.

- *Selected contact*: The contact you have selected will appear in blue lettering.

- *Contacts view button*: Click this button to switch back and forth between single contact view and group contacts view. Single contact view will display the address book as a single page showing only the selected contact's card and not a list of others in that contact's group.

- *Add contact*: This + button allows you to add a contact.

- *Edit contact*: This button allows you to edit an existing contact.

- *Share contact*: This button allows you to quickly e-mail the contact's vCard to someone.

- *Selected contact*: On the right-side page, you'll see the selected contact's information. The information displayed can be detailed or just a single e-mail address. Adding information to a contact's card will be covered later in this chapter.

- *Switch between group and contact view*: Clicking this red ribbon allows you to enter the group so you can see individual contact cards.

Creating a New Contact

Now that you understand the layout of the address book, let's take a look at creating a new contact. You can create as many contacts as you want. To get started, make sure you are inside a group. If you don't have any groups, double-click the All Contacts group. It will always be listed by default.

To create a contact, follow these steps:

1. Click the + button at the bottom of the contacts list (see Figure 8–3). Alternatively, you can select **File ➤ New Card**.

2. On the new contact card that appears (Figure 8–4), fill in any of the fields you want, including name, company, phone numbers, e-mails, and addresses.

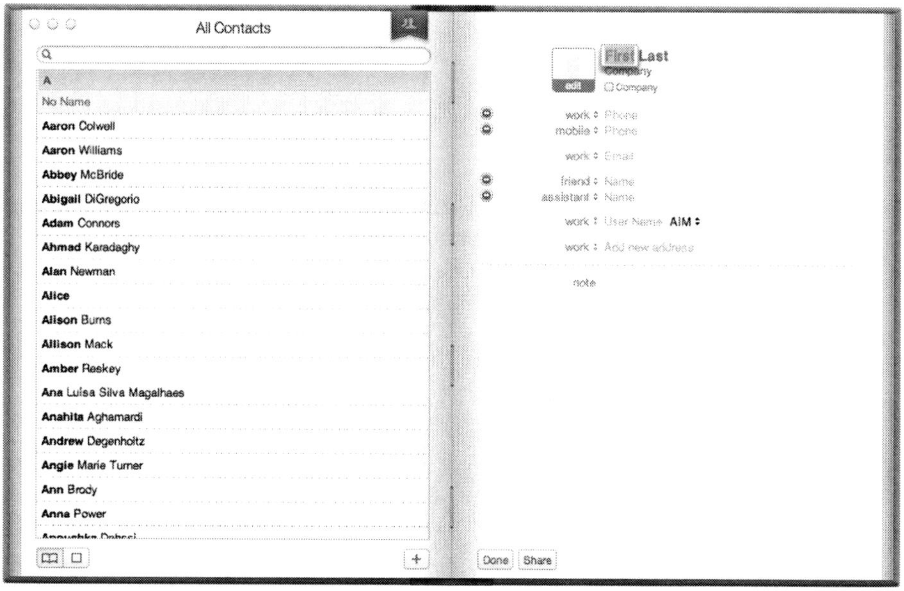

Figure 8–4. Creating a new contact

3. (Optional) You can add additional fields on the card by selecting **Card ➤ Add Field** from the menu bar and then selecting the type of field you want to add. As you can see in Figure 8–5, the options are numerous.

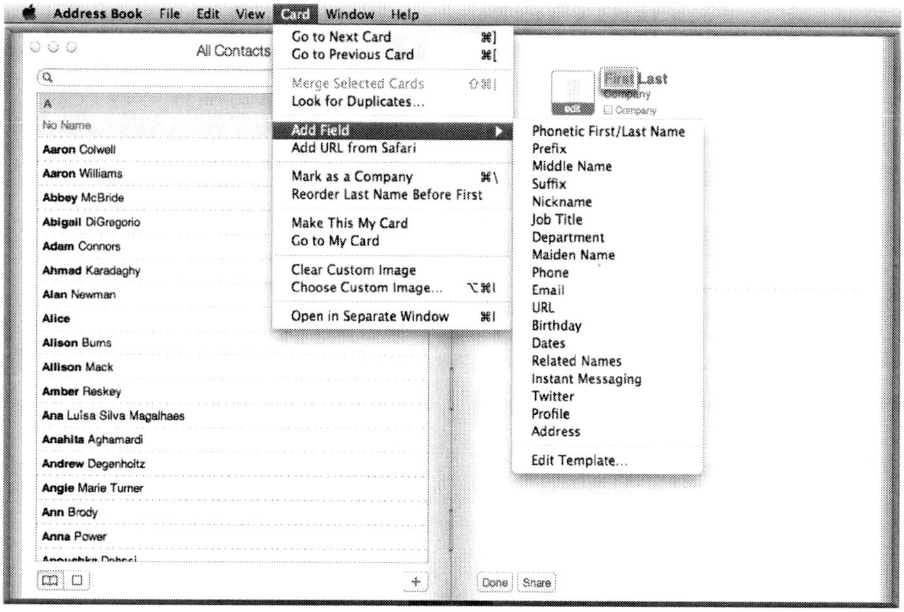

Figure 8–5. Adding additional fields to a contact's card

4. When you finish adding all the fields and information to the card, click the Done button.

Creating Groups

You can create two types of groups in Address Book: regular and smart. A regular group is one you add contacts to manually. You might have a group called Family, for example, or even Fun People. A smart group is one that is automatically updated with contacts based on certain criteria, say geographical location, or a group can be based on people who all work at the same company.

Regular Groups

Let's get started with creating a regular group. You can think of a regular group as a drawer that you can add or remove your contact's business cards at will.

To create a regular group, follow these steps:

1. From the groups page (see Figure 8–2), click the Add a Group button.

2. In the field that appears in your groups list, type in the name of your group. In Figure 8–6 you can see I've named the group New Group. Press the Return key on your keyboard, and the group will be created. Groups are automatically sorted alphabetically.

Figure 8–6. Creating a new group

After you've created a regular group, it remains empty until you manually add a contact to it. You can add as many or as few as you want, and the same contact can be in multiple groups.

To add contacts to a regular group, follow these steps:

1. Select the All Contacts group so that you have a full list of all your contacts.

2. Now, select any contact you want and drag that contact's card on top of the group to which you want to add it. You can select more than one contact at a time by Command-clicking each name. In Figure 8–7 you can see I am adding six contacts to the New Group group.

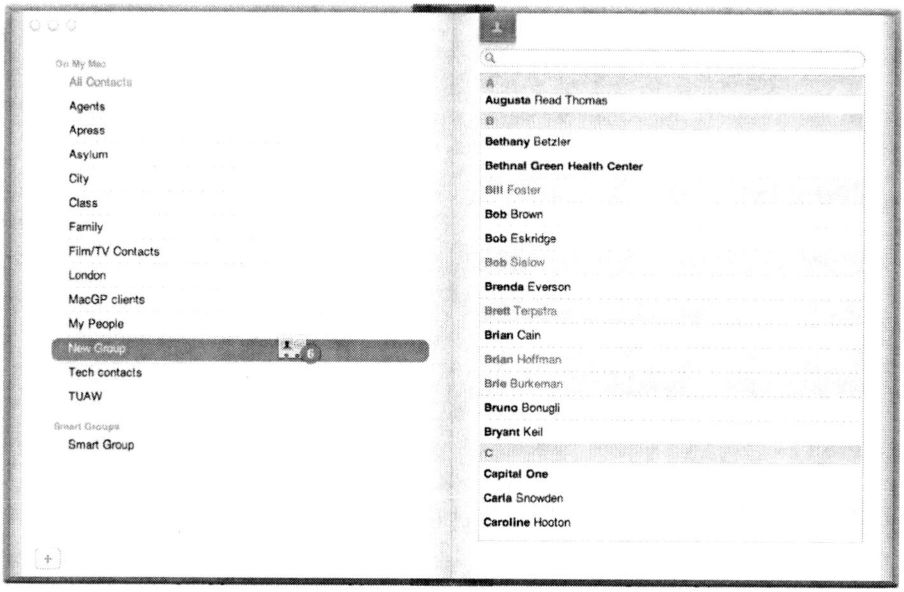

Figure 8–7. Adding contacts to a regular group

If you want to remove a contact from a group, select the group the contact is in. Then follow these steps:

1. Click the name of the contact.

2. Press the Delete key on your keyboard.

3. In the dialog box that appears (Figure 8–8), click Remove from Group. The contact will remain in your address book and in any other groups the contact is in. The contact will be removed only from the selected group.

4. To delete the contact from Address Book entirely, click Delete. The contact and all the related information will be deleted from your address book.

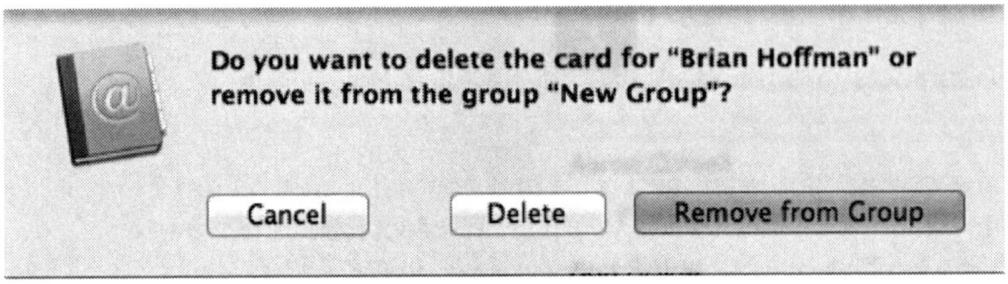

Do you want to delete the card for "Brian Hoffman" or remove it from the group "New Group"?

Cancel   Delete   Remove from Group

Figure 8–8. Removing a contact from a regular group

Smart Groups

There may be instances where you don't want to manually create groups. For example, you might want to quickly organize all the people who work at a specific company into one group or put all the people who live in a certain city into one group. If you have hundreds of contacts, that could be a big task. Thankfully, smart groups allow you to create groups based on criteria you define.

To create a smart group, follow these steps:

1. Choose File ➤ New Smart Group from Address Book's menu bar.

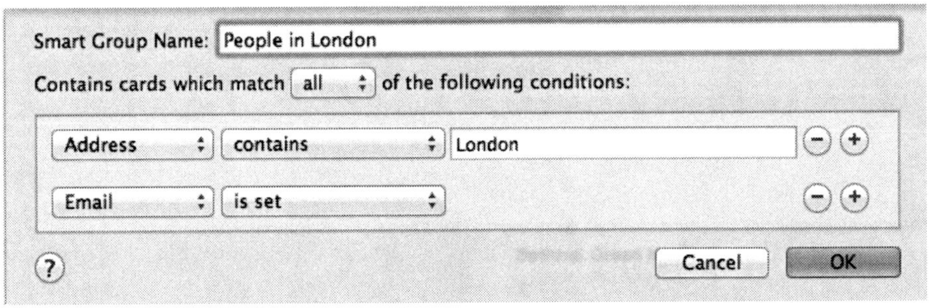

Smart Group Name: People in London

Contains cards which match all ⁑ of the following conditions:

Address ⁑   contains ⁑   London ⊖ ⊕

Email ⁑   is set ⁑   ⊖ ⊕

(?)   Cancel   OK

Figure 8–9. The smart group creation dialog box

2. From the smart group dialog box (Figure 8–9), enter the name of the smart group.

3. Choose a filter from the first drop-down menu. A filter is a specific criterion that must be matched for Address Book to determine whether the particular item fits into one of your smart groups. A filter can be a keyword, a birth date, whether the contact has an e-mail address, or even the area code of a phone number.

4. Once you have selected a filter, choose a verb from the verb list. Common verbs in this list are "Is," "Is not," and "Contains."

5. Finally, enter a requirement in the conditions list, such as a company name or a specific city.

6. To add additional criteria, click the + button and choose additional criteria based on whatever you want. Then select whether any or all of the multiple criteria must be met. When you are done, click OK, and the smart group will appear under the groups list in Address Book under the Smart Groups label.

In Figure 8–10 I've set up a simple smart group named People in London with the criteria: City contains London.

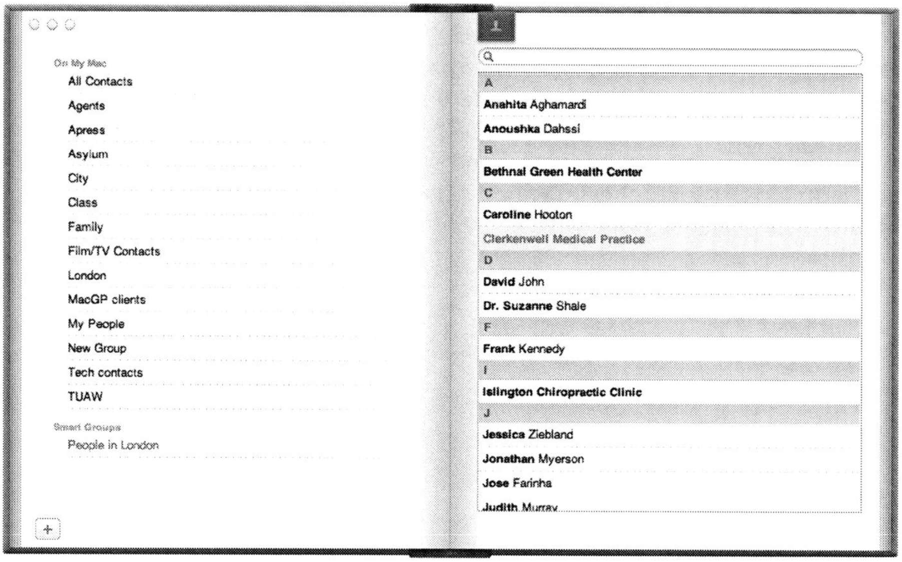

Figure 8–10. A smart group containing all the cards with "London" in the address field

> **NOTE:** You cannot manually remove contacts from a smart group. To remove a contact, you must change the smart group parameters. To do this, right-click the smart group's name and click Edit Smart Group. Also, if you remove the information from an individual's vCard that matched the parameter, they will be removed from the smart group. For example, if David is in the smart group London because an address with London in it is the smart group's paramiter and you change David's address to somewhere in Chicago, David's vCard will automatically be removed from the smart group because it doesn't match anymore.

Some Tips and Tricks for Using Address Book

Believe it or not, like with most things in Mac OS X Lion, an entire book could be written about Address Book. I could go into everything you can do with Address Book here, but then there wouldn't be room for anything about iCal, which is an incredible application in its own right. Earlier I covered the basics of what you need to know to get the most out of Address Book, but before we move on, I wanted to touch on a few cool tips and tricks you can do with Address Book.

Add a Picture to Your Contacts

Adding a picture to your contacts is cool for many reasons. When you get an e-mail from the contact, their picture will show up in the e-mail's header in Mail. Also, their picture will show up in iChat and FaceTime and other places throughout the OS where you interact with them. To add a picture, click the edit button on the contact's card and then drag and drop a picture into the small box labeled "edit." You can then resize and crop the photo to your liking (Figure 8–11).

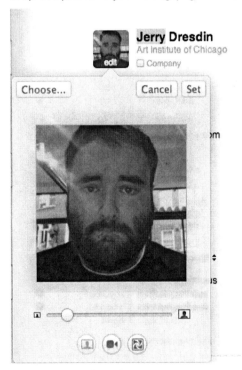

Figure 8–11. Adding a picture to a contact

View Phone Numbers in Large Type

Yeah, this sounds kind of strange at first, but it's one of the most helpful features of Address Book. It's irritating when you need to squint to read someone's phone number in your address book. Instead, just click the label by a contact's phone number (such as "home" or "work") and select Show in Large Type from the context menu. The contact's phone number then appears in giant type across your screen (Figure 8–12), which makes it easy to read when dialing the contact's number on a landline.

Figure 8–12. Viewing a phone number full-screen

Tweet Someone from Your Address Book

Twitter is the hottest thing going nowadays, and Apple has baked some Twitter functionality right into Address Book. If you've added your contact's Twitter handle, all you need to do is click the Twitter label on their card and click Send Tweet from the contextual menu (Figure 8–13). Your web browser will open to Twitter.com with a new tweet all ready to go, even adding an @mention to your contact.

Figure 8–13. Sending a tweet via Address Book

View a Google Map of Your Contact's Address

For any contact that has an address, simply click the "address" label and click Map this Address on the contextual menu. Your web browser will open displaying the address on Google Maps.

Some pretty cool tips, huh? Address Book—and all of Lion actually—is full of neat little tricks like the previous ones. Don't be afraid to click things, because you never know what cool features you might find!

Working with iCal

Apple has redesigned the look of iCal in Lion. Gone is the old brushed metal industrial interface. In its place is a calendar app that looks remarkably like an old Day-Timer. To launch the iCal, just single-click its icon (Figure 8–14) in the Dock or on the Launchpad or double-click its icon in the Applications folder. The day and date are current and update every day in iCal's icon in the Dock and Launchpad. Its icon in the Applications folder, however, will always show July 17.

Figure 8–14. The iCal icon

Switching Calendar Views

iCal offers four views to navigate your appointments: Day, Week, Month, and Year. To move between the different views, click the Day/Week/Month/Year tabs in iCal's header (Figure 8–15). Let's take a look at each view.

Day View

The view shown in Figure 8–15 is the Day view, which on the right displays an hour-by-hour listing of what's going to happen during the current day. See that pinhead with the line across from it at about 7:45 p.m.? That indicates the current time so you can see at a glance how much time you have until your next appointment.

On the top of iCal in Day view, there's a handy month calendar that lets you jump to any day just by clicking its date. On the left side of Day view you'll see a list of all the appointments scheduled that year. Scroll through the list and then click an appointment to display the entire day on the right side.

Figure 8–15. iCal's Day view

To move forward a day at a time in this virtual appointment book view, click the right arrow at the top of the page. Moving to the previous day just requires clicking the left arrow.

If all of this moving around in iCal causes you to get lost, there's a Today button in between the next and previous day buttons that allows you to quickly jump to the current day.

Week View

The Week view (Figure 8–16) is helpful in mapping out what tasks need to be accomplished during a specific week. Any items listed at the top of the calendar are all-day events, while colored boxes denote the time and duration of your meetings. The days of the week are listed across the top, with the hours of the day on the left side. To scroll earlier or later in the day (by default the calendar shows only 12 hours of each day at a time), use your mouse or trackpad to scroll up or down.

> **NOTE:** You can change the total number of viewable hours in a day by choosing iCal ➤ Preferences from the menu bar and then clicking the General tab. You can select to show anywhere between six and twenty-four hours of each day at a time.

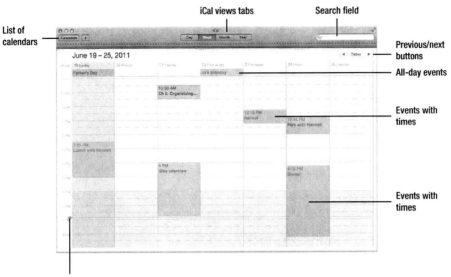

Figure 8–16. iCal's Week view

Month View

The Month view (Figure 8–17) provides the look of those "Month at a Glance"–style calendars that have been sold for years as desk pads. Here, every appointment during the month is displayed on its particular day.

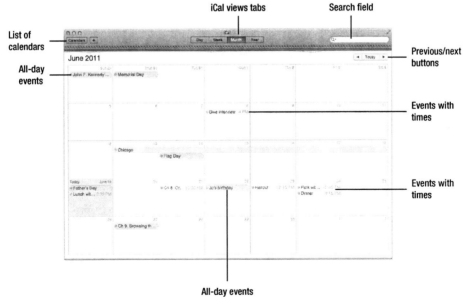

Figure 8–17. iCal's Month view

Year View

The Year view (Figure 8–18) gives you a heat map of all your events in the selected year. The color of the square tells you how many events you have on that day. White date squares have no events scheduled. Yellow date squares have one event. Orange date squares have two events. And red date squares have three or more events.

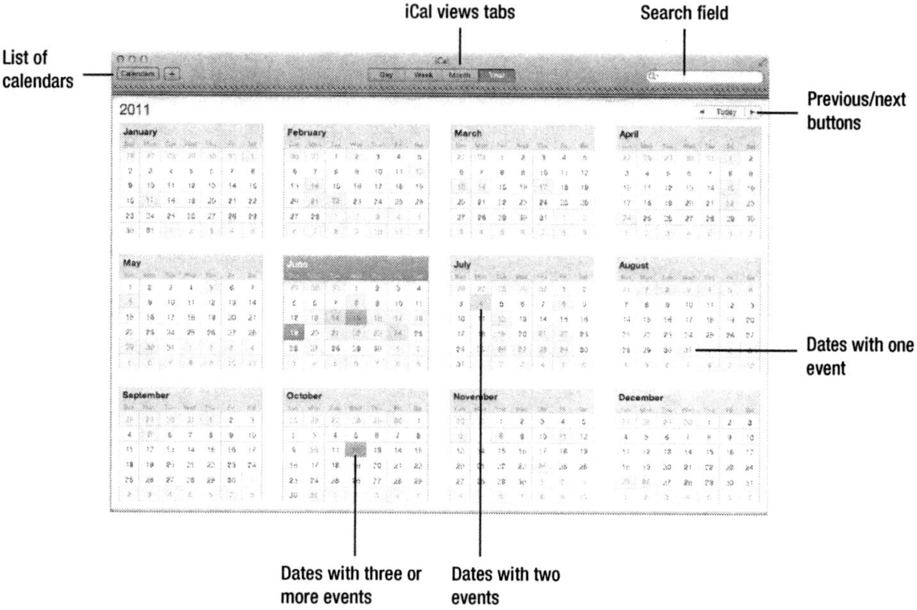

Figure 8–18. *iCal's Year view is a color-coded heat map.*

The Today Button

Clicking the Today button in any view automatically jumps you back to the display for the current day but preserves whichever view you are using. So, you'll see the current month for Month view or a recentered list in Day view.

The Calendars Button

The Calendars button (Figure 8–19) at the top left of iCal's header allows you to choose which calendars you want to show. A calendar with a check mark will show events in any of the calendar views. To hide a certain calendar, tap it to uncheck it.

Figure 8–19. The Calendars button and pop-up menu

Creating Calendars

By default iCal has two calendars: home and work. They are distinguished by different colors. However, you can add an unlimited number of calendars in iCal. You can even subscribe to calendars from the Web. Creating different calendars for different events helps you organize your event and easily tell what kind of event it is by looking at the color of it in any calendar view.

To create a calendar, follow these steps:

1. Choose File ➤ New Calendar ➤ On My Mac from iCal's menu bar.

2. In the pop-up menu that appears below the Calendars button, enter the name of your new calendar (such as "Writing project"). The calendar will be assigned a color that is not in use by other calendars. You're done after this step if you're happy with the color of the calendar. Now any event you add can be added to the new calendar. However, if you want to change or add any details to a calendar, continue with the following steps.

3. Right-click the calendar name in the pop-up menu (Figure 8–19) and choose Get Info.

4. From the drop-down menu that appears (Figure 8–20) you can rename the calendar, change the color associated with the calendar, and add a description to the calendar.

5. Click OK when you are done making your changes.

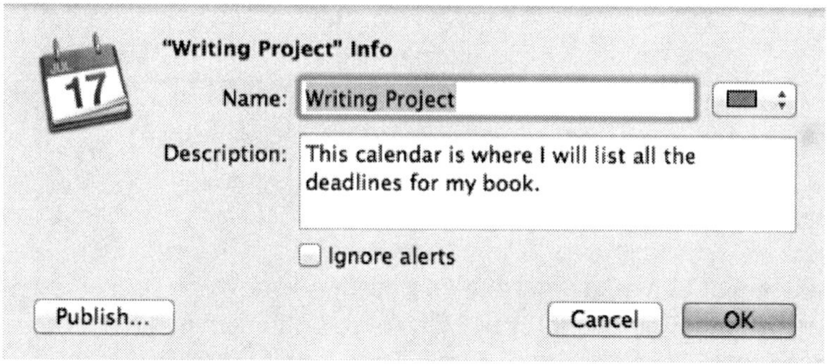

Figure 8–20. Calendar settings

Grouping Calendars

Sometimes you may have multiple calendars that you may want to group together. For example, you may have multiple project calendars that you all want to put into a master "work" calendar. Creating a calendar group like this allows you to see all events for a group of calendars in one place.

To create a calendar group, follow these steps:

1. Choose File ➤ New Calendar Group from iCal's menu bar.

2. Enter the name of the group in the pop-up calendar menu.

3. Drag other calendars to the group's name in the pop-up list.

Creating Events

Adding events to iCal is probably the number-one thing you will do with the app. You can add events to iCal no matter what calendar view you are in. I like working in Month view, so I'll describe how to add events there. Just remember that the steps to adding events in any other view are the same.

To create an event, follow these steps:

1. Double-click the date square (if in Month view) to which you want to add the event. If you are in Week or Day view, double-click the day to which you want to add the event.

2. When the new event item appears (Figure 8–21), enter a name for it.

Figure 8–21. Adding a new event

3. Double-click the new event to see its information pop-up window. To change or add information to the event, click Edit. As you can see in Figure 8–22, you have many settings for an event. Let's look at them next.

Setting the Details of an Event

An event's information window shows you myriad details about the event. It's also where you can add more details. Simply click the Edit button in the information pop-up window after you open an existing event. Then you can update the event name and/or location, and you can specify when the event starts and ends, whether it repeats, who is invited to your event from your contact list, when to play an alert to notify you about the event, and what calendar the event should appear on (Work, Bills, and so on). You can also set your availability to "busy" or "free." In addition, you can add a note about the event, an attachment, and a web URL. Customize any or all of these options, as described in the following sections, and then click Done to finish adding the event.

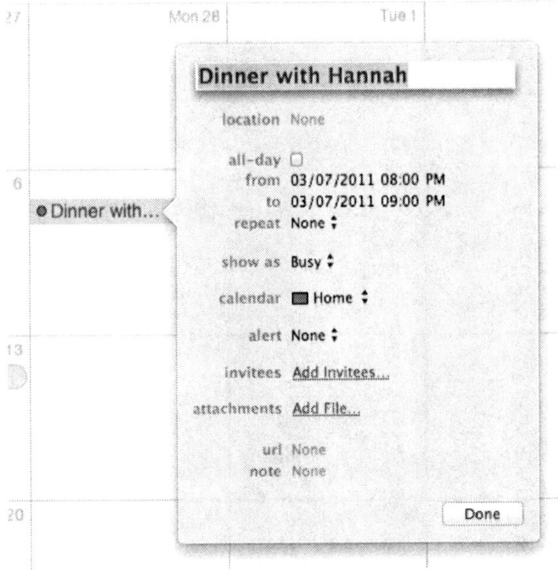

Figure 8–22. An event's information settings

Updating an Event Name or Location

Click the event name or location line to update the event's name and location text. You can enter any text you want.

Setting the Event Start and End Dates and Times

In the From/To fields, enter the date and time the event begins and ends. You can also manually drag the event's bubble in Day or Week view to adjust the time of the event.

Setting a Repeating Event

When your event repeats, you can select from a standard list that defines how often: Every Day, Every Week, Every Month, or Every Year. To make this happen, click the drop-down menu by the Repeat label and select a repetition interval. Select Custom to customize when the event repeats (such as on the 17th of every month).

Setting Your Availability

To set you availability for an event, click the drop-down menu next to the "show as" label. Set your availability to "busy" or "free" during any specific event. This is handy when you have an event on your calendar that lists, for example, a child's field trip. The child would be busy during this event, but you would be free to attend other events.

Assigning Event to a Specific Calendar

You can select which calendar the event is assigned to by clicking the Calendar drop-down menu and then selecting which calendar the event belongs on from the list.

Adding Alerts

You can add event alerts to notify you when an event is coming due. For example, you may want a one-hour notice for those dental appointments and a two-day notice for your wedding anniversary. iCal provides a nice selection of options. These include messages with sounds, e-mails, automatic file opening, and more. Click the drop-down menu by the Alert label to set an event alert.

Once you've added your first alert, iCal offers you the option to add a second one. This allows you to remind yourself both a day before an event and a few minutes before you need to leave. This is a particularly useful feature for people who need extra reminders.

Adding Invitees

You can mark the people who will be at an event by adding their name to the Invitees list. Click the Add Invitees link by the Invitees label and then start typing the name of the people who will be at the event. After each name, click Return, and then start typing the next name. Names will autofill for the contacts already in your address book.

Adding Attachments

You can add attachments to iCal events. Attachments can be any file on your computer. For example, you can attach a PDF of the upcoming sale at your local Apple Store. Click the Add File link by the Attachments label and then select the file you want to attach from Finder. Now any important file related to your event is easily accessible just by clicking it in the iCal event.

Adding URLs

You can add URLs to events, such as `www.apple.com`. Adding a URL to an event is handy when the event has some online connection. For example, your child's baseball league might have a web site with updated news. Adding the web site's URL to the event is a great way to remind yourself to check their web site for the latest information or to see whether any games have been canceled.

Adding Notes

You can also add a free-form note to your event. Click the Notes field at the bottom of event information window to enter any text you like, such as phone numbers or directions.

Editing and Removing Events

After you've set your parameters for events, you can always go back and change them. Simply double-click any event in any view (Day, Week, Month, or Year) to edit it. This opens the event's information window where you can edit any of the settings described previously.

To remove any event, select it by clicking it once and then press the Delete key on your keyboard. The event will be deleted immediately.

Some Cool iCal Tips and Tricks

This section describes some of the advanced iCal tips and tricks you might find interesting. iCal has many other hidden features like these (enough to fill a whole book), but these are some of the coolest ones.

Subscribing to Calendars

You aren't limited to using only the calendars you create in iCal. You can subscribe to thousands of calendars on the Web. The best sites to find calendars to subscribe to are www.icalshare.com and www.apple.com/downloads/macosx/calendars/. On both those sites you can find calendars for virtually anything, from national holidays to a calendar that tracks the release dates of Xbox 360 games.

When you find a calendar you want to subscribe to, download its .ico file (a universal calendar file format) and double-click it. The calendar subscription will automatically be added to iCal.

Always Show the Event Information Window

Do you hate that you have to double-click an event to see its pop-up information window? You don't have to. From iCal's menu bar, simply select Edit ➤ Show Inspector to show a free-floating information window (Figure 8–23). The window displays the information of any event you click.

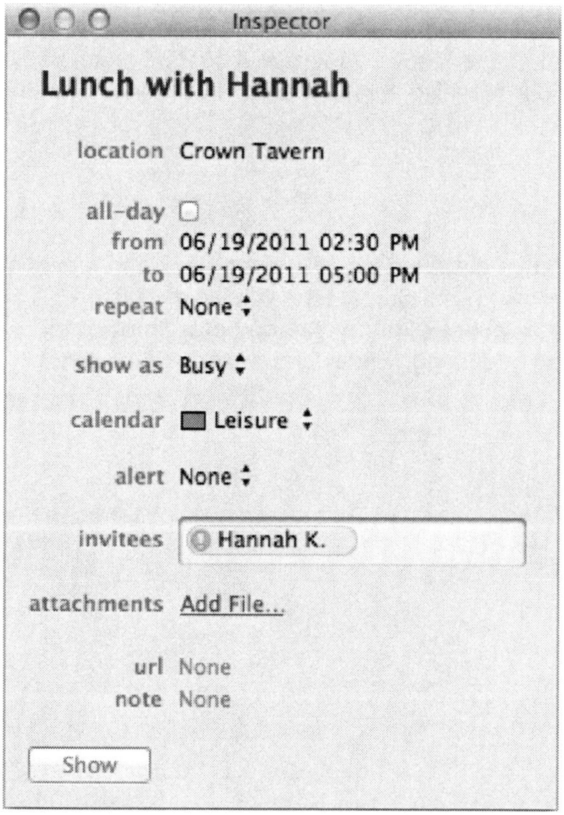

Figure 8–23. The free-floating information window

Create Reminders

Sometimes you don't know when something will occur, but you want a reminder to do it. Maybe that something is picking up the groceries or a reminder to schedule an event. iCal allows you to create reminders that are viewable in a sidebar right under the search field (Figure 8–24).

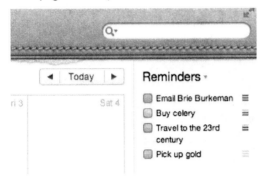

Figure 8–24. Reminders in iCal

To create a reminder, select **File ➤ New Reminder** from iCal's menu bar. Then simply enter the name of the reminder. If you right-click the reminder, you'll see a context menu that allows you to link the reminder to a calendar and also set its priority: low, medium, or high.

Create a Quick Event

There's a + button right next to the Calendars button in iCal's header. Click it to create a quick event (Figure 8–25). Quick events allow you to simply type "Movie at 7pm on Friday," and iCal will automatically create an event with the parameters of "movie" for event name, "7pm" for event time, and the upcoming "Friday" for the day of the event. Pretty cool, huh?

Figure 8–25. Creating a quick event

Summary

iCal and Address Book are two powerful apps included in Lion. Together with Mail, these incredibly useful tools can help you organize your life. Get used to them and all they can do because you won't find two better apps to manage your contacts and events. Here are some tips to remember before moving on to the next chapter:

- Address Book's smart groups are a great way to organize your contacts automatically.

- Removing a contact from a group does not delete that contact from your address book.

- There are four ways to view iCal: Day, Week, Month, and Year. All have their own benefits.

- Once you understand how to add an event in one iCal view, you know how to add an event in all iCal views.

Search the Web for calendars to which you want to subscribe. There are some really good ones at www.icalshare.com!

Chapter 9

Browsing the Internet with Safari

The number-one most-used app on any computer—whether it's a Mac or Windows computer—is the web browser. The many different web browsers go by many different names, including the following: Internet Explorer, Firefox, and Chrome. But my favorite web browser is the one that ships on every Mac: Safari.

In this chapter, you'll discover how to get the most from Safari with all its awesome powers. You'll learn how to navigate web pages, manage bookmarks, and search the Web. You'll also discover some great Safari-only features including Top Sites, Reading List, and Reader. Read on for all this and more.

Getting Started with Safari

To launch Safari, just click its icon (Figure 9–1) in the Dock or on the Launchpad or double-click its icon in the Applications folder. Once launched, the Safari application opens a new window.

Figure 9–1. *The Safari icon*

Safari's Browser Window

Many elements in the Safari window may look familiar, especially to anyone experienced in using other popular web browsers. Familiar elements include the address bar, the Refresh button, and the history navigation arrows. Figure 9–2 shows a typical Safari browser window.

Figure 9–2. *The Safari window displays many familiar features, including the address bar and the back, forward, and bookmarks buttons.*

Let's look closer at the top of a Safari page. Atop every Safari window you'll see the navigation bar (see Figure 6-3). The navigation bar contains common buttons and tools found in any modern web browser. Clockwise from left to right, they are as follows:

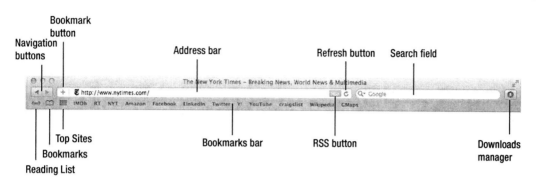

Figure 9–3. *The Safari navigation bar*

- *Navigation buttons*: These buttons take you back or forward one page in your browsing history.

- *Bookmark button*: This + button allows you to add the current page to your bookmarks, Top Sites, or Reading List.

NOTE: When the back and forward buttons are grayed out, you haven't yet created a history. The arrows turn from light gray to dark gray after you start browsing, and you can move back and forth through your history to the previous and next pages. Each page maintains its own history.

- *Address bar*: Use the address bar at the top center of the Safari window to enter a new web address (web addresses are uniform resource locators [URLs]).

- *Refresh button*: The arrow bent in a semicircle in the address bar field is the Refresh button. Click it to refresh the current screen.

- *Search field*: Enter text here to search using Google, Bing, or Yahoo!

- *Downloads Manager*: Click this to see all your current and past downloads.

- *RSS button*: Click this button to see the RSS feed of the current web site.

- *Bookmarks bar*: This is an optional bar that shows you some of your most-visited bookmarks.

- *Top Sites*: Click this button to reveal your Top Sites list.

- *Bookmarks*: Click the book-shaped button to open your Bookmarks screen. The Bookmarks screen also contains your complete browsing history for Safari.

- *Reading List*: Click the eyeglass button to reveal the Reading List sidebar.

Navigation Basics

Safari lets you do all the normal things you expect to do in a browser, so if you've used any browser in the past, you know how to use the most basic features of Safari. We'll quickly run through navigation basics next before we get to the meat of Safari—the features it has that other browsers don't and the places where Safari does something differently.

Entering URLs

This is the most basic function of any web browser—entering web addresses, or URLs (for example, www.google.com). Double-click in the address bar (see Figure 6-3) and type any URL you want to go to; then press Return on your keyboard, and Safari navigates to the address you've entered.

If the current URL field is empty, simply click it and begin typing. Don't worry about typing http:// or even www; Safari adds these elements automatically.

As you type, Safari matches your keystrokes to its existing collection of bookmarks and history. A pop-up field displays a list of possible matches from both your bookmarks and your history. To select one, just click it. Safari automatically navigates to the selected URL.

> **TIP:** You can refresh the web page you are currently on by clicking the Refresh button.

Searching the Web

From any Safari window, you are just a click away from a web search. As shown in Figure 9–3, a search field is located just to the right of the URL field. It initially appears marked with a spyglass with light gray text saying *Google*, *Yahoo!*, or *Bing*, depending on what search engine you've selected. Click this search field to bring up the keyboard and enter a term you want to search for, and then press Return on your keyboard to be taken to the search engine results web page.

As you can see in Figure 9–4, after you type a word or two, a pop-up box appears with autosuggested search terms based on what you've typed. To select one of the autosuggested terms, simply click it in the list, or just finish typing what you are looking for and press Return on the keyboard. Safari will navigate to the search engine results page (no matter what page is currently displayed) and search for your queried term.

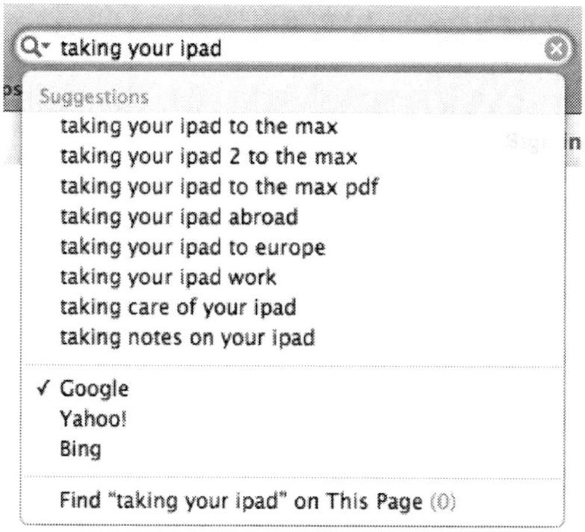

Figure 9–4. *The search field complete with suggested keywords*

If you'd rather use Bing or Yahoo! search than Google, you can select them from the search list. Click the magnifying glass icon in the search field and choose which search engine you want. A check mark will appear next to your search engine of choice.

Searching for Text on a Web Page

Safari also allows you to search for specific text on a web page. To search for text, simply enter that text in the search field and then click where it says "Find [your selected text] on This Page" (shown at the bottom of Figure 9–4). You'll then see the Find toolbar displayed below the address bar but above the web page (see Figure 9–5).

After the Find bar is displayed, Safari will locate the first occurrence of the text you are looking for and highlight it in yellow (see Figure 9–5). Then, using the Find bar, you can tap the forward or back button to find the next or previous instances of the text on that web page. You can also refine your keyword search using the search field in the Find bar at the bottom of the page.

Finally, when you click the magnifying glass in the search field in the Find bar, you can choose to find text that either starts with or contains the text you entered. When you are done searching for text, click the Done button in the Find bar.

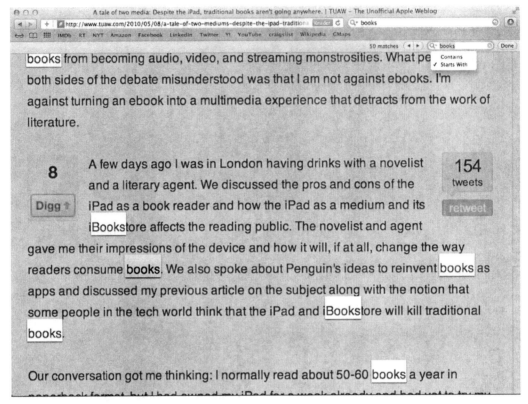

Figure 9–5. *Searching for text on a web page*

Working with Tabs

Most modern browsers have tabs, and Safari is no exception. Tabs allow you to have multiple web pages open in a single browser window. This reduces clutter on your desktop. When you have multiple tabs open, they appear below the address field in Safari's header, as shown in Figure 9–6.

Figure 9–6. *The tab bar in Safari*

In Figure 9–6, four tabs are open. The selected tab (the London Wikipedia entry) displays that page's content. To navigate to another tab, simply click that tab, and that page's content will be displayed in the Safari window.

You can use any of the following options to open tabs in Safari:

- Choose **File ➤ New Tab** from Safari's menu bar.

- Press Command-T on your keyboard.

- Right-click a link on a web page and then select "Open page in new tab" from the context menu.

- If the tab bar is already displayed, click the + button in the right corner (Figure 9–6).

Navigating with Gestures

To give iPad and iPhone users a more familiar feel when using a Mac, Apple has baked in some multitouch gestures to Safari. In Safari in Lion, you can use your MacBook's trackpad, your Magic Mouse, or your Magic Trackpad to perform the following gestures:

- *Tap to zoom:* Double-tap (rather than double-click) your Magic Mouse or trackpad to zoom in on an image or a column of text. The image or text scales up nicely without becoming pixelated. This is perfect for web sites that have small font sizes or if you have less than perfect eyesight. Figure 9–5 shows a column of text that was enlarged using the tap to zoom feature.

- *Pinch to zoom:* This is similar to tap to zoom, but it gives you more precise control of what you're zooming in on.

- *Swipe to navigate:* Swipe left or right on your Magic Mouse or trackpad to go backward or forward one page in your browsing history. You can use this gesture as an alternative to using Safari's navigation buttons (see Figure 9–3).

Eliminating Clutter with Reader

Safari has an awesome built-in feature that most other web browsers lack. It's called Reader (not to be confused with Reading List—another awesome feature covered later). Reader allows you to eliminate all the clutter on web pages—the ads, the comments, the links—and read the content of that page as if you were reading it from a piece of paper. You can see Reader in action in Figure 9–7.

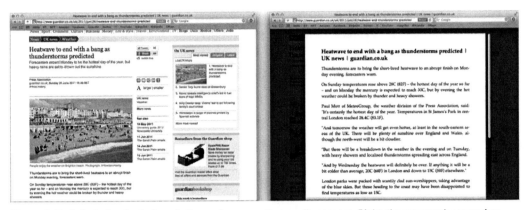

Figure 9–7. *Safari's Reader feature. Left: a web page as it normally appears. Right: the same web page when viewed through Reader.*

As you can see in Figure 9–7, viewing the text on a web page through Reader is much easier because all the distractions are eliminated. To activate Reader, click the gray Reader button that appears in the address bar. The Reader document will slide up onto the screen. To exit Reader mode, click the now purple Reader button in the address bar. Notice that the Reader button appears only when you are on a web page that has a single article. You will not see a Reader button on the front page of the *New York Times* web site; you'll see it only when you view single articles on the site.

Checking Your Sites at a Glance Using Top Sites

We all have our list of favorite web sites we like to visit frequently. However, sometimes when we visit those sites, they offer nothing we haven't already seen. Wouldn't it be great if a simple visual feature alerted us when new content was available on our favorite sites? Well, that feature is called Top Sites.

In Figure 9–3 you'll see a little button that looks like it's made up of 12 little boxes. This is the Top Sites button. Click it to reveal the Top Sites screen, shown in Figure 9–8.

Top Sites shows you 6, 12, or 24 of your favorite web sites at a glance. You can see thumbnails of their current pages, but more importantly, you'll see a star in their upper-right corners if there is new content on the site. You'll see this star only if new content has been added since you last visited. To navigate to one of these sites, simply click its thumbnail.

By default, Safari will start populating your Top Sites list with sites based on your browsing history. However, you can easily set up your own Top Sites and even arrange them in the order you want. To add a site to Top Sites, while on that site, click the + Bookmark button shown in Figure 9–3 and then select to save the page as a Top Site. To edit the order of your Top Sites and select how many you want to show, go to the Top Sites screen and then click the Edit button in the lower-left corner. The Top Sites edit screen will appear, as shown in Figure 9–9.

Figure 9–8. *Top Sites*

Figure 9–9. *Editing and arranging your Top Sites*

Once on the edit screen, you can simply drag your Top Sites to put them in the order you want them to appear. Top Sites with a blue pushpin are the ones you have manually bookmarked. If the pushpin is black, it means it is one that Safari is suggesting based on your browsing history. To keep the suggestion in your Top Sites list, click its pushpin. To remove a Top Sites suggestion or one you bookmarked, click the X button on its thumbnail. In the lower-right corner you'll see buttons labeled Small, Medium, and Large. Clicking any of those will switch between displaying 6, 12, or 24 Top Sites. Click Done when you are finished editing your Top Sites list.

Working with Bookmarks

Bookmarks are a feature that everyone is familiar with. A bookmark is a saved link to a particular web page (sometimes bookmarks are called *favorites*). Bookmarks let us quickly jump to saved spots on the Web. And though they're definitely still handy, I find myself using fewer bookmarks nowadays since Apple added the Top Sites and Reading List (discussed later) features to Safari.

Adding Bookmarks

Adding a bookmark is simple. When you have found a web site you want to bookmark, all you have to do is click the + bookmark button (see Figure 9–3), and a drop-down menu will appear (Figure 9–10). From this drop-down menu you can choose where you want to save your bookmark, whether it's to Top Sites, Reading List, your bookmarks list, or a specific folder in your bookmarks list.

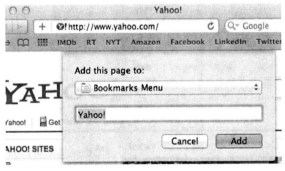

Figure 9–10. *Adding a bookmark*

After you have decided where you want to save the bookmark, click the Add button.

Managing Bookmarks

A bookmarks collection can contain hundreds of individual URLs, which is why people will really appreciate Safari's simple bookmarks browser (see Figure 9–11). When you click the bookmark button in the navigation bar (Figure 9–3), the bookmarks browser appears. It uses a folder structure that allows you to easily sort bookmarks into folders.

In the bookmarks sidebar in Figure 9–11, you can see I've created dozens of folders to sort my bookmarks. These folders are listed under the BOOKMARKS header. Click any folder to see its enclosed bookmarks to the right. You can create a folder for bookmarks by clicking the + button in the lower-left corner of the bookmarks screen and then drag any existing bookmark you want into the folder, or you can simply save a new bookmark directly to that folder using the previous steps.

Figure 9–11. *Safari's bookmarks manager*

In addition to folders in the bookmarks manager, you'll see another header labeled Collections. The Collections header contains your browsing history, bookmarks bar, bookmarks menu, Address Book links, Bonjour links, and RSS feeds.

- *Browsing history:* This contains links to every site you've visited since you last cleared your browsing history. To clear the history, choose **File ➤ History ➤ Clear History**.

- *Bookmarks bar:* Any bookmarks placed in this folder will appear in the bookmarks bar located below Safari's address field (shown earlier in Figure 9–3).

- *Bookmarks menu:* This is the default spot bookmarks go that aren't sorted into folders. From the Bookmarks menu you can drag bookmarks into folders.

- *Address Book:* Any URLs you have listed in any of your contacts address book cards show up here.

- *Bonjour:* If you are on a shared networked, shared bookmarks will show up here.

- *All RSS feeds:* If you subscribe to any RSS feeds, the links to those feeds will show up here.

Managing Downloads

One of the main things we do with a web browser is find things to download. However, we often lose track of the download's progress, or we don't even know where it was downloaded to. That's where Safari's Downloads manager comes in.

When you download anything in Safari, the status of the download is always shown in the Downloads manager (Figure 9–12). All you have to do is click the Downloads manager's button, which looks like a downward arrow with a progress bar beneath it, to see a list of all your past and current downloads.

Figure 9–12. *Safari's Downloads manager*

Current downloads show a progress bar and an estimated time remaining until the download is finished. You can stop a current download by clicking the X. Past downloads also show up in the list.

You can find where any download on your computer is by opening the Downloads manager and then clicking the magnifying glass next to the download. A Finder window will open showing you the exact location of the download. You can also drag a completed download out of the Downloads manager right to your desktop for quick access to the file.

To clear the Downloads manager history, click the Clear button.

Building Up Your Reading List

Reading List is another new feature of Safari in Lion. It allows you to save web pages to read when you have the time. I know, that sounds a lot like adding a bookmark, right? It's similar, but Reading List is more of a temporary bookmark. It's for that cool article you find about a small town in Andorra that you want to read but don't have time right now. It's not a bookmark you want to keep forever; it's just something you want to make sure you read.

To activate Reading List, click the eyeglasses icon in Safari's navigation bar (Figure 9–3). The Reading List panel will slide open in your browser window (Figure 9–13).

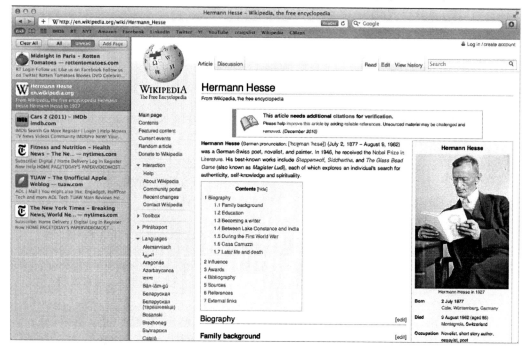

Figure 9–13. *Safari's Reading List*

The Reading List panel contains all the web articles you've added to it. You can select a tab to see all the articles you've added or just the ones you haven't read yet. Simply select an article in the Reading List to read the saved web page.

When you are on the page you want to save to your Reading List, you can save it by taking any of the following actions:

- Click the eyeglasses button and then click the Add Page button in the Reading List panel.

- From the menu bar, choose **Bookmarks ➤ Add to Reading List**.

■ Click the add bookmark (+) button (Figure 9–10) and then choose Reading List from the drop-down menu.

Any saved page will disappear from Reading List after you have scrolled through its entirety. You can also remove pages from Reading List by clicking the X that appears when you move your mouse over their label in the Reading List. Finally, you can clear all Reading List pages by clicking the Clear All button in the Reading List panel.

One of the best features about Reading List is that it is synced across all your computers and iOS devices (such as the iPad and iPhone) that use Safari. This allows you to find an interesting article on Safari on your iPhone, save it to Reading List, and then read it on your iPad or Mac when you get home. Just open Safari, and the article will appear in Reading List no matter what device you are on. It does this by syncing Reading List via your MobileMe or iCloud account.

Extending Safari with Extensions

Safari is an ultra-modern web browser. That means it's not limited to doing just what Apple says it can do. You see, Apple built extension support into Safari. This means other people can write small programs—or extensions—that add features to Safari.

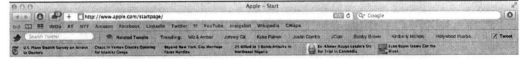

Figure 9–14. *Safari with multiple extensions*

Look at Figure 9–14. Notice anything different? You should. Look at all those extra toolbars and buttons. There's a Twitter toolbar that shows Twitter updates, a *New York Times* toolbar that shows top stories, a weather button that shows severe weather alerts when clicked, and an ad blocker button. And those are just four of the dozens of extensions available for Safari.

You can view all the Safari extensions available by going to the Safari Extension Gallery at www.extensions.apple.com. There you can search extensions by category and install them with one click.

To manage your extensions, choose **Safari ➤ Preferences** from the menu bar. In the preferences window that appears, select the Extensions tab (Figure 9–15). From this tab you can enable or disable certain extensions, turn off extension support entirely, and check for updates for any of your extensions.

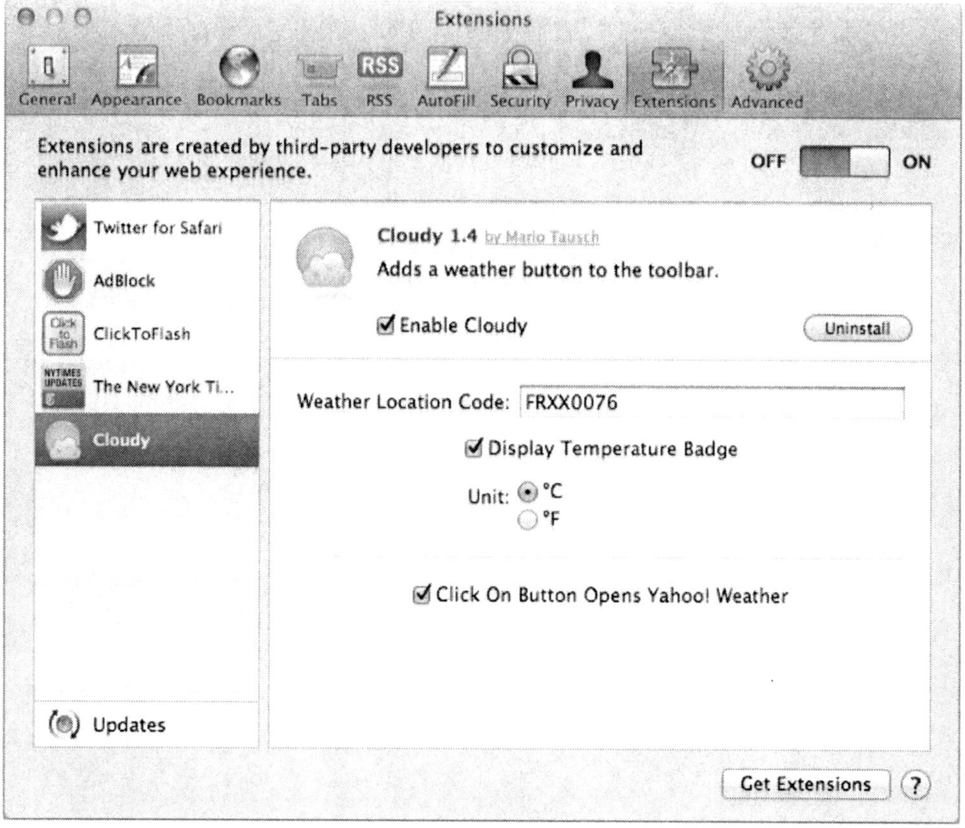

Figure 9–15. *Managing extensions in Safari's preferences*

Summary

As you can see, Safari is far from your average web browser. It offers a host of features the other ones don't, and best of all it's the one standard browser that's available on PC, Mac, iPad, iPhone, and iPod touch.

Here are a few tips to keep in mind as you move on from this chapter:

- Don't confuse Reader and Reading List. Reader lets you strip away ads and read a web page's text as if you were reading a newspaper. Reading List allows you to save interesting articles to come back to at your leisure.

- Tabs are a great and fast way to manage several web pages at once. Get used to them!

- Top Sites is an amazing feature that lets you quickly check at a glance whether your favorite web sites have been updated with new content since your last visit.

■ Extensions can add a lot of features to Safari. Don't be afraid to add them. You can always disable them from Safari's preferences.

If you own a Mac or PC and also an iPad or iPhone, there's no reason not to be using Safari as your main browser. Not only will all your bookmarks sync across devices, so will all your saved Reading List articles!

Chapter 10

Communicating in Real-Time with iChat and FaceTime

It seems like there's no shortage of ways to communicate nowadays. We have mobile phones, e-mail, instant messaging, Facebook, texting, VoIP, and even old-fashioned letters. Included with Lion are two built-in apps that allow us to communicate in many of the ways listed. First, there's iChat, which allows you to IM your friends as well as audio and video chat with them.

Then there's FaceTime, Apple's newest communications technology. FaceTime is similar to iChat in that it allows you to video call your friends. But that's all FaceTime does: video calling. However, as you'll see in this chapter, there is a very important difference between the type of video calls you make using iChat and those you make using FaceTime. Read on to discover how to take advantage of both apps and learn all about the advantages and disadvantages of each one.

Communicating with iChat

iChat has been part of Mac OS X for a long time, although Apple has added several improvements to it in Lion. When iChat was first introduced (you can see its icon in Figure 10–1), it was strictly an instant messaging application. Instant messaging is a form of communication where you add friends to a buddy list, and when both you and your friend are online at the same time, you can type messages to each other in real time. I'll refer to instant messaging by its most frequently used term "IM" or "IMing" throughout this chapter.

Figure 10–1. *iChat's icon*

As iChat evolved, Apple added other features to it. One of those features was audio chatting. As long as your computer had a built-in microphone (as well as your friend's), you could skip writing messages and simply speak to each other through iChat as if you were making a phone call. After Apple added audio, it decided to add video chatting. Again, as long as both you and your friends have video cameras attached to your computers, you could both hear and see each other.

As you'll see in this chapter, iChat does a lot of things. However, for all of iChat's features, it does have one big drawback: iChat is limited to computer-to-computer communication. You can't use iChat to make an audio call to a mobile phone or make a video call to an iPad. As you'll see in the second half of this chapter, that's what FaceTime is for.

Setting Up iChat

To launch iChat, just click its icon (Figure 10–1) in the Dock or on the Launchpad or double-click its icon in the Applications folder. If you've never used iChat before, the first time you launch it you'll be taken through a setup procedure that allows you to use your existing IM accounts with the app. iChat supports instant messaging accounts from AOL Instant Messenger (AIM), MobileMe, Google Talk, Yahoo! Messenger, or Jabber accounts.

From the setup screen (Figure 10–2) you can add your primary IM account. If you don't have one, click the Get an iChat Account button, and you'll be taken to the Web where you can register for a free AIM account. After you've added your account, iChat's buddy list will appear, as shown in Figure 10–3. The buddy list is the main window in iChat.

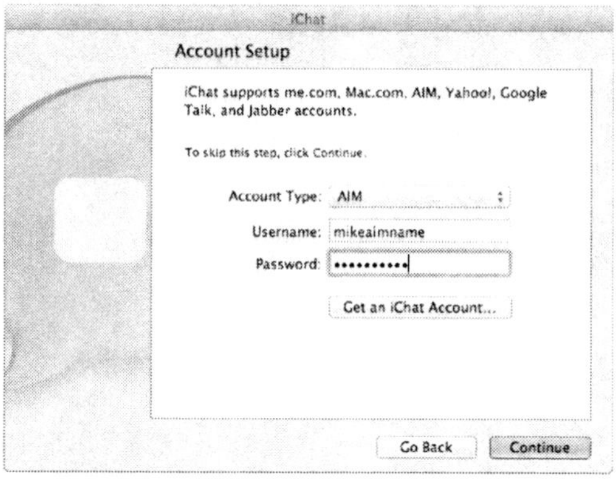

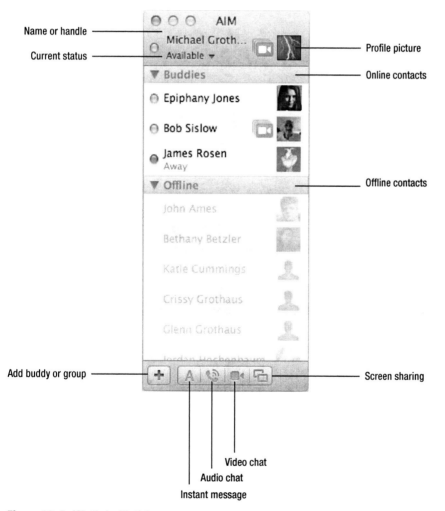

Figure 10–2. *iChat's setup screen*

Figure 10–3. *iChat's buddy list*

As you can see in Figure 10–3, the iChat window contains several important elements:

- *Name or handle*: This shows either your full name (such as Michael Grothaus) or your IM handle. A *handle* is your IM name that you log in with (such as mikerocks86).

- *Current status*: Select this drop-down menu to change your current status to a predefined one (such as "available" or "away") or create a custom one. There is even a predefined status that shows your buddies what song you're currently listening to in iTunes.

- *Profile picture*: This is the image that appears next to your name in your friends' buddy lists. Click the image to change the picture.

- *Online contacts*: The Buddies group lists all your contacts that are currently online. You can see their names, profile pictures, and status.

- *Offline contacts*: The Offline group lists all your contacts that are currently offline.

- *Add buddy or group*: Click the + button to add a new buddy or create a new group of buddies.

- *Instant message*: Click this A button to start a text chat.

- *Audio chat*: Click this button with a phone icon to start an audio chat.

- *Video chat*: Click this button with a camera icon to start a video chat.

- *Screen Sharing*: Click this button to enter screen-sharing mode.

About Multiple Accounts and iChat

Before we delve into what makes iChat iChat, it's important to mention that you aren't limited to using just one account in iChat. Let's say you have two AIM accounts: one for work and one for friends. You can log into both of them in iChat at the same time. Likewise, if you have a Google Talk account and a Yahoo! Messenger account, you can log into both those accounts (in addition to any others) in iChat at the same time. As a matter of fact, about the only instant messaging accounts you can't use iChat with are MSN Messenger and Skype.

To add accounts other than the one you first set up when launching iChat, select iChat ➤ Preferences from iChat's menu bar and then click the Accounts tab. At the bottom of the Accounts screen you'll see a + button. Click it to enter the iChat setup screen again (as shown in Figure 10–2). Repeat as necessary until you've added all your IM accounts.

Also, don't think that iChat users can communicate only with people using iChat. iChat is simply an instant messaging client. That is, it's just a program that allows you to talk to each other using other instant messaging programs. So, you can be using iChat on your Mac and talking to a friend who is using AOL Instant Messenger on his Windows computer. It doesn't matter what clients you are using; you just need to be on each other's buddy lists.

Using Buddy Lists

iChat's buddy list lets you sort your friends into different groups. As you can see in Figure 10–3, by default you will have two groups: Buddies and Offline. *Buddies* contains all of your friends that are currently online. They may be away (signified by a red dot) or idle (signified by a yellow dot), but they are at least logged in and online. *Offline* contains all your buddies you have added to your IM account, but they aren't actually logged in to the account at the moment.

Adding Buddies

Adding buddies to your list is easy. Simply click the Add Buddy or Group + button at the bottom of iChat's window (see Figure 10–3). Select Add Buddy, and in the drop-down menu that appears (see Figure 10–4), enter your friend's account name (or handle). You can then select which of your groups you want to add the friend to and also enter their real first and last names if you want. Click Add, and your new friend will appear on your buddy list.

Figure 10–4. *Adding a friend to your buddy list*

Adding Groups

iChat allows you to sort your friends into multiple groups. This enables you to divide everyone on your buddy list into more manageable lists. For example, you can create a group called Work People and put all your colleges into that group. You can have another group called Family that's just for your closest relatives.

To create a new group, click the Add Buddy or Group + button at the bottom of iChat's window (see Figure 10–3). Select Add Group, and in the drop-down menu that appears, enter the name of your new group. Click Add, and your new group will appear on your buddy list. However, at this time, your new group will be empty. You still need to put people into it.

Adding people to groups is easy. Simply click a name from wherever it resides in your buddy list and drag it onto the group header to which you want to add it. That's it. You've added that person to the group. Newly added buddies will not actually appear in the group unless they are online. If they are offline, they will appear only in the offline group. When they come online, they will jump from the offline group to the group that you have selected to put them in. Figure 10–5 shows you a buddy list with multiple groups.

Figure 10–5. *You can create multiple groups for your buddy list.*

As you can see in Figure 10–5, I've created three new groups in addition to the default Buddies and Offline groups. One is called Europe, and the others are Work People and Family. As mentioned, you can move people from one group to the next simply by dragging their names around. However, besides the Offline group, a friend can reside in only one other group at a time. Using Figure 10–5 as an example, if I added Epiphany Jones to the Family group, she would automatically be removed from her current Europe group.

Text Chatting

Initiating a text chat with someone (also known as an *instant message*) is easy. Simply double-click their name in the buddy list, and a new instant message window will open (Figure 10–6). You can also click a friend in your buddy list to highlight their name and then click the A instant message button at the bottom of iChat's buddy list to open a new instant message window; however, it's generally faster just to double-click your friend's name in the buddy list.

To begin chatting to someone, simply enter text in the text field at the bottom of the instant message window and then press Return on your keyboard. Your text will be displayed in a colored speech bubble on the right side. When the person who you are chatting with replies, their text will be shown in a different-colored speech bubble on the left side.

You'll also note that there is a smiley face icon in the text entry field. Click this to display a drop-down menu of emoticons (commonly known as *smilies*) into your text chats.

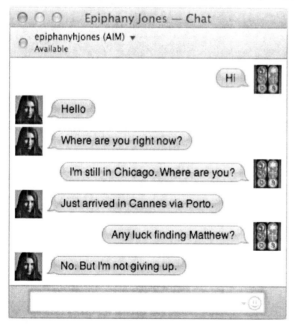

Figure 10–6. *An instant message window*

Another cool feature of iChat is that it incorporates all your different chats into one tabbed window, even if one of those chats is from your Google Talk account and one is from your AIM account. As you can see in Figure 10–7, all your open chats are displayed in the same window, and to switch from one to the next, simply click the name of the person in the tabbed sidebar.

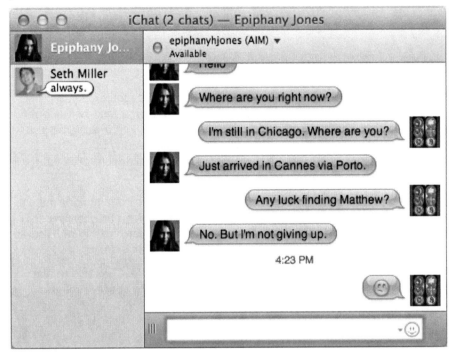

Figure 10–7. *Tabbed chats in iChat*

Audio Chatting

Initiating an audio chat with someone is even easier than text chatting because you don't have to do any typing! To start an audio chat, you first need to select a buddy who is using the same IM service as you (such as AIM or Google Talk). You then need to make sure they have a microphone on their computer. If they do, you'll see a green phone icon next to their name in the buddy list. If you see a green video camera icon next to their name in the buddy list (as shown in Figure 10–3), that means they have a camera and microphone.

To begin an audio chat, simply click the telephone icon next to the friend you want to chat with. Alternatively, you can click the friend's name in the buddy list so that their name is highlighted and then click the Audio Chat button at the bottom of iChat's buddy list to initiate the call; however, it's generally faster just to click the telephone icon next to the friend's name.

As you can see in Figure 10–8, an audio chat window appears when your friend has accepted your invitation to talk. As you speak, the audio meter increases and decreases in response to sound. This lets you know that you are indeed connected. You can add more people to your audio chat by clicking the + button and then selecting their names from your buddy list. You can also mute your side of the call by clicking the mute button. Finally, you can adjust the volume of the call, separate from your Mac's system volume, by moving the volume slider.

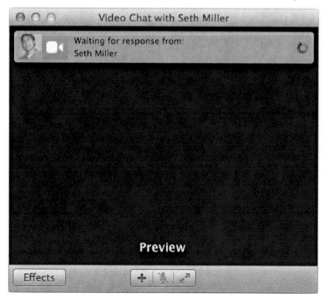

Figure 10–8. *An audio chat window*

Video Chatting

To initiate a video chat, simply click the video camera icon next to the friend you want to video chat with. Alternatively, you can click the friend's name in the buddy list to highlight their name and then click the Video Chat button at the bottom of iChat's buddy list (Figure 10–3) to initiate the call; however, it's generally faster just to click the video icon next to the friend's name.

When you initiate a video chat with someone, the video chat window appears (Figure 10–9). You'll see a message that says "Waiting for response from: [name of friend]." This message persists until your friend accepts the video chat invite. When they do, the video chat window appears (Figure 10–10). The main body of the window displays the video feed of the friend to whom you are talking. The box in the corner displays you, or whatever the person on the other end of the video chat is seeing. You can click and drag the picture-in-picture window to any other corner so that it doesn't obstruct what you are seeing.

Figure 10–9. *Initiating a video chat*

Figure 10–10. *A video chat window*

The buttons at the bottom of the video chat window give you additional options. To add more people to the video chat, click the + button and then select their names from your buddy list. You can also mute your side of the video call by clicking the mute button. If you want to video chat full-screen, click the button of the two arrows that are pointing in opposite directions. Finally, you can add effects to your video calls for some fun. Apple has included more than 40 special effects that let you set custom backdrops, morph your image, and add filters to your video. To see all the effects, click the Effects button at the bottom of a video chat window. The Video Effects pop-up (Figure 10–11) will appear, allowing you to browse all the effects. Find the one you want and click it to apply it to the video chat.

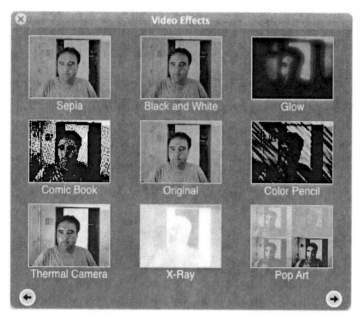

Figure 10–11. *Optional effects for a video chat*

iChat Theater and Screen Sharing

Apple has built some nice sharing features into iChat. The first is called iChat Theater, and it's basically a remote presentation function. With iChat Theater you can present web pages, files, and photos in a video chat window. However, unlike for video chatting, you don't need a video camera for iChat Theater.

To initiate an iChat theater presentation, all you have to do is simply drag any file onto an open video chat window, and the person you are video chatting with will see it instead of you on their screen. If you don't have a video chat in progress, you can select File from iChat's menu bar and then choose either Share a file with iChat Theater, Share a Webpage with iChat Theater, or Share iPhoto with iChat Theater (Figure 10–12) and then simply select the file, web page, or photo you want to share.

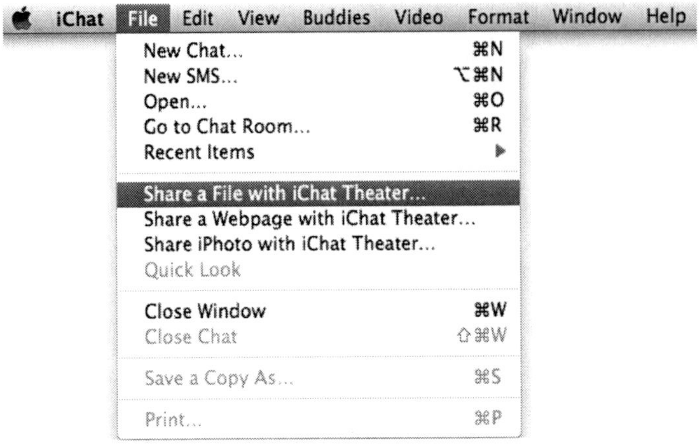

Figure 10–12. *Sharing files via iChat Theater*

Screen sharing is another feature of iChat. It allows you to create a shared desktop with anyone in your buddy list. What that means is that, during screen sharing, both you and the person you are sharing your screen with will have full access to your computer. They can open and edit files and even delete them if they want.

> **CAUTION:** Obviously, privacy and security are big issues with the screen-sharing feature of iChat, so share your screen only with those people on your buddy list that you absolutely trust!

To initiate screen sharing, click a friend's name in your buddy list so that the name is highlighted. Then, click the Screen Sharing button at the bottom of the buddy list window (Figure 10–3). Screen sharing will start, and an iChat audio chat will automatically commence so you can speak with the person you are sharing your screen with.

The Differences Between FaceTime and iChat

Now that you understand what iChat is and does, let's move on to FaceTime. But before we do, now is a good time to talk about the differences between the two apps. iChat is an excellent tool for text, audio, and video chatting with people *between computers*. To use iChat, you must be on a computer, and that's its biggest limitation. Why? Because today many of us have iPads and iPhones and while we may be at our computers, the person we want to communicate with might be out and about with their iPhone.

That's where FaceTime comes in. FaceTime doesn't let you text or only audio chat with people. FaceTime is strictly a video chatting platform. But the beauty of it—and here is how it differs from video chatting in iChat—is that with FaceTime you can video chat from Mac to iPad or from iPad to iPhone. In short, FaceTime supports a wide array of devices, so you aren't limited to video chatting with people only when they are at their computers. As you'll see, FaceTime is a technology that brings easy and intuitive video calling to the masses.

Getting Started with FaceTime

With the FaceTime app in Lion, you can video call anyone with an iPhone 4, an iPad 2 or newer, a fourth-generation iPod touch or newer, or a Mac that has a FaceTime HD or iSight camera and is running 10.6.8 or newer with the FaceTime app installed.

Apple wants to make FaceTime the de facto standard for video calling, and to do so, it has made the FaceTime technology an open standard, which means that other phone manufacturers can build the technology in their phones so that one day you'll be able to FaceTime video call on your iPod to someone on an Android phone.

To use FaceTime in Lion, besides your Mac, you'll need to have a Wi-Fi Internet connection and an Apple ID. The person who you are calling must also have a Wi-Fi connection, even if you are calling them on an iPhone 4. At this time, iPhone 4 owners can use FaceTime only over Wi-Fi, not over their service provider's 3G network. Most likely, it was the service providers that put this limitation in place. Streaming live video over a 3G network takes a lot of bandwidth, something that is very costly for a service provider. It's also very taxing on the network.

Signing In

To begin using FaceTime, just click its icon (Figure 10–13) in the Dock or on the Launchpad or double-click its icon in the Applications folder. If this is the very first time you've launched the app, you'll be presented with the FaceTime sign-in screen (Figure 10–14).

Figure 10–13. *The FaceTime icon*

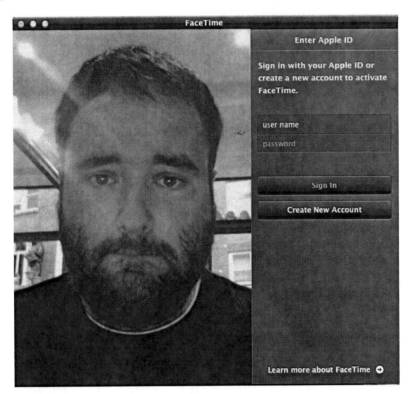

Figure 10–14. *The FaceTime sign-in screen*

Signing In with Your Existing Apple ID

To sign in with your existing Apple ID, simply fill in the user name and password fields and click Sign In. You already have an Apple ID if you use the iTunes Store, the App Store, or the iBookstore. You also have an Apple ID if you have a MobileMe account.

When you sign in for the first time, Apple notifies you that people will call you using your e-mail address (Figure 10–15). They ask you which e-mail address you would like to use. You can keep the same e-mail address that is your Apple ID, or you can enter another e-mail address.

Figure 10–15. *Choosing which e-mail address you want to act as your FaceTime "phone number"*

Once you have selected which e-mail address you want associated with FaceTime calls, click the Next button. A short verification notification will appear as Apple verifies that your e-mail address is authentic, and Apple will ask you to check your e-mail. Look for an e-mail with the subject "Please verify the contact e-mail address for your Apple ID" and then click the Verify Now link in the e-mail. A Safari window will open that takes you to the My Apple ID page. There you'll need to enter your Apple ID and password to verify your FaceTime e-mail address. Once you are presented with the "E-mail address verified" web page, return to the FaceTime app, and you can sign in.

Please be aware that this authorization procedure for FaceTime, which is subject to change, was in effect at the time this book was written. Apple could change its account creation and authorization process in the future.

Creating an Account

If you don't have some form of Apple ID, you can create one by clicking the Create New Account button (Figure 10–14). The New Account panel opens (Figure 10–16). In this panel you will enter your first and last names, your e-mail address (which will become your new Apple ID), and a password of at least eight characters. This password does not have to be the same as the password for your e-mail account.

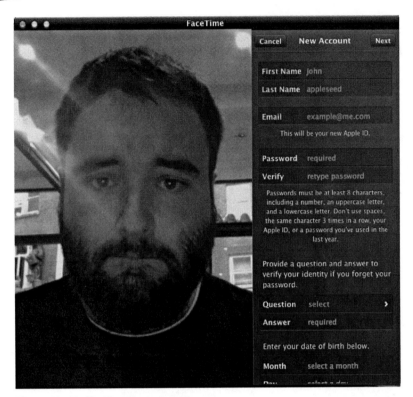

Figure 10–16. *The New Account panel*

On the New Account screen you'll also need to choose a question and enter the answer. This question/answer is used in case you forget your Apple ID password. Finally, enter your month and day of birth, choose which country you reside in, and select whether you want to subscribe to the Apple e-mail list.

Once you have entered this information, click the Next button. You'll be returned to the Sign In screen with your Apple ID and password already entered, and signing in will commence. A short verification notification will appear as Apple verifies that your e-mail address is authentic, and Apple will ask you to check your e-mail. Look for an e-mail with the subject "Please verify the contact e-mail address for your Apple ID," and then click the Verify Now link in the e-mail. A Safari window will open that takes you to the My Apple ID page. There you'll need to enter your Apple ID and password to verify your FaceTime e-mail address. Once you are presented with the "E-mail address verified" web page, return to the FaceTime app, and you can sign in.

Once you are presented with the "E-mail address verified" web page, return to the FaceTime app. You'll automatically be presented with the standard FaceTime screen (Figure 10–14), which you'll see every time you launch the app.

Navigating Your FaceTime Contacts

When you sign into FaceTime, you will always see your image (or whatever is in front of your camera) on the left, while the right-side panel in the app will show you all your contacts (Figure 10–17). The Contacts panel is divided into three sections, accessible by clicking the buttons in the contact bar at the bottom of the screen.

- *Favorites*: This panel allows you to add your favorite contacts to it. It's handy as a shortcut to the people you call the most.

- *Recents*: This panel lists the recent FaceTime calls you've made or received.

- *Contacts*: This panel lists all the contacts in your Mac OS X Lion Address Book.

Let's look closer at each of these contact sections.

Favorites

The Favorites panel (Figure 10–17) allows you to create and maintain a list of your favorite contacts. Favorite contacts generally encompass anyone you call the most, such as family and friends and important work contacts. This panel acts as a shortcut to their FaceTime e-mail addresses or phone numbers.

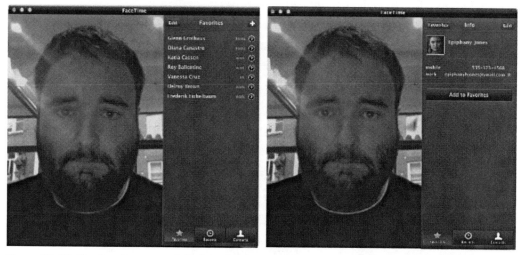

Figure 10–17. *The Favorites screen (left). Selecting the e-mail or phone number of a Favorites contact (right).*

- *Adding a contact to Favorites*: Click the + button in the upper-right corner and then select your contact from the Address Book list that slides up on screen.

- *Choosing the contact's FaceTime info*: From your selected contact's info screen, click the FaceTime e-mail address or phone number for the contact. If your contact is using an iPod touch or iPad, you must choose their associated FaceTime e-mail. If you contact is using an iPhone 4, you must choose their iPhone 4 phone number. Once you have chosen your contact's FaceTime info, a blue star (Figure 10–17) will appear by their FaceTime e-mail or number.

■ *Calling a Favorite*: Once you have set up your favorites, simply click their name in the Favorites list, and a FaceTime call will be initiated.

You can click the blue and white arrow next to a favorite's name to view or edit their contact information.

Recents

The Recents panel (Figure 10–18) lists the recently made or received FaceTime calls. This list can be sorted into two categories via the tabs at the top of the screen:

■ *All*: Shows you all the FaceTime calls you have made, received, or missed. Missed calls show up in red. The time of the call is shown to the right of the name of the person called. You can click the blue and white arrow next to a favorite's name to view or edit their contact information.

■ *Missed*: Shows only the FaceTime calls you have missed.

To clear your Recents list, click the Clear button in the upper-right corner of the screen.

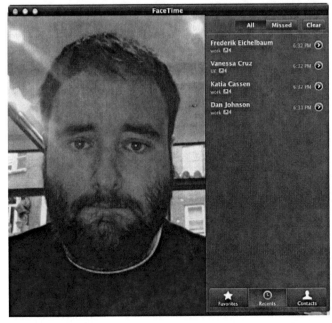

Figure 10–18. *The Recents list*

Contacts

The Contacts panel features your entire address book (Figure 10–19). You can navigate it by all the contacts or by selecting just a group of contacts.

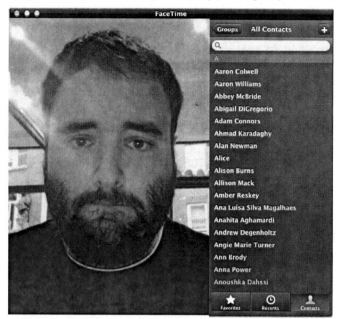

Figure 10–19. *The Contacts panel*

When you find the contact you want to call, click their name, and their contact information card will be displayed. Select their FaceTime e-mail or FaceTime phone number, and your FaceTime call will begin.

Making a FaceTime Call

To make a FaceTime call, simply select a contact from your Favorites, Recents, or Contacts list. As stated earlier, if you are selecting a contact from your Favorites or Recents list, simply clicking their name will initiate the FaceTime call (Figure 10–20, left). To start a call using your Contacts list, you'll need to click the contact's name and then choose their FaceTime phone number or e-mail. To cancel a call before the person has picked up, click the END button.

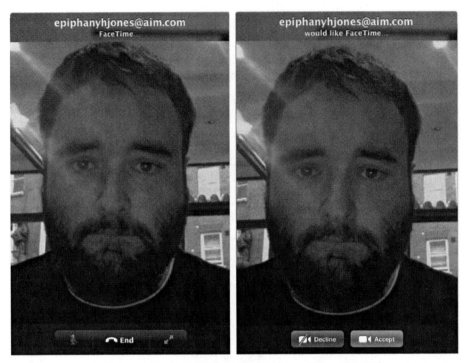

Figure 10–20. *Initiating a FaceTime call (left) and receiving a FaceTime call (right)*

When you receive a FaceTime call, the FaceTime app will appear on the screen telling you that a friend would like to FaceTime with you (Figure 10–20, right). To accept, click the green Accept button. To reject the call, click the red Decline button.

Figure 10–21 shows you what it looks like when you are in a FaceTime call. The speaker's image takes up a majority of the screen, while your image appears in a rectangle at the corner of the screen. You can drag the little rectangle around so it's not blocking the view. Also, notice that the FaceTime call window shown in Figure 10–21 is in portrait mode. If the person you are FaceTime calling with is using an iPhone or Pad and they adjust their device's orientation, the orientation of your FaceTime call window on your Mac will change as well.

Figure 10–21. *A FaceTime video call*

> **NOTE:** Watch out for bright backgrounds! If light is glaring in through the window behind you, it's likely to cause your viewer to see you in silhouette. To fix this, turn your Mac's camera just slightly away from the light source.

At the bottom of your FaceTime call window is the FaceTime control bar. This gives you several options:

- *Mute*: Click the microphone icon to switch between muting and unmuting a call. While you call is muted, you can still hear the person you are calling, but they cannot hear you. While a call is muted, the other person can still see you, so be careful what you do!

- *Ending the call*: To end a FaceTime call, click the End button.

- *View the call in full-screen*: If you want your FaceTime call to appear full-screen on your Mac, click the button with the two arrows pointing away from each other.

FaceTime Preferences

FaceTime has several preferences. Select FaceTime ➤ Preferences in FaceTime's menu bar to see the FaceTime preferences panel, as shown in Figure 10–22.

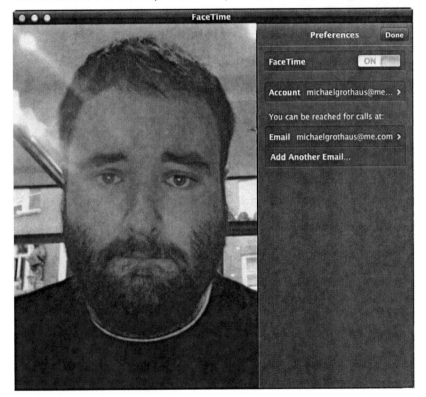

Figure 10–22. *FaceTime preferences*

- *Turn FaceTime on or off*: Click the FaceTime switch to ON or OFF. While it's off, you cannot make or receive FaceTime calls.

- *Change your FaceTime geographic location*: Click your Account e-mail. From the pop-up menu, click Change Location. Choose your location's new region from the list of regions.

- *View your FaceTime account settings*: Click your account e-mail. On the next panel, click View Account. After you confirm your account password, the Account Settings screen will appear. Click any field to change your account settings, such as your name or security question.

▓ *Sign out of FaceTime*: Click your account e-mail. On the next panel, click Sign Out. This will immediately sign you out of FaceTime without any more warnings. To sign back in, reenter your Apple ID password on the Sign In screen.

▓ *Remove a FaceTime email address*: You can deassociate your FaceTime e-mail address by clicking it and then clicking the Remove This Email button.

▓ *Adding more email addresses*: FaceTime allows you to associate more than one e-mail address with your FaceTime account. This is handy if you use more than one e-mail, one for friends and one for work colleagues, for example. If multiple e-mails are associated with your FaceTime account, people can initiate a FaceTime video call with you using any of your e-mails.

▓ To add additional e-mails, click the Add Another Email field, and then enter your other e-mail address. Repeat this step for each e-mail address you have. With each e-mail added, you'll need to check that e-mail account for the FaceTime verification e-mail from Apple and click the link in that e-mail before the e-mail address can be added to your FaceTime account.

When you are done changing FaceTime preferences, click the Done button.

Summary

As you can now see, Lion includes two great apps for real-time communication. Both have their advantages. iChat allows you to communicate with other people in a number of ways, including by text, audio, and video. FaceTime is an awesome app in itself because it allows you to not only communicate Mac to Mac but Mac to iPad and iPhone as well, and its popularity is sure to grow as more devices become FaceTime-compatible. In this chapter, you learned how to set up your iChat and FaceTime accounts and send and receive audio chat, instant messages, and video calls. Here are a few tips to take away with you:

▓ iChat is an great instant messaging client. Don't forget that you can add multiple IM accounts to it so that you can see all your online friends in a single buddy list!

▓ Sometimes it's quicker to talk than type. Take advantage of iChat's audio calling features. It's fast and easy, plus it will save you the cost of long-distance phone calls!

▓ With FaceTime you aren't limited to computer communication. You can talk to anyone with a compatible iPhone, iPad, or iPod touch using your Mac. Also, since FaceTime is an open standard, more devices should be compatible with it in the future.

FaceTime is an amazing feature for those who can't speak. The screen resolution is crisp enough where sign language can easily be read.

Chapter 11

System Preferences

The System Preferences application is one of the most powerful tools on your Mac. The app is the control pane through which you fine-tune your Mac to work the way you want it to work.

System Preferences still has the same icon (Figure 11–1) you may have come to know and love in earlier versions of Mac OS X, and some of the individual preference files haven't changed significantly. In this chapter, I'll highlight the changes to System Preferences that are important in Mac OS X Lion.

Figure 11–1. *The System Preference Dock icon, the gateway to total control over the look, feel, and actions of your Mac*

The layout of System Preferences is identical to that in Mac OS X 10.6 Snow Leopard (Figure 11–2). The preferences are laid out in five rows:

- *Personal*: These settings are used to personalize the look and feel, language, security, and accessibility of your Mac.

- *Hardware*: These preferences control the input and output devices used with your Mac and provide a way to control your Mac's energy usage.

- *Internet & Wireless*: These preferences allow you to tweak network connection settings, share your Mac with other users, and synchronize your Mac with the new iCloud service and the service it is replacing, called MobileMe.

- *System*: You can use these controls to add users and groups to your Mac, to keep kids from making unwanted changes or deleting files, to get system software updates, and to make adjustments to backups, time, and the disk your Mac starts up from.

- *Other*: Not discussed in this chapter, this row contains preferences for third-party applications that are closely integrated with Mac OS X.

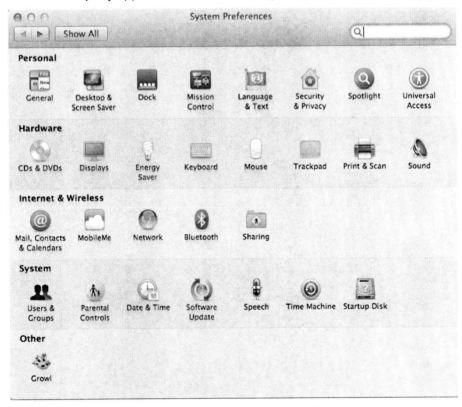

Figure 11–2. *System Preferences hasn't changed much in terms of layout, but some of the individual settings are new or provide different functionality for Lion.*

In the rest of this chapter, I'll discuss only those System Preferences items that have changed markedly from earlier versions of Mac OS X. Let's get started.

Personal

In the Personal row, the General, Dock, Mission Control, Security & Privacy, and Universal Access preferences are either new, have updated features, or have been moved a new location compared to Mac OS X 10.6 Snow Leopard.

General

The General preference (Figure 11–3) was previously known as Appearance, because many of the settings deal with the overall look of buttons, menus, windows, selected text, scroll bars, and how many items show up in a "recent items" list.

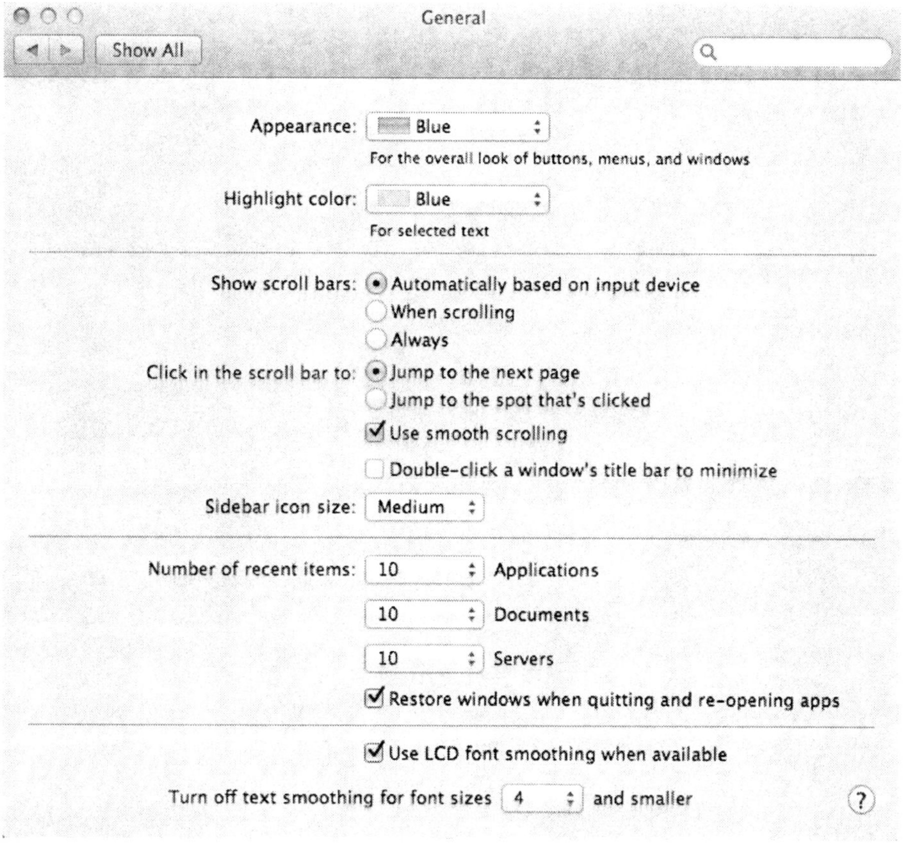

Figure 11–3. *The General preference pane in System Preferences under Mac OS X Lion*

The major changes in the General preference pane deal with scroll bars and windows. In the scroll bar section, Lion's switch to disappearing scroll bars (described in Chapter 2) takes precedence. If you find yourself missing permanent scroll bars in Finder windows and many Mac apps, switch "Show scroll bars" to Always to display them all of the time.

Another addition is the ability to select the size of icons in the Finder window sidebar. By default, Lion uses a medium-sized icon but also provides both smaller and larger icons to accommodate personal preference and less than perfect eyesight.

One very useful new feature is the check box to restore windows when quitting and reopening apps. Imagine that you're using Microsoft Word 2011 for Mac and have three or four documents open, all in different phases of completion. With the box checked by default, quitting Word and then restarting it later results in all of those documents opening as well.

Dock

The Dock preference pane (Figure 11–4) has changed just a little bit from Snow Leopard. The only change to the Dock in Mac OS X Lion is that the small glowing indicator lights that appear under applications that are open and running can be turned off.

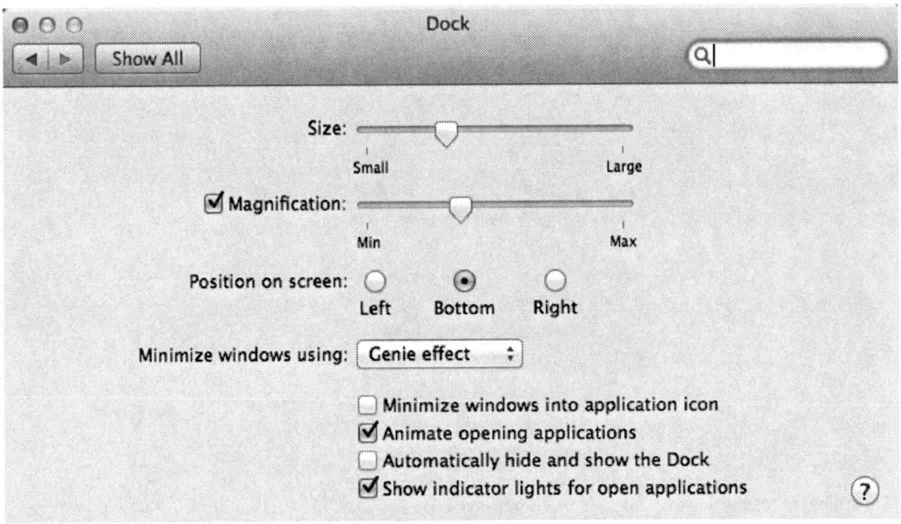

Figure 11–4. *The Dock preference adds only one check box to show or hide the indicator lights for open applications.*

Checking the "Show indicator lights for open applications" box is the default setting and is the way that the lights were used in Mac OS X 10.6. With the box unchecked, the indicator lights are turned off even when applications have been launched and are running.

Mission Control

The Mission Control preference pane replaces the Exposé & Spaces pane in the previous version of Mac OS X. Exposé provides a way to view all open windows or the windows of the current application with a single keystroke. It also hides all windows to make finding files or folders on the desktop a snap. As described in Chapter 5, Spaces is a way to organize applications and windows into groups that are activated with a keyboard shortcut.

Apple took Exposé and Spaces and melded them into the new Mission Control (see Chapter 6) to simplify navigation and control of windows with new trackpad gestures and the same familiar keyboard shortcuts. As a result, the Mission Control preferences (Figure 11–5) are much more streamlined than the old Exposé & Spaces preferences.

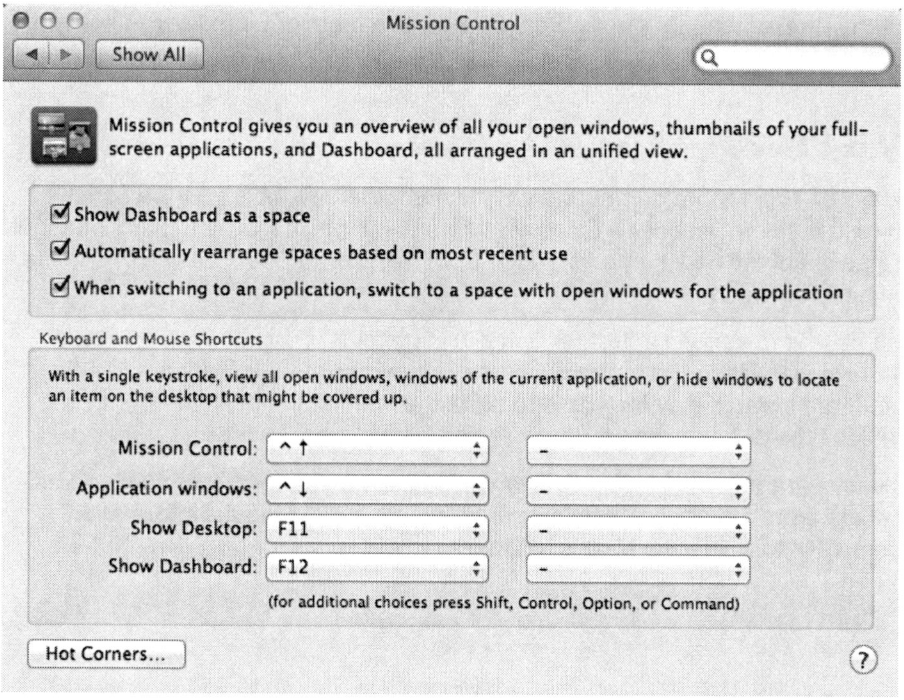

Figure 11–5. *The new Mission Control preference pane provides fine control of how spaces, keyboard shortcuts, and gestures are used to manipulate windows and applications.*

By default, Mission Control shows the Dashboard as a separate space that is usually navigated to by swiping right with three fingers on a trackpad. Some Mac users have never gotten in the habit of using Dashboard widgets, so they may want to simplify their Mac usage by removing the Dashboard space. Unchecking the first box on this pane does that.

The second check box defines how spaces are listed in Mission Control. By default, the spaces are automatically arranged with the most recently used space just to the right of the desktop space and progressively "older" spaces listed further right or down the grid of spaces. If that automatic arrangement throws off your use of Mission Control, uncheck the box to disable this function.

The third check box is used to disable (or reenable) the default setting of switching to a space with open windows for an application when switching to that app.

The lower portion of the preferences pane is very similar to the Exposé preferences in Snow Leopard, providing a way to set the shortcut keys or mouse buttons used to hide or show windows. The old controls to set active screen corners (placing the cursor into a corner performs a specific action) are now accessed with a single button titled Hot Corners.

Mission Control is Lion's powerful new tool for quickly jumping between workspaces on the Mac, and the simplicity of the new preference pane for Mission Control is an indication of the level of thought the Apple user interface team put into how to interact with your computer.

Security & Privacy

Apple's dedication to a secure computing environment that respects your personal privacy shows in the new Security & Privacy preference pane. In fact, the major changes visible in the pane are the new name (changed from Security in Snow Leopard) and the new Privacy tab on the pane.

The FileVault pane is described in further detail in Chapter 2 of this book; the biggest change to note is that FileVault now encrypts the entire disk of your Mac, not just the home folder. There's also a way for Apple to store the special "recovery key" that is created to unlock the disk in case you can't remember your password.

The new Privacy pane (Figure 11–6) provides you with a way to keep everything about your Mac private, from the applications that are running and diagnostic information about the computer to where the Mac is located.

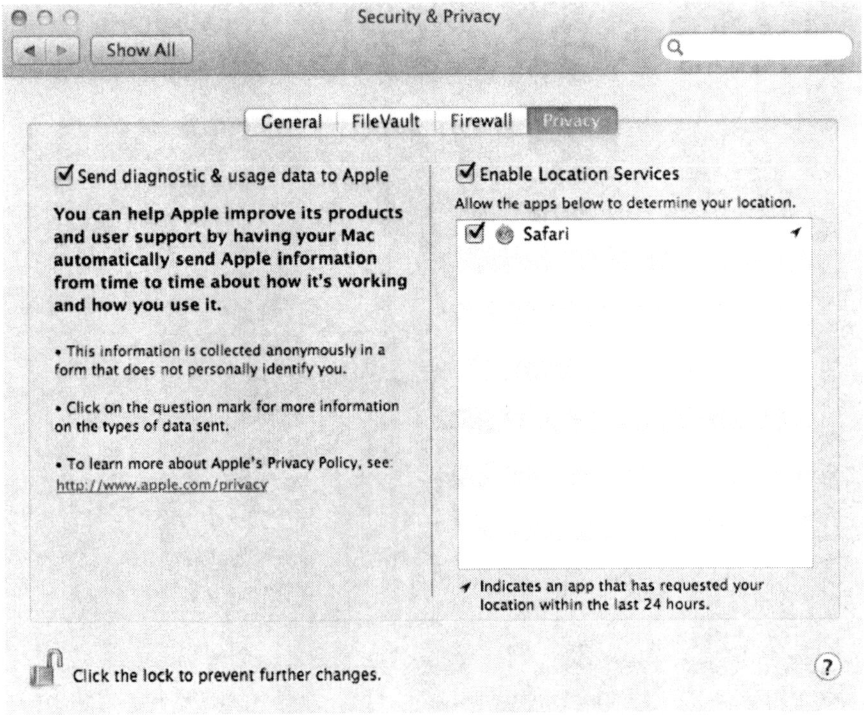

Figure 11–6. *Apple wants you to have control of your private information.*

Although the diagnostic and usage information sent to Apple and app vendors on those rare occasions when an app crashes is anonymous, some Mac users may choose to not send that data. To disable the sending of diagnostic information, uncheck the box on the left side of the Privacy pane.

The right side of the pane is something completely new in Mac OS X Lion. A growing number of applications can discern the location of your Mac, even though no current models have built-in GPS receivers. Through the use of Wi-Fi geolocation services, apps can now determine the approximate location of your Mac. The Find My Mac service described in Chapter 2 uses exactly this type of service to figure out where your lost or stolen Mac is.

Some Mac users may not want to allow apps to know where they currently are, so Apple has provided both a general control and fine-tuning for location services. If you don't want *any* location services to run on your Mac, uncheck the Enable Location Services box.

If you'd like to keep location services running for the purposes of Find My Mac but want to have more choice as to which applications are asking for and using your location, there's a list of applications that have requested your location in the last 24 hours. It's not a bad idea to take a look at this list from time to time if you're concerned about keeping your location information private. Any apps that you want to keep your location information from should be unchecked on the right side of the Privacy pane.

Universal Access

The Universal Access preference pane has moved from the System row in previous versions of Mac OS X up to the Personal row. The only major changes to Universal Access are on the Mouse & Trackpad pane (Figure 11–7), where you can fine-tune the control of your Mac with either a mouse or a trackpad.

In Figure 11–7, the Trackpad Options button has been clicked to reveal the new control options for the Magic Trackpad, built-in trackpads on MacBooks, or third-party Bluetooth trackpads.

Adjusting the double-click speed on your Mac trackpad to be slower can be a lifesaver for those who need some extra time to make a second click. Likewise, slowing down the scrolling speed on your Mac is useful for those with impaired eyesight.

"Scrolling with inertia" is a new Lion feature that came over from iOS devices like the iPhone and iPad. If you have one of these devices, you're familiar with how a flick of a scrolling window causes the window to "coast" for a while before scrolling stops. It's a handy feature, but it can be difficult for those with motor control issues to scroll to the point where they need to stop. Disabling "Scrolling with inertia" by unchecking the box can be a big help to some Mac users.

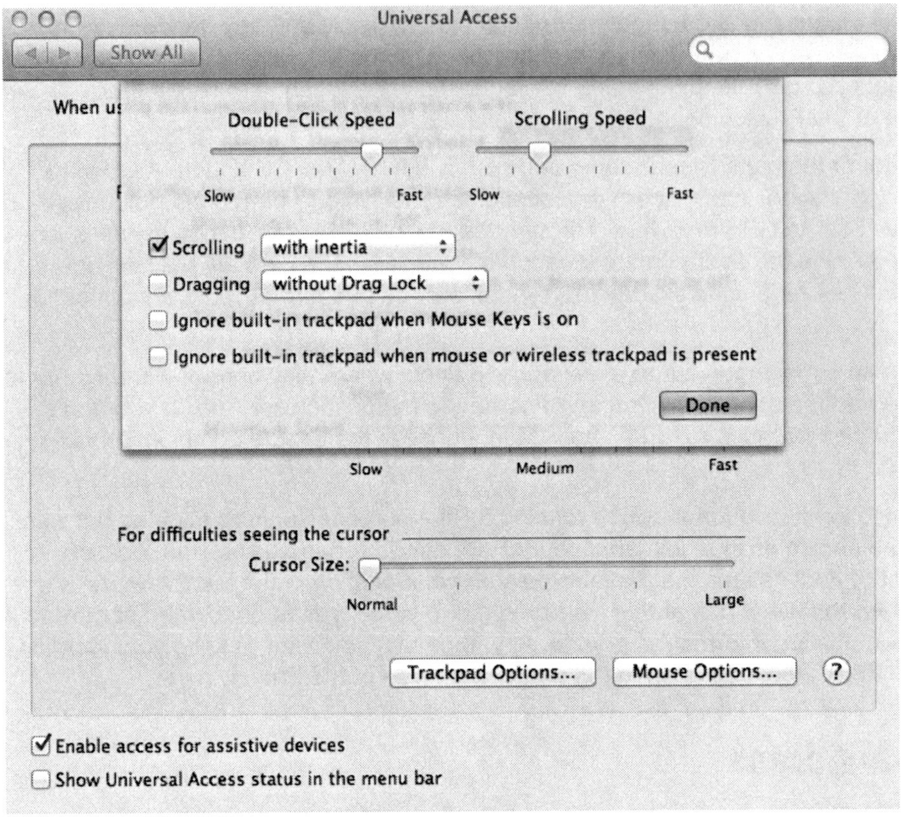

Figure 11–7. *Trackpad and mouse options allow open accessibility to the new Lion user interface gestures.*

Dragging with Drag Lock is actually a carryover from the first Mac trackpads. When enabled by checking the check box and selecting Dragging with Drag Lock from the drop-down menu, this provides a way to drag an item around the screen while still being able to lift a finger off of the trackpad and then place it back on to continue dragging.

The next check box provides a way to ignore the built-in trackpad on a MacBook when using Mouse Keys, which allows use of the keyboard arrow keys instead of a mouse or trackpad. For Mac users who have special adaptive mice or trackpads they'd rather use, the final check box (when checked) ignores the built-in trackpad when you're using another device.

The Mouse Options button provides access to double-click and scrolling speed adjustments for Apple and third-party wireless mice. Through the use of Apple's Universal Access controls, all Mac users have a way to make their favorite computer work the way they need it to work.

Hardware

The next row in System Preferences is Hardware. Here you find controls for all of the built-in hardware as well as external peripherals that are used with your Mac. What has changed in the Hardware row in Mac OS X Lion? The Energy Saver, Keyboard, Mouse, Trackpad, Print & Scan, and Sound preference panes have all changed, some dramatically and some with barely discernable differences. Let's explore those changes.

Energy Saver

The primary difference between the Energy Saver preference pane in Mac OS X Lion and Snow Leopard is the addition of a new item in the list of check boxes: "Restart automatically if the computer freezes."

As much as Apple tries to keep your entire Mac from locking up because of a software glitch, it does happen on occasion. Checking this new box enables a function that detects situations where a Mac has completely stopped responding and then restarts the computer automatically.

By default, this is unchecked (Figure 11–8) and therefore disabled. I prefer to keep it unchecked because there are often troubleshooting steps I want to perform before my computer decides to restart, and I can always shut my Mac down completely by holding down the power button for ten seconds if I need to force a restart. The choice to enable this feature is left up to the discretion of the user.

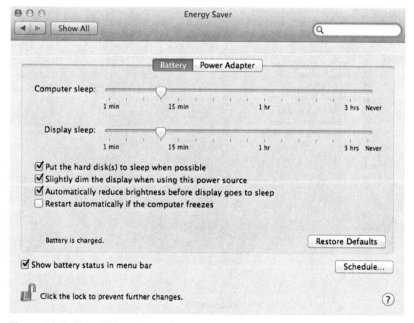

Figure 11–8. *The addition of an option to restart your Mac automatically in the event of a total system lockup is the only change to the Energy Saver preferences.*

Keyboard

As with the Energy Saver preferences, very little has changed in the Keyboard preferences (Figure 11–9). The only significant changes are the addition of two new Lion features—Launchpad and Mission Control—to the list of keyboard shortcuts.

For Launchpad, which is covered in detail in Chapter 5, the ability to show or hide Launchpad with a keyboard shortcut has been added. The big changes are for Mission Control (Chapter 6), which has a number of powerful keyboard shortcuts enabled by default.

Remember, though, that you don't have to use keyboard shortcuts for many actions in Lion. In many cases, if your Mac has a built-in trackpad or you're using an external Magic Trackpad, there's a gesture that can accomplish the same action without having to remember a key combination. For example, the keyboard shortcut for viewing Mission Control (Option-up arrow) provides the same results as swiping three fingers up the trackpad, and the Dashboard can be displayed with a three-finger swipe to the right on a trackpad instead of pressing F12.

Apple is very good about providing choices in how you use your Mac, so if keyboard shortcuts are more compatible with the way you work, you'll want to use them. If the new user interface paradigm of gestures is more your style, you can choose to work that way as well.

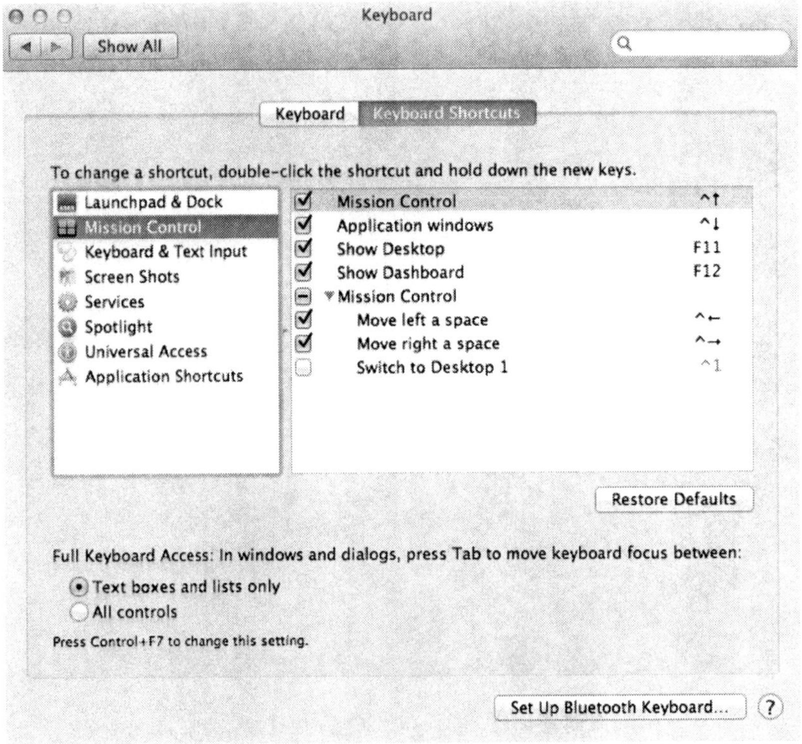

Figure 11–9. *Lion introduces new keyboard shortcuts for Launchpad and Mission Control.*

Mouse

I like what Apple did to the Mouse preferences in Mac OS X Lion. Depending on the mouse you're using, the preferences change. Figure 11–10 shows a very generic preference pane that was displayed when I connected a third-party two-button mouse to my Mac via Bluetooth.

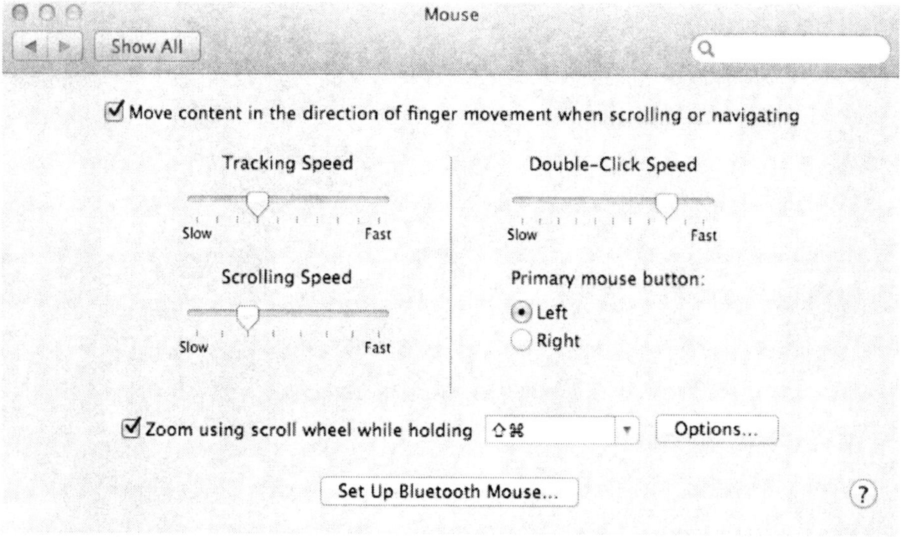

Figure 11–10. *Mouse preferences for a third-party two-button mouse*

All of the standard settings for mice, including tracking, double-clicking, and scrolling speed, have their individual sliders for controlling sensitivity. There's also a set of radio buttons to specify which mouse button—left or right—is the primary button, which might be very important to left-handed Mac users. Finally, the "zoom using scroll" function is enabled by checking the appropriate box and specifying modifier buttons (in this case, Shift-Command) to be pressed along with the scroll wheel action.

Things look a lot different when you have an Apple Magic Mouse connected to your Mac over Bluetooth. Figure 11–11 shows that Apple chose to demonstrate how the various gestures for controlling Lion work by including a small color movie on the right side of the preference pane.

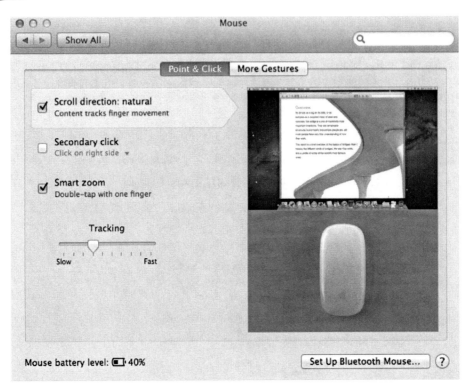

Figure 11–11. *Small movies demonstrate how the Apple Magic Mouse can be used with Lion on your Mac for gesture control of apps and Finder.*

Not only does this preference pane let you set up regular "point-and-click" functions such as a right-click capability, but the More Gestures tab opens up a number of gestures that are specific to Lion, such as swiping between pages or full-screen applications or opening Mission Control.

One of my fellow TUAW bloggers was frustrated by Lion's default scrolling direction, which is the opposite of what Mac users have been using for almost 30 years. With the new "natural" scroll direction that was borrowed from the iPhone and iPad, the content tracks your finger or mouse movement. You swipe up, the content moves up, and vice versa. The old scrolling method that most people are used to works in the opposite way. You swipe up on a trackpad or roll a mouse up, and the content moves down.

I pointed my blogging buddy to the Mouse Preferences pane, which allowed her to uncheck the scroll direction box and go back to the traditional scroll. As for me, I find that my heavy use of the iPad has made me a fan of the natural scroll direction implemented by Apple. It's all about personal preference, and fortunately Apple is good about giving Mac users a choice.

Trackpad

The Trackpad preference pane for Snow Leopard was complex and cluttered. In Lion, Apple has organized the Trackpad preferences into three main headings: Point and Click, Scroll and Zoom, and More Gestures. Each of the screens features no more than six trackpad settings and includes movies to demonstrate each of the gestures.

Apple is definitely moving in the direction of making trackpads the pointing device of the future, because many more gestures are available for the built-in and Magic trackpads than for the Magic Mouse or third-party mice.

Point & Click

The first pane, Point & Click (Figure 11–12), describes what the title suggests—settings that control how you point your cursor.

Figure 11–12. *The Point & Click pane of the Trackpad preferences*

"Tap to click," when enabled, allows a single tap the trackpad to act as a mouse click. I prefer to have this turned off, instead using a press on the trackpad to make a click because the latter provides audible and tactile feedback. "Secondary click" refers to right-clicking to view a context-sensitive menu. Enabling this gives you an action similar to right-clicking a mouse by clicking the trackpad with two fingers.

"Look up" is something new to Lion. Enabling this feature brings a dictionary lookup to compatible apps such as Safari and TextEdit by double-tapping a word with three fingers (Figure 11–13).

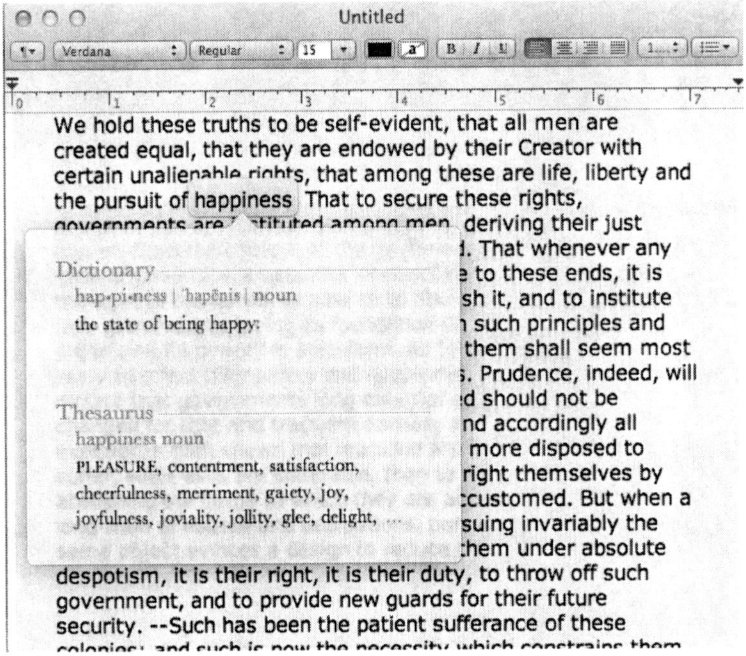

Figure 11–13. *"Look up" brings the Mac's Dictionary app to your fingertips.*

This feature is very useful to anyone who writes for a living and who needs to frequently check the meaning of words.

The last check box on the Point & Click pane is "Three finger drag." When this is enabled, moving three fingers on the trackpad drags any selected window around the Mac screen. Enabling this feature changes the swipe between full-screen apps and Mission Control gestures to four-finger gestures.

Scroll & Zoom

A look at the Scroll & Zoom pane (Figure 11–14) shows that it is primarily concerned with the gestures used to scroll, zoom, and rotate items on the Mac screen.

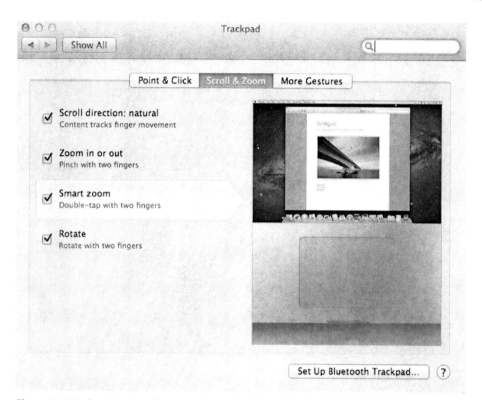

Figure 11–14. *Control of scrolling, zooming, and rotation with a trackpad is done through the Scroll & Zoom pane.*

Remember the comment about setting up scrolling with a mouse so that it followed the traditional Mac scrolling method? If you prefer the old-school method, uncheck the Scroll direction: natural box. Those who are coming to a Mac from an iPhone or iPad might prefer the natural scrolling direction.

The common iOS zoom gesture of using a pinch or "reverse pinch" to zoom out and in is enabled by checking the "Zoom in or out" box. This works only with compatible applications such as Safari, TextEdit, and iPhoto, and it may not be supported by third-party apps. There's also a "Smart zoom" option that is very familiar to iOS users. When enabled, double-tapping with two fingers zooms in on a compatible app. A second double-tap zooms out, showing more of a web page or document.

One gesture I've really enjoyed on the iPad is the ability to rotate objects with two fingers. Enabling Rotate by checking the last box on this pane brings that ability to compatible apps such as iPhoto.

More Gestures

Many of the new gestures that have been added to Mac OS X Lion are found in the last pane, More Gestures (Figure 11–15).

Figure 11–15. *Mission Control, full-screen app swiping, and Launchpad are among the Lion features accessible with gestures set up on the More Gestures pane.*

The first gesture, "Swipe between pages," is used in Safari to scroll to previous or next pages in a specific tab. This is very useful for looking at your browsing history by swiping left or right with two fingers.

"Swipe between full-screen apps" is a three-finger gesture that allows for quick switching between apps that are available in full-screen view. If you've enabled this and you also have the Dashboard activated, a three-finger swipe to the right on the trackpad displays the Dashboard and its widgets.

The default gesture used with a trackpad to display Mission Control is a three-finger swipe in the upward direction. If you prefer to use four fingers instead, you can change that setting here.

Although the App Exposé gesture isn't set by default, swiping down with three fingers displays the active application and any open documents. The App Exposé gesture is very useful when working with multiple documents in one app because it's easy to switch between those documents with as swipe and a tap.

Another gesture new to Lion is a pinch with the thumb and three fingers to display Launchpad. It's a fast way to get to your apps, especially if you hide your Dock or work in full-screen applications.

Finally, the More Gestures pane is used to enable or disable the Show Desktop gesture. It's a "reverse pinch" that is the opposite of the Launchpad gesture described earlier. This gesture displays all open applications and all full-screen apps as well. Once again, it's a very fast way to move between applications.

Print & Scan

Other than an external backup hard drive, the peripherals most Mac users are likely to own are printers and scanners. Printers let you get a hard copy of your documents or print labels, while scanners provide a wonderful way to avoid the need for a fax machine. The Print & Scan preference pane has changed subtly in Lion; it was previously called Print & Fax, but the move away from fax machines and toward scanning and e-mailing documents has made the word "fax" a bit outdated.

There's one other more significant change in the Print & Scan preference pane (Figure 11–16). In previous versions of the pane, clicking the plus sign icon to add a printer opened an Add Printer dialog that gave choices of Default (Bonjour-compatible printers that were on the same network), Fax, IP, and Windows. In Lion, those default printers are immediately visible in a drop-down menu.

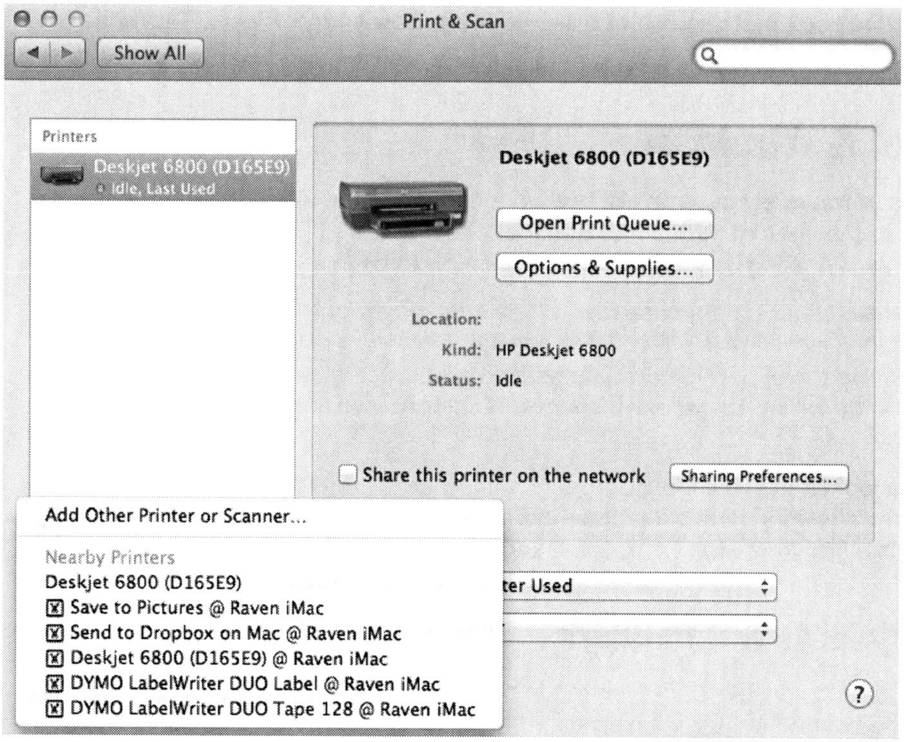

Figure 11–16. *Printers that are available on the local network can be selected for addition to your list of printers with a click.*

The nearby printers on my network in Figure 11–16 include a Wi-Fi enabled HP Deskjet printer and a number of shared printers available on my iMac. Those shared printers are not visible when the iMac is turned off. Shared scanners on a network appear under a separate Nearby Scanners heading on the same drop-down menu.

For printers or scanners that are not visible in the Nearby Printers list, clicking Add Other Printer or Scanner displays the familiar Add Printer dialog from Snow Leopard and earlier versions of Mac OS X.

Sound

The only change in the Sound preference pane is so minor that it doesn't deserve a screenshot. Mac OS X Lion no longer includes Front Row, an application that was used in earlier versions of the Mac OS to provide a way to view video content on your Mac or listen to music. Older Macs came with an infrared remote control that brought up Front Row with a click and then let you choose the type of media you wanted to watch or listen to.

Apple's new tack is to send Mac and iOS device video and audio to a $99 Apple TV, where it can be pumped to a large-screen HDTV. The Sound preference pane in Lion is missing a check box that enabled or disabled Front Row sound effects. That's the only change.

Internet & Wireless

These days, Macs rarely operate without a connection to the Internet. Whether you're connected to the Internet through an Ethernet cable or a Wi-Fi network or you're using a 3G/4G cellular tethering connection, it's uncommon to be in an unconnected situation.

The Internet & Wireless preference row will be changing slightly in the future. Currently, one of the icons is for Apple's MobileMe service. Beginning in the autumn of 2011, Apple is moving to the new iCloud data sharing and syncing service. At the end of June, 2012, MobileMe will no longer exist, and the MobileMe icon is destined for the trash heap.

Let's take a look at the new Mail, Contacts & Calendars preference pane and the minor change in the Network pane. All of the other Internet & Wireless preference panes remain unchanged from Mac OS X Snow Leopard.

Mail, Contacts & Calendars

The Mail, Contacts & Calendars preference pane (Figure 11–17) is new to Lion, and it is critical to the setup of e-mail accounts and the syncing of contacts and calendars between multiple devices (Macs, PCs, iPhones, and iPads).

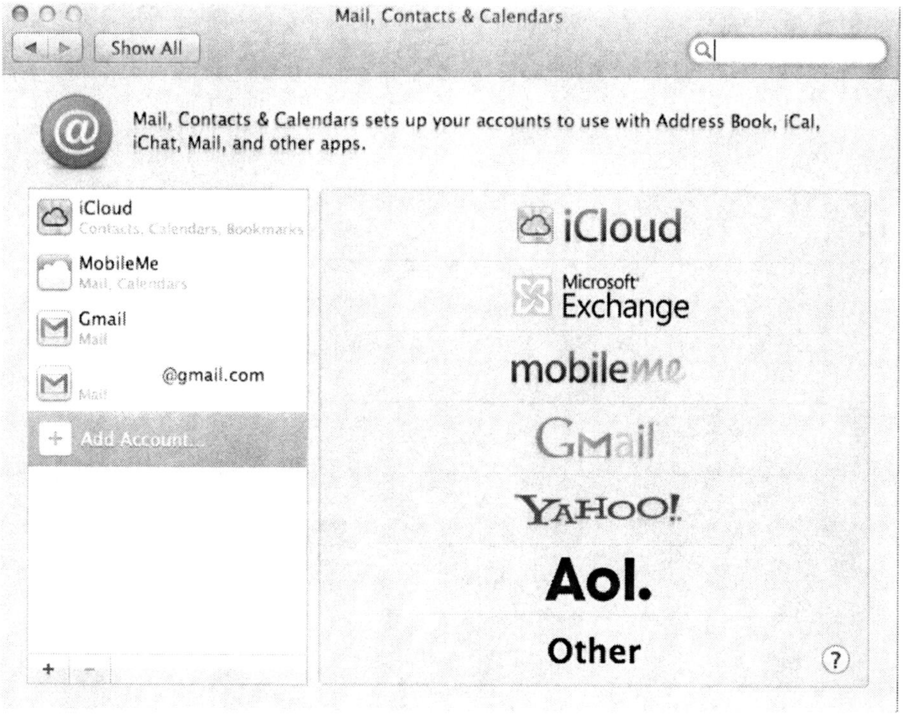

Figure 11–17. *The Mail, Contacts & Calendars preference pane is used to set up accounts for use with various Mac apps to interface with a number of online services.*

Adding an account to your Mac has been simplified with this preference pane. If you're adding a mail account, you may want to do that in the Mail application (Chapter 7). For services such as iCloud and Gmail that offer multiple services, such as address books, shared calendars, and e-mail, the Mail, Contacts & Calendars preference pane gives you a way to set up all of the services at once.

The Add Account button is highlighted by default on this pane and displays the list of services on the right side of the pane. Clicking one of the services generally displays a dialog that requests your full name, e-mail address, user ID or user name, and account password. With few exceptions, that information is enough to set up mail, contact, and calendar services. In those few exceptions where the easy setup fails, you'll be asked to continue to the Mail app to enter more details about the mail account.

For services that you've already set up, the Mail, Contacts & Calendar preference pane is useful for remembering what services you have set up, account names, and e-mail addresses.

Network

The Network preference pane has a very minor change. With Mac OS X Lion, Apple has replaced the internal brand name for Wi-Fi products—AirPort—with the term Wi-Fi.

Under earlier versions of Mac OS X, a Wi-Fi network connection was shown as "AirPort," a term that was confusing to new Mac users. The new name for those wireless network connections is good old Wi-Fi.

System

The final row of System Preferences that I'll describe is System. (The row titled Other doesn't always appear on every Mac.) System preference panes that have changed since Mac OS X Snow Leopard include Users & Groups, Date & Time, and Time Machine.

Users & Groups

The former Accounts preference pane has a new name: Users & Groups (Figure 11–18).

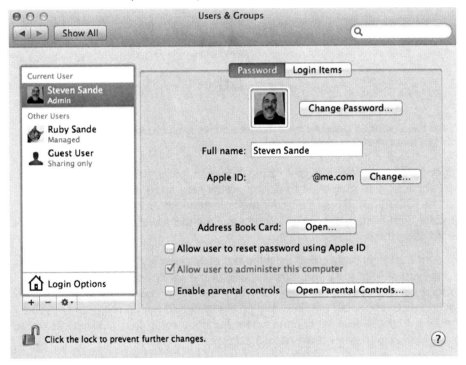

Figure 11–18. *The Password pane of the Users & Groups preferences pane*

The main change on the Password pane is in preparation for iCloud and also to provide a new feature. Rather than asking for a MobileMe user name, Lion now asks for an Apple ID. This is the ID that is used to log into the Mac App Store, iTunes, and other services provided by Apple.

The new feature is a check box that enables the ability to reset a Mac password by using an Apple ID. This could be very handy in situations where someone has deliberately or inadvertently changed your account password and either doesn't remember what they used as a password or doesn't want to tell you. Now you can change the password on your Mac with your Apple ID instead.

Date & Time

There's only one tiny change on the Date & Time preference pane. The map for Time Zone was previously a rather busy-looking color map that used NASA imagery to show deserts, mountains, and other geographical markers. It's now a uniform gray map showing the outlines of the Earth's continents. The functionality of the pane is unchanged.

Time Machine

The final System Preference pane I'll be describing is the one for Apple's built-in backup utility, Time Machine. The basic appearance of the pane is unchanged, but some differences appear when the Select Disk and Options buttons are clicked.

When Select Disk is clicked, a slightly different dialog appears than you're probably used to (Figure 11–19).

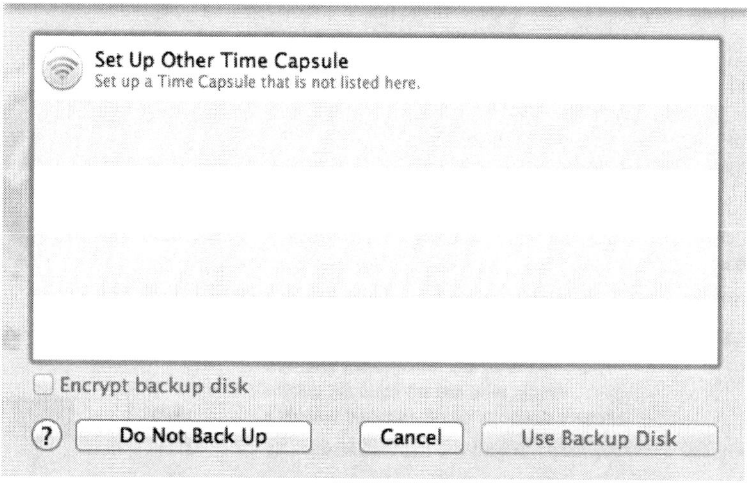

Figure 11–19. *The revised Time Machine Select Disk dialog*

Previously there was a separate button for setting up an Apple Time Capsule. Now, by default, a button to set up an additional Time Capsule appears. This is useful if you purchase a second Time Capsule for extra backup security and want to set it up for backups from your Mac as well.

There's a new security feature in Mac OS X Lion that allows encryption of your entire backup disk. The "Encrypt backup disk" button provides a way to completely encrypt the backup disk and keep your files safe from tampering or theft. This wasn't available in previous versions of Mac OS X, which meant that files that had been backed up to an external drive were unencrypted. If your backup drive was ever lost or stolen, your files were wide open to inspection.

Now let's look at the Options dialog (Figure 11–20).

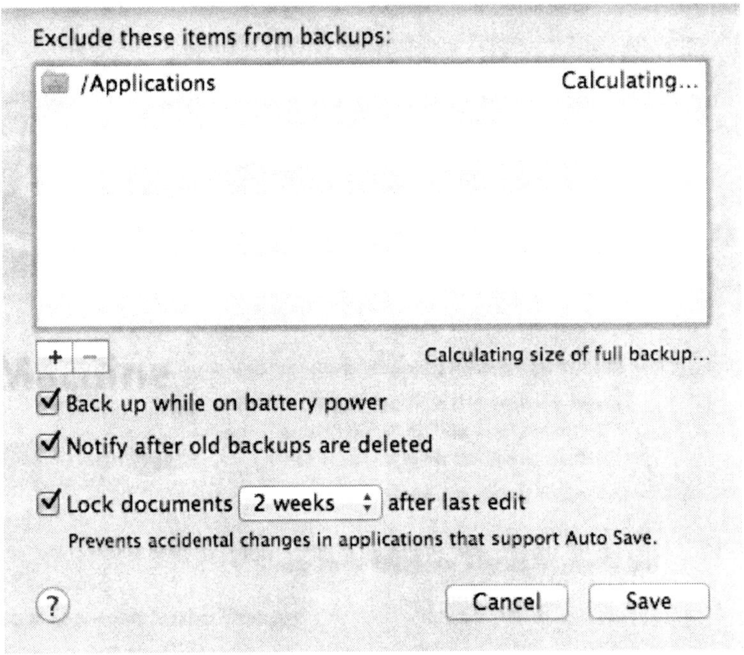

Exclude these items from backups:

/Applications   Calculating...

+ −   Calculating size of full backup...

☑ Back up while on battery power

☑ Notify after old backups are deleted

☑ Lock documents 2 weeks ⬍ after last edit
   Prevents accidental changes in applications that support Auto Save.

(?)   [Cancel]   [Save]

Figure 11–20. *A new feature for the Options dialog in Time Machine*

The new feature here, "Lock documents after last edit," helps prevent accidental changes in Mac applications that support Lion's new Auto Save function. By locking documents after a specified amount of time, Auto Save won't save changes automatically over an old document that you may not want to have changed. It's just a good way to ensure that you always have a chain of the changes that were made to your documents over time.

Summary

In this chapter, I've outlined the changes to the System Preferences for Mac OS X Lion. In some cases, those changes are subtle; in other situations, the changes are rather involved. Let's review the System Preference changes that make the largest impact:

- Lion's "disappearing scroll bars" are brought back to life with the check of a box on the General preference pane.

- The old Exposé & Spaces preference pane is gone, replaced by a completely new way (Mission Control) to organize and reveal apps, documents, and Finder.

- Since Lion now supports many new iOS-like gestures to perform actions, it's a good idea to get familiarized with the revised Mouse and Trackpad preference panes.

- Mail, Contacts & Calendars is the new way to set up mail, address, and calendar accounts with a variety of service and is your gateway to the new iCloud service.

- Lion users are able to change a lost or unremembered Mac password using an Apple ID.

- Time Machine now encrypts the backup disk, protecting your personal information in your backup.

Chapter 12

OS X Lion Server

The day that OS X Lion was announced, Apple surprised the Mac community with the announcement of OS X Lion Server. Previously, the server version of OS X was a completely separate operating system that provided many collaborative services while still maintaining the ease of use of the Mac OS. That power came with a price tag: Snow Leopard Server cost $499 for an unlimited user license.

Apple has changed all that with OS X Lion Server. At just $49.99 for an unlimited user license, Server is now an application that is purchased from the Mac App Store and installed on a Mac to give it the ability to act as a workgroup or home server. In this chapter, I'll provide background on what a server is and what it can do, how to install and configure OS X Lion Server, and how to make the best use of the various components of Lion Server.

What's a Server?

A *server* is a computer program running to serve the needs or requests of other programs (or clients) that may or may not be running on the same computer. A server can also be a physical computer dedicated to running services to serve the needs of other computers on the same network.

When talking about OS X Lion Server, I'm referring to a computer program running on a Mac that provides a set of services to other Macs, iPads, iPhones, and PCs. These services include the following:

- *Network Management:* To make the server easily accessible by users, administrators need to configure the network settings and host name. This varies depending on whether the server is a local host or is intended to be an Internet server.

- *User and Group Management:* An administrator can create user accounts and organize those users into logical or organizational groups. Depending on the groups a user is member of, the user has access to particular services and is denied access to others.

- *Address Book Server:* This service provides you with an excellent choice for sharing an address book between Mac users in your office or home.

- *File Sharing:* A necessity for most businesses, servers provide a common repository for files used by workgroups.

- *iCal Server:* Sharing calendars among members of a workgroup is possible with iCal Server. It's also possible to add resources to calendars, such as meeting rooms, projectors, or pool cars.

- *Time Machine Server:* Rather than giving each Mac on a network a separate external hard disk for backups, Time Machine Server creates a shared space on the server for all machines to point Time Machine to.

- *Web Server:* Some companies or individuals want to host their own web sites. The Apache web server built into the OS X Lion Server app makes configuring and updating those sites easy.

- *Wiki Server:* Many organizations like to use wikis for collaborative creation and storage of documents. Think of a small-scale version of Wikipedia.org containing process documents for your organization, and you've got the idea of what Lion Server's wiki tools can do.

Each service described in the preceding list is covered in more detail in this chapter. The following additional services handled by OS X Lion Server won't be covered here:

- *Mail Server:* Small businesses often benefit from having their own e-mail server on-site instead of outsourcing e-mail to another company.

- *Podcast Server:* For schools or other organizations wanting to create and host podcasts, Podcast Server works hand in hand with the Mac Podcast Capture application (found in the Utilities folder) to record, edit, and broadcast content.

- *VPN Server:* Remote or traveling workers need secure access to their office network. VPN Server provides that secure connection.

- *Device Management:* Mac users on a network with a Lion Server can use the Mail, Contacts & Calendar preference pane to automatically configure their Macs to use services provided by the server.

- *iChat Server:* Apple's iChat service comes to the family or workgroup through iChat Server, which hosts a private chat group.

Apple has been making a concerted effort over the last few versions of Mac OS X to simplify setting up and maintaining a server. With OS X Lion Server, that effort has paid off. Apple is now targeting home offices, businesses, schools, and hobbyists with capabilities that used to require a trained administrator and dedicated hardware. Now any Mac that is capable of running Mac OS X Lion can be set up as a server.

Configuring a server properly for access over the Internet can be frustrating and is best left to those who are familiar with the details of name servers and DNS resolution. For the remainder of this chapter, I'll focus on configuring a local server that is providing limited shared services to a single internal network.

Purchasing and Installing OS X Lion Server

To purchase OS X Lion Server, you must have an Apple ID that you've used with the Mac App Store or iTunes before. If you don't, no worries; you can set up a new account easily through the Mail, Contacts & Calendars preferences pane (Chapter 11).

Launch the Mac App Store, and then use the search field in the upper-right corner of the store to search for *Mac OS X Lion Server*. When it appears in the search results, click the price ($49.99), and the button turns green and displays the words *Buy App*. Click that button, provide your Apple ID password if required, and Lion Server begins to download and install itself.

The first indication that installation is beginning is a cheerful Welcome to Server splash screen (Figure 12–1).

Figure 12–1. *After the Server app is downloaded from the Mac App Store, installation begins with this splash screen.*

If you'd like to install Server at a later time, click the Quit button. Like all other apps on your Mac, Server is stored in your Applications folder. Click the Continue button to start installing and configuring Server.

The installer requests that you agree to the terms of the software license agreement. Upon clicking the Agree button, you get to see one more screen; this one has the words *Install Software* on it. Click the Continue button one more time to move closer to having Server installed on your Mac (Figure 12–2).

Figure 12–2. *OS X Lion Server downloads and installs additional software to your Mac as part of the configuration process.*

The time it takes to download the additional files depends on the speed of your Internet connection, but it generally takes less than ten minutes for most broadband connections. Once the installation is completed, another splash screen (this one containing a green circle with a check mark in the center) appears, letting you know that you're ready to go. Click the Finish button, and the Server user interface appears (Figure 12–3).

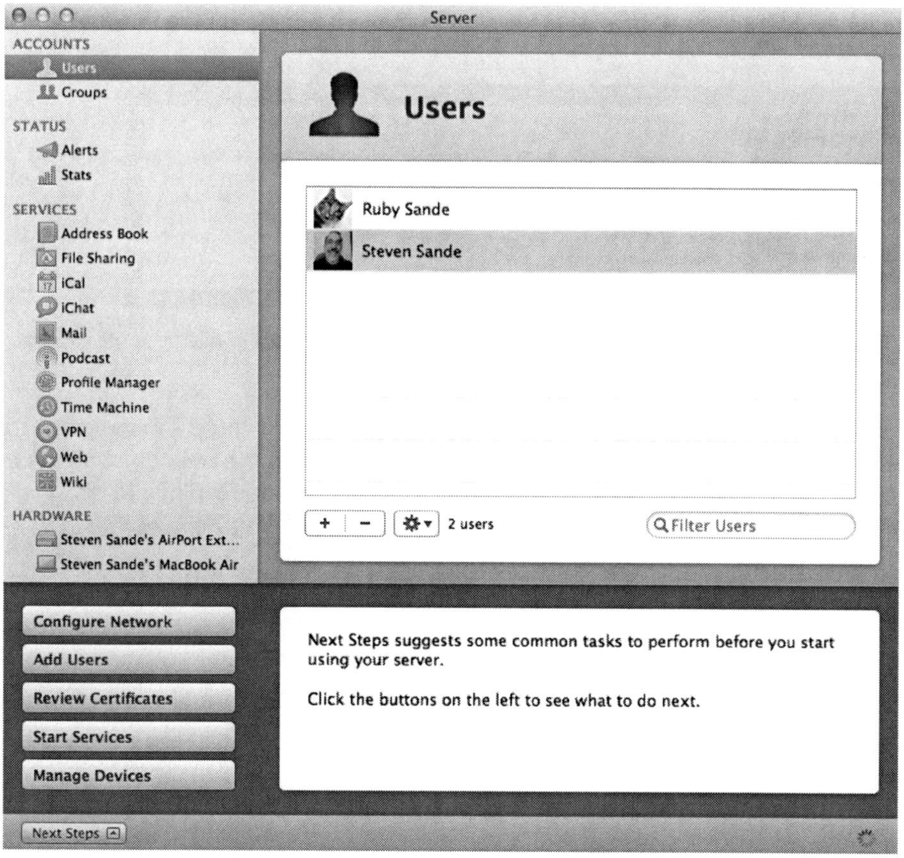

Figure 12–3. *The Lion Server user interface, with Next Steps listed at the bottom of the window to help configure and set up the server*

Configuration of Lion Server

The first step in setting up your server is to configure your network settings. On the bottom of the Lion Server window are five buttons that describe the next steps you should take in the setup. The buttons can be hidden by clicking the Next Steps button at the bottom of the window and can be brought out for review again with one more click of the button. I'll describe the function of four of these five buttons in the remainder of this chapter, detailing some of the services provided by Lion Server.

Configure Network

Network settings are critical to server success. As mentioned, in this chapter I'll be setting this server up in the simplest way—as a local shared resource on a single network. Clicking the Configure Network button displays a short explanation of how the server is presently configured and what is needed to make it usable on the Internet (Figure 12–4).

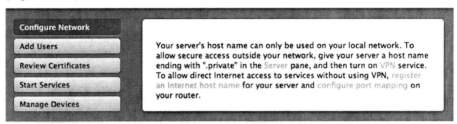

Figure 12–4. *The Configure Network button provides a quick path to the proper setup of your server on the local network.*

As shown in Figure 12–4, the default configuration is just what is wanted—a server on the local network. To set this up for secured external access from the outside, it needs a `.private` host name. Clicking the Server link in this window provides a place to change the host name. The network settings for the server are displayed (Figure 12–5).

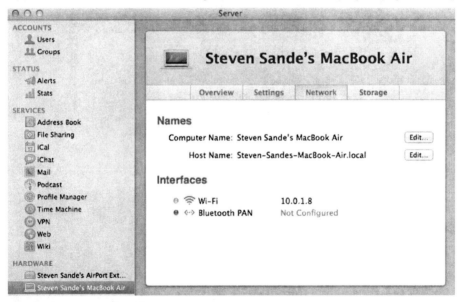

Figure 12–5. *The network settings for your hardware provide a way to change the server's host name.*

Since most office servers receive a lot of network traffic, it's best to make sure your server has an Ethernet connection. For home servers, a Wi-Fi connection, as shown in Figure 12–5, should be more than adequate. It is also recommended that a static IP address be set up so that the server is always at the same network address.

To change the name of the computer, you can click the Edit button at the right of the Computer Name listing to bring up an edit window in which you can easily change and save the name.

Change the Host Name

Editing the host name isn't as simple. Clicking that Edit button displays a configuration assistant for changing the host name. After you get a warning that changing a server's host name may affect services running on the server, you're asked to click Continue, which displays a Host Name panel describing your choices (Figure 12–6).

Figure 12–6. *Select the type of server you want to set up. Choices include a local server, a local server that can be accessed remotely via a virtual private network (VPN) connection, or an Internet-connected server.*

Three choices of host name are available: host names for a local network, a private network, and the Internet. For the purposes of this chapter, I've selected the local network before clicking the Continue button to go to the next screen (Figure 12–7).

On this screen are fields for the computer name and host name. For example, I'll change the computer name to Home Server so that other users on my network see that name in the Finder. For the host name, I'm going to retain the name provided by the Server app.

Server

Connecting to Your Mac

Users will connect computers and mobile devices to your server by using the server's name or address.

Computer Name: Home Server

Enter a name that users will see in their Finder sidebars and may click to connect for file sharing, such as "My Company Server".

Host Name: server.local

Enter a host name ending in ".local", such as "server.local".

Network Address: 10.0.1.8 on Wi-Fi   Change Network...

Figure 12–7. *The server name and host name are defined on this screen, and the network settings are accessible by clicking the Change Network button.*

Remember the recommendation earlier to use a static IP address for your server? That address can be entered and saved with a click of the Change Network button shown in Figure 12–7. Once the computer and host name changes are committed with a click of the Continue button at the bottom of the window, you're returned to the server network configuration pane.

For readers who are setting up either private servers or Internet-connected servers, clicking the appropriate links in the Next Steps description for configuring your network displays other configuration assistants to walk you through the required steps.

Add Users

The next button on Next Steps is Add Users (Figure 12–8). Similar to adding users to a stand-alone Mac, what you're doing here is creating user accounts and passwords for other people who are going to use the services provided by the server.

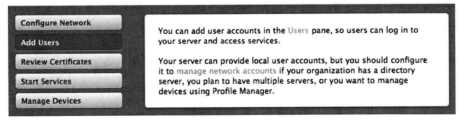

Configure Network
Add Users
Review Certificates
Start Services
Manage Devices

You can add user accounts in the Users pane, so users can log in to your server and access services.

Your server can provide local user accounts, but you should configure it to manage network accounts if your organization has a directory server, you plan to have multiple servers, or you want to manage devices using Profile Manager.

Figure 12–8. *The Add Users button in the Next Steps window provides links for setting up user accounts, setting up network accounts, and connecting to a directory server.*

A few paragraphs about network accounts and directory services are in order, since I won't be discussing them in detail. A directory service is software that stores and organizes information about a network's users and resources and that allows network administrators to manage users' access to the resources.

Apple recommends that if you have a directory server, if you plan to have multiple servers at some point, or if you want to be able to manage devices on your network, you should configure this server to manage network accounts. Clicking the "manage network accounts" link visible in Figure 12–8 launches a Configure Networks and Groups configuration assistant to walk you through the necessary steps.

If you're setting up a Lion server in an existing enterprise environment that already provides directory services and login authentication through Apple's Open Directory or Microsoft's Active Directory, your server can be connected to those directories. A "connect to it" link, not visible in Figure 12–8, launches the Configure Networks and Groups configuration assistant to set up the directory services.

In this example, the server is being configured for local user accounts. To add and edit those accounts, clicking the Users link displays the Users pane. Click the plus sign (+) icon to add a new user (Figure 12–9).

New User

Full Name:	David Caolo
Account Name:	davecaolo
Email Address:	afakeaddress@gmail.com
Password:	••••
Verify:	••••

☑ Allow user to administer this server

Cancel   Done

Figure 12–9. *Adding a new user to the server*

Each new user requires a minimal amount of information for setup—their full name, an account or "short" name that can also be used for logging in, their e-mail address, and a password. The key to the right of the password field in Figure 12–9 is useful for generating strong random passwords that can then be sent or given to the new user.

There's also a powerful check box on this setup dialog. Allowing a user to administer the server is giving them the keys to the castle; they'll be able to turn services on and off, change settings, add and remove users, and more. It's good to have a person or two designated as a backup network administrator, but be sure that person knows exactly what the responsibility entails. By clicking the Done button, the user is added to the local directory.

Add Groups

One more thing you might want to do with your users is to add them to groups. Groups are very helpful in making sure that certain users have access to some folders but not others or are allowed to use a specific service while others are denied.

At the top of the sidebar of the OS X Lion Server app is an Accounts section where administrators can add or edit user information and also create groups. Clicking the plus sign (+) icon at the bottom of the New Groups window displays a dialog that asks for a unique full name (for example, Finance) and creates a group name that can be changed if desired.

Once a group has been created, it's time to add members to it. Double-clicking the group name displays a dialog (Figure 12–10) in which group services are defined and members are added or removed.

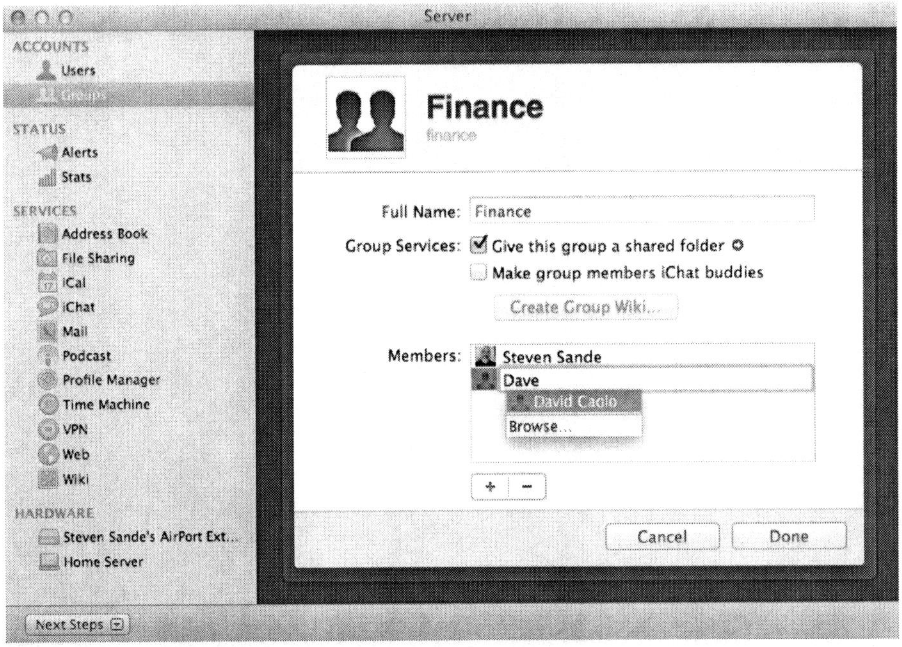

Figure 12–10. *Adding members to a group and defining group services*

As visible in Figure 12–10, you don't need to type the full name of a user to add them to a group; the short name (in this case, Dave) works fine and displays the full name from a drop-down list.

At the top of this dialog are several group services that may be enabled. First, selecting "Give this group a shared folder" creates a Finance folder that only members of the Finance group have read and write access to. By default, the shared folders are stored at the root level of the server boot drive in a Groups folder.

The next check box adds all the group members to an iChat buddy list. This is useful if you're planning to enable iChat as a service and want to facilitate communications in workgroups. There's a Create Group Wiki button that is grayed out in Figure 12–10; that button becomes usable if the Wiki Server service is enabled.

Review Certificates

The next item in the Next Steps pane is Review Certificates. Digital certificates provide a way to encrypt information being transferred between users and the servers and are critical if your server is on the Internet, being set up to host a virtual private network (VPN), or hosting web pages for e-commerce.

Although this chapter doesn't include details on how to obtain certificates or how to use them with Lion Server, clicking the links in the Next Steps description provides that information for you. Digital certificates obtained from a certificate authority usually have a fee associated with them, must be renewed annually, and may require that you send documentation about your business to the authority.

Push notifications are familiar to anyone who has an iPhone or iPad. What notifications provide is a way to be alerted to new e-mails, incoming calendar events, and so on. If you want to enable push notifications from your server, Apple provides a way to obtain a special certificate through the Server app that requires only an Apple ID and a password.

Start Services

At this point, the basics of a server have been installed and users and groups have been created, so it's time to start sharing services with those users. In this section, I'll describe how several of the services are enabled and what it takes for other devices on the network to connect to those services.

Address Book

Apple describes the Address Book service as providing a "consolidated, server-hosted contact list." To get full details on how the service works for both a local server as described in this book and for an Internet-connected server, select Help ➤ Server Help, click Collaborate, and then choose "Provide centralized contact information."

To start the Address Book service, select the service from the Server app sidebar and click the On/Off switch so that it slides to the On position. It may take a few moments for Address Book to start up, but once it is ready, a small green dot appears next to the app name in the Server app sidebar.

If you choose to make the Address Book service available to users over the Internet, some extra steps are involved that aren't described here. Those steps are outlined in a series of Apple manuals downloadable from `http://support.apple.com/manuals#macosxserver`. Although the manuals for OS X Lion Server were not yet available at publication time, many of the manuals for Snow Leopard Server also have detailed information about how to configure your server for Internet access.

For homes or businesses with Apple AirPort Extreme Wi-Fi routers, those devices can be managed by the Server app to provide the port forwarding that is necessary to make services visible to Internet users.

Connecting to Address Book Server from a Mac

To connect to a user's address book on Lion Server from a Mac, launch the Address Book application, select **Address Book ➤ Preferences** from the menu bar, and then click the Accounts button. By clicking the plus sign (+) button at the bottom of the Address Book preferences, an Add Account dialog appears (Figure 12–11).

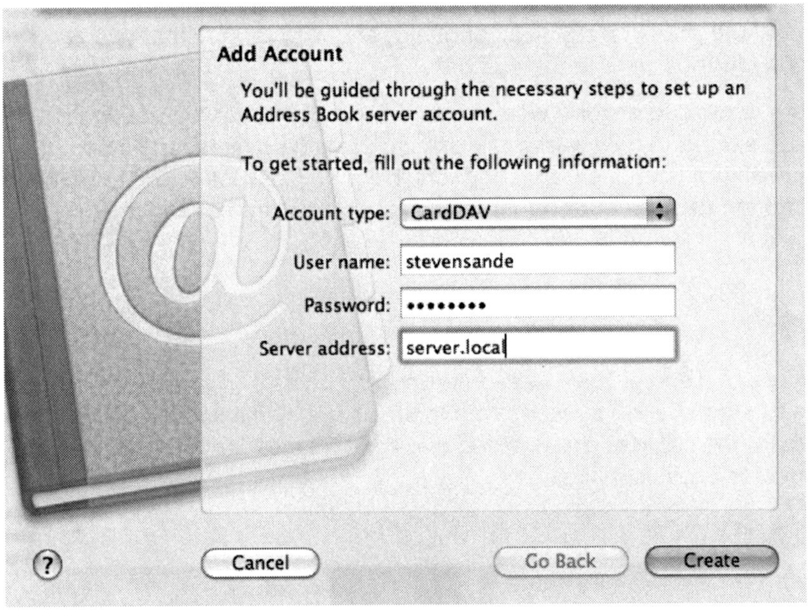

Add Account

You'll be guided through the necessary steps to set up an Address Book server account.

To get started, fill out the following information:

Account type: CardDAV

User name: stevensande

Password: ••••••••

Server address: server.local

Cancel   Go Back   Create

Figure 12–11. *Adding an Address Book server account*

The Account Type option is already set as CardDAV, the protocol used by Address Book Server. For the user name, enter the "short name" of the user. For example, my full name is listed as Steven Sande, but the user name or short name is stevensande. That's an important distinction to remember, because entering your full name results in an error message. Enter the user password, and then enter the host name of your server, which in this case is server.local. Click Create, and the account is added to Address Book.

In the situation shown in Figure 12–11, I would be able to access only the address cards for my user name. For a shared organizational or family address book, create a shared user account—something like "sharedaddressbook"—and a password that can be given to everyone. As individual users add their cards to the shared user account, everyone is able to view and edit them.

The OS X Lion Mail, Contacts & Calendars preference panel is another way to add a server-based address book. Click Add Account... and then click the Other button. Select "Add a CardDAV account" from the list of account types, and then click Create.... Enter the same user name, password, and server address information discussed previously, and click Create... again to finish creating the account.

Connecting to Address Book Server from an iOS Device

One of the more exciting features of OS X Lion Server is the built-in support for iOS devices. Any iPad, iPhone, or iPod touch on a network can connect to Address Book Server for access to a shared or single-user address book hosted on the server.

To connect to Address Book Server from an iOS device, launch the Settings app and then tap the Mail, Contacts, Calendars button. Tap Add Account, and then tap Other. Tap Add CardDAV Account, and a screen appears where you can enter your server and user information (Figure 12–12).

Figure 12–12. *Entering CardDAV account and server information to link an iPhone to Address Book Server*

Entering the iOS Contacts app, the connection to the server is listed at the bottom of the list of groups. Tapping the server connection displays only the address cards stored on the server, while All Contacts displays address cards stored locally, shared via MobileMe or iCloud, shared with other services (Gmail, for example), and stored on the server.

File Sharing

One of the classic uses of servers is to let users store and share folders and files on the server. OS X Lion Server gives Mac, Windows, and iOS device users access to file shares without the need to run any special software. Select the File Sharing service in the Server app sidebar and click the On/Off switch to start the service. Once File Sharing is enabled, a green dot appears in the sidebar, and a list of the share points appears as well (Figure 12–13).

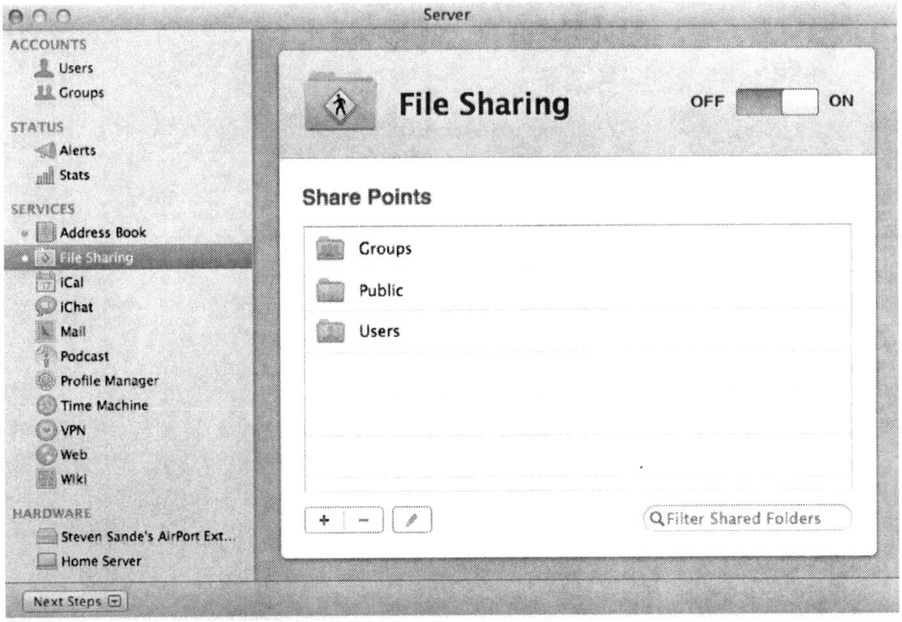

Figure 12–13. *File sharing is enabled, and the three standard share points are visible.*

Three standard share points are visible when File Sharing is enabled: Groups, Public, and Users. Groups contains files and folders available for sharing by one or more of your groups. Public contains information that is openly available to anyone on your network; think of this as an open dropbox for unsecured shared information. Users is the repository for private folders for individual users.

Share Point Access Controls and Settings

Each of the share points has a set of top-level access controls and settings that are available by double-clicking the share point (Figure 12–14).

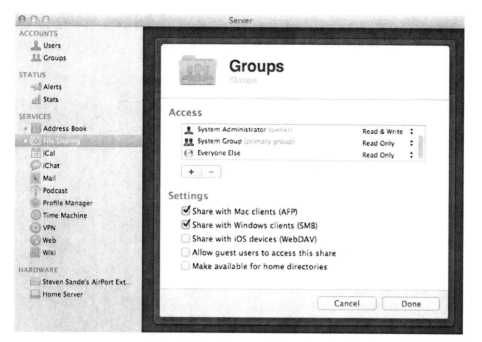

Figure 12–14. *Double-clicking a share point reveals access controls and settings.*

For these high-level share points, it's not a bad idea to leave the default access permissions, to keep users from creating new, unwanted shared folders. By default, the systems administrator has complete control over the share point, while everyone else can view what's in the share but not do much else. A description of how individual folder permissions are applied is coming up shortly.

The settings check boxes are useful for deciding what kind of devices can access the share points. By default, files and folders are shared with Mac and Windows clients. To make the share points available to iPhone, iPad, and iPod touch users, check the "Share with iOS devices" box. Sometimes you may want to allow guest users to access a share without needing a user name and password, and checking the "Allow guest users to access this share" box provides that capability.

The last settings check box is an interesting one because it gives the share point the ability to host home directories for server users. What does this mean? Rather than keeping the home directory of a user on a specific computer, it can be stored in a share point. The advantage of this is that the user can move from one Mac to another, and that computer appears the same to them on each Mac. All of their settings, documents, and personal applications show up on any machine once the user signs into the server. Storing home directories on a server is not discussed further in this book, but information on how to do so is available in Apple's downloadable manuals at http://support.apple.com/manuals#macosxserver.

Connecting to Shared Folders from Mac OS X

Now that the server is set up with shared folders, I'll show you how to get to those folders from another Mac on the network. The examples shown here are from an OS X Lion machine, but the process is essentially the same on earlier versions of OS X. You have a couple of ways to connect to the shared folders.

The first way involves clicking the server icon in the Shared category of the Finder Sidebar. If the Finder window shows that you're "Connected as Guest," then you have access only to shared folders that have provided full read and/or write access to all users. To log in as a registered user, click the Connect As button, and a standard login dialog appears (Figure 12–15).

Enter your name and password for the server "Home Server".

Connect as: ○ Guest
            ⦿ Registered User
            ○ Using an Apple ID

Name: stevensande

Password: ••••••••

☐ Remember this password in my keychain

Change Password...   Cancel   **Connect**

Figure 12–15. *Logging into a server as a registered user*

This dialog provides several choices: connecting as a guest, connecting as a registered user, or using an Apple ID to connect. There's a check box for saving the password in the Mac OS X keychain, and a user also has a way to change his or her password from the dialog.

Once connected, the user sees all shared folders that they have been given permission to. Files or folders that cannot be read or opened by the user because of insufficient permission are marked with a small red circle on the lower-right side of the file or folder icon.

The alternative method of connecting to shared folders is to select Go ➤ Connect to Server from the Finder menu bar. In the Connect to Server dialog that appears, enter the server host name and click Connect. The same dialog shown in Figure 12–15 appears, but after connecting to the server, a new dialog appears (Figure 12–16).

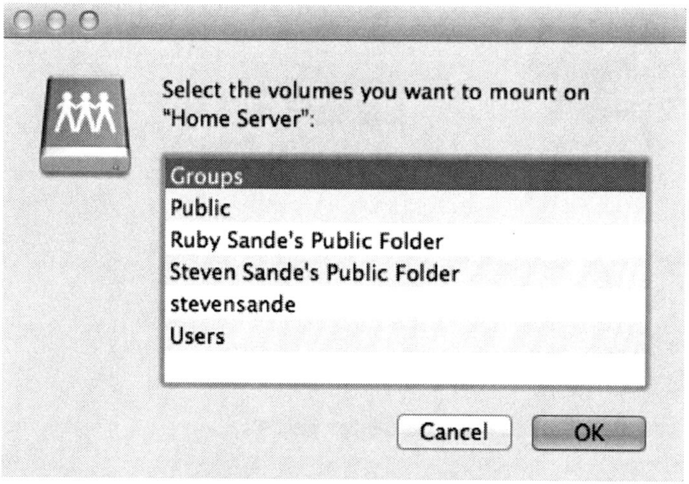

Figure 12–16. *The dialog for selecting volumes to mount on your Mac*

After you've selected a volume (shared folder) or several and then clicked the OK button, the volumes are opened in Finder windows for browsing.

Connecting to Shared Folders from iOS Devices

One of the settings visible in Figure 12–14 is a check box for enabling sharing with iOS devices through WebDAV, a protocol for sharing files over a standard web HTTP connection. Using that capability, any app on your iOS devices that uses WebDAV can connect to your server for saving and retrieving files.

For businesses, this means employees have instant, secure access to content such as shared presentations, document templates, process manuals, or even medical records or imagery. Around the home, imagine having access to a shared library of digitized movies on the server, available to watch on your iPhone, iPod touch, or iPad.

As an example, I'll grab a Pages document from the server and open it in Pages on the iPhone. On the opening screen of Pages, there's a plus sign (+) in the upper-left corner to add a new document. Users can either create a totally new document or copy one that has been imported from iTunes, is stored on iDisk, or is located on a WebDAV server. Since my document is stored on the server, I tap the WebDAV button. A WebDAV sign-in screen is displayed (Figure 12–17).

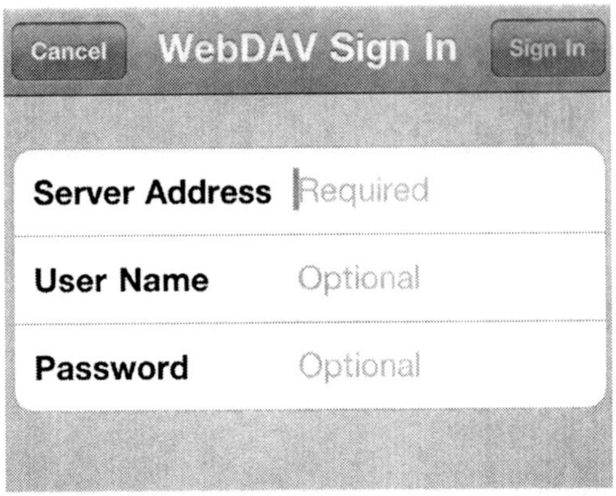

Figure 12–17. *The sign-in screen for a connection to a shared folder through WebDAV*

As with most sign-ins, the trick here is to use the proper server address along with your user name and password. The server address will be in the following format:

```
http://[server host name]/webdav//[path]
```

In my example, the server host name is server.local, and the documents are stored inside a folder named Development stored in the Groups share. The server address is entered as follows:

```
http://server.local/webdav//Groups/Development
```

The user name is once again the short name described earlier. Once I've entered the account password and tapped the Sign In button, I see the contents of the folder (Figure 12–18).

Figure 12–18. *The documents stored on the server. Grayed-out items cannot be opened by the current application.*

Document types supported by the current iOS application show up in black, while those that aren't supported are listed in gray. With a tap, the document is copied to Pages for editing.

Moving documents from iOS devices to the server is just as easy. In Pages, tapping the Share and Print "wrench" icon reveals a Copy to WebDAV button. If you've logged in to the server previously to download a file, you are connected to the server immediately. This last observation brings up an important security point; users should remember to sign out of the server when they're not actively copying or saving files to prevent unauthorized access by others.

iCal Server

Connecting to a shared calendar on the server is similar to connecting to the shared address book. As with the previous shared resources, Address Book and File Sharing, iCal Server is enabled by clicking the iCal service in the Server app sidebar and then clicking the Off/On button. Once the green light appears, you're ready to go.

Although I won't elaborate here, the iCal Server settings provide a way to allow invitations using e-mail addresses. That requires that the mail service be up and running on your server as well, since iCal requires the creation of an e-mail address to respond to those invitations. Server administrators are also able to create locations and resources—things like offices or PC projectors—that can be scheduled using iCal.

Connecting to Shared Calendars from Mac OS X

To connect to a calendar that is shared or hosted on the server, the process is quite similar to what I described for Address Book. Launch iCal, select **iCal ➤ Preferences** from the menu bar, and then click the Accounts button. After clicking the plus sign (+) button at the bottom of the Address Book preferences, an Add Account dialog appears (Figure 12–19).

When connecting to the server, select CalDAV as the account type, instead of Automatic, because you need to enter a server user name. By entering the same user name, password, and server address (host name) that was entered for Address Book, you are connected to the server in moments after clicking the Create button.

If I log into iCal Server with the settings shown in Figure 12–19, I would be able to access the calendar only for my user name. For a shared organizational or family calendar, create a shared user account—something like "sharedcalendar"—and a password that can be given to everyone. As individual users add their appointments to the shared user account, everyone can view and edit them.

The OS X Lion Mail Contacts & Calendars preference panel is another way to add a server-based calendar. Click Add Account... and then click the Other button. Select "Add a CalDAV account" from the list of account types and then click Create.... Enter the same user name, password, and server address information discussed previously and click Create... again to finish creating the account.

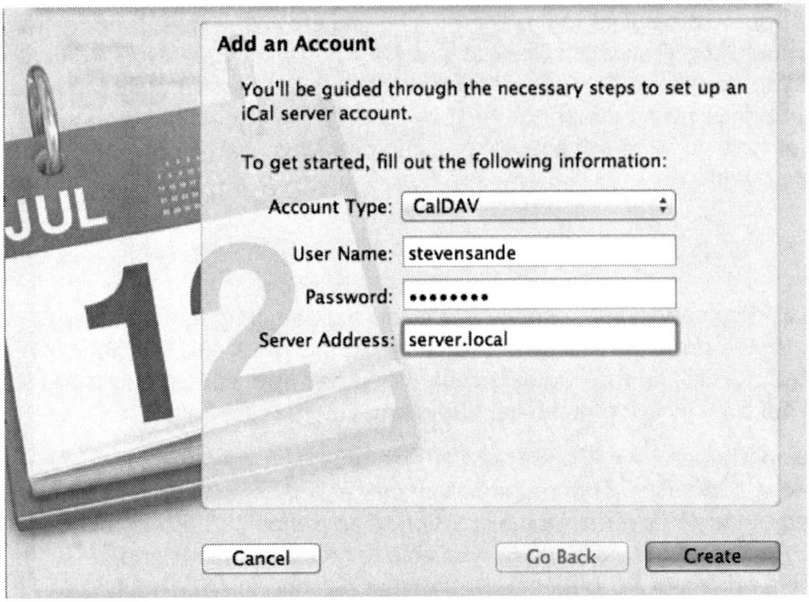

Figure 12–19. *Adding an iCal server account in OS X Lion*

The added calendar appears in the sidebar in iCal. To add an event to the shared calendar, double-click the day on which the event occurs to create a blank event and then fill in the pertinent start time, end time, alarm, and other information associated with a calendar event. Anyone logged into a shared calendar sees the new event immediately.

Connecting to Shared Calendars from iOS Devices

Shared calendars are even more useful if you view them from any Apple device, including your iPad, iPhone, or iPod touch. Much in the same way that shared address books are added to iOS devices, those same devices can connect to an iCal Server.

To connect to iCal Server from an iOS device, launch the Settings app and then tap the Mail, Contacts, Calendars button. Tap Add Account and then tap Other. Tap Add CalDAV Account, and a screen appears for entering your server and user information (Figure 12–20).

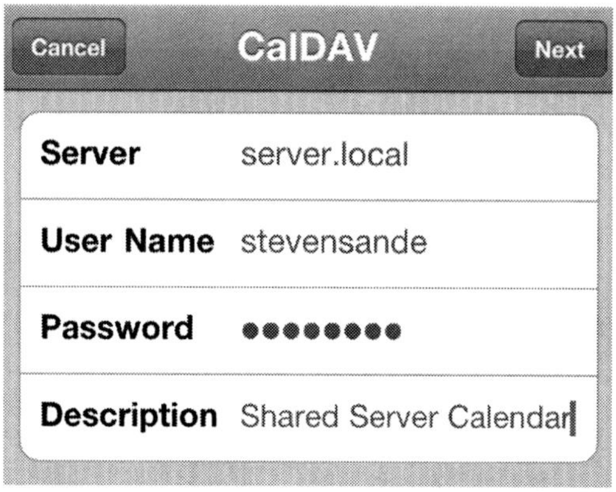

Figure 12–20. *Signing into the iCal Server from an iPhone*

The same information that was entered for the shared address book is entered here: the server host name, the short user name, and the user password. Tapping Next makes the connection and adds the server-shared calendar to the list of calendars on the iOS device.

Time Machine

Another use of Lion Server in small businesses or homes is to create a shared Time Machine backup point. This has its advantages (there's only one drive or array to take care of, instead of one for each Mac), but it also has a several big disadvantages. Time Machine backups expand to the amount of space available on a hard drive, so even a relatively small group of Macs backing up to a server can overwhelm its capacity quickly. The other issue is that Macs connected over Wi-Fi connections take a very long time to complete the initial backup to the server. It is recommended that Ethernet networks be used in situations where multiple workstations are backing up to a server.

To set up a Time Machine server to accumulate the backups from all the Macs at your location, turn on the Time Machine service by selecting it from the Server app sidebar and then clicking the On/Off button. The service requests a backup destination, which is generally an external drive or RAID array that is linked to the server with a fast FireWire 800, Thunderbolt, iSCSI, or fiber-optic connection.

How much disk space do you need to back up a bunch of Macs? A good rule of thumb is to add up the disk capacities of all Macs being backed up and then double it. It's also a good idea to set the Time Machine options so that applications and system files are not backed up; those items can be reinstalled from the Mac App Store and application disks if needed and don't need to be taking up space on your backup drive.

Once the service is running, as signified by the green light next to the service name in the Server app sidebar, the Time Machine server is visible to any Mac on the network (Figure 12–21).

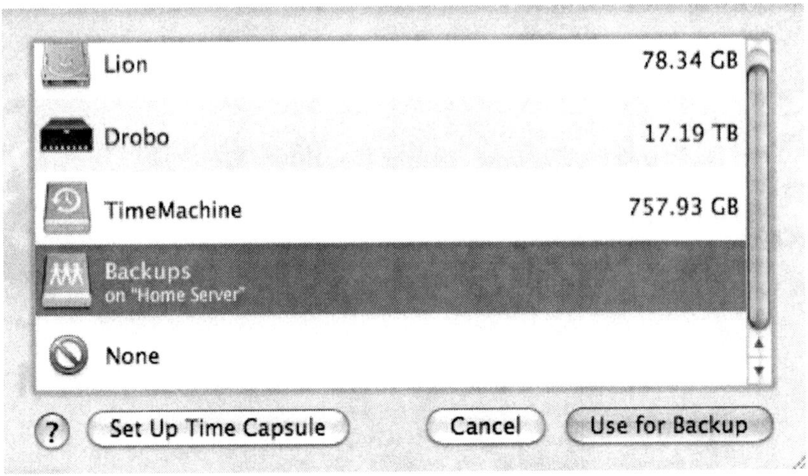

Figure 12–21. *The backup drive connected to the server Home Server is available for use as a Time Machine target for all Macs on the network.*

To ensure that Time Machine backups continue unabated even after the network backup drive is nearing capacity, it is recommended that the "Notify after old backups are deleted" option in the Time Machine options on the workstations be unchecked. This way, Time Machine automatically removes older backups without causing undue worry for users on the network.

Web

Although the examples in this chapter are for a local server, enabling the Web Server service on your OS X Lion Server is still a good idea. For a small business, an internal web site makes an excellent intranet, providing up-to-date information and news to employees. For a home server, a family web site containing important information is useful for making sure that information is available to everyone with a click.

Like the other services discussed in this chapter, the Web Server service is enabled by clicking it in the Server App sidebar and then clicking the On/Off button. When the service is running, a green light appears in the sidebar. Your Mac is now a web server. I recommend checking the "Enable PHP web applications" box (Figure 12–22), because that allows your web server to host many powerful applications through the PHP scripting language.

There's a sample web site hosted by default on your server, and it is listed on the Web Server page of the Server app. To see what the sample web site looks like, there's a View Server Web Site link at the bottom of the Web Server page, or the page may be visited from a Mac on the network by typing the server host name (in this case, server.local) into the address bar of a web browser.

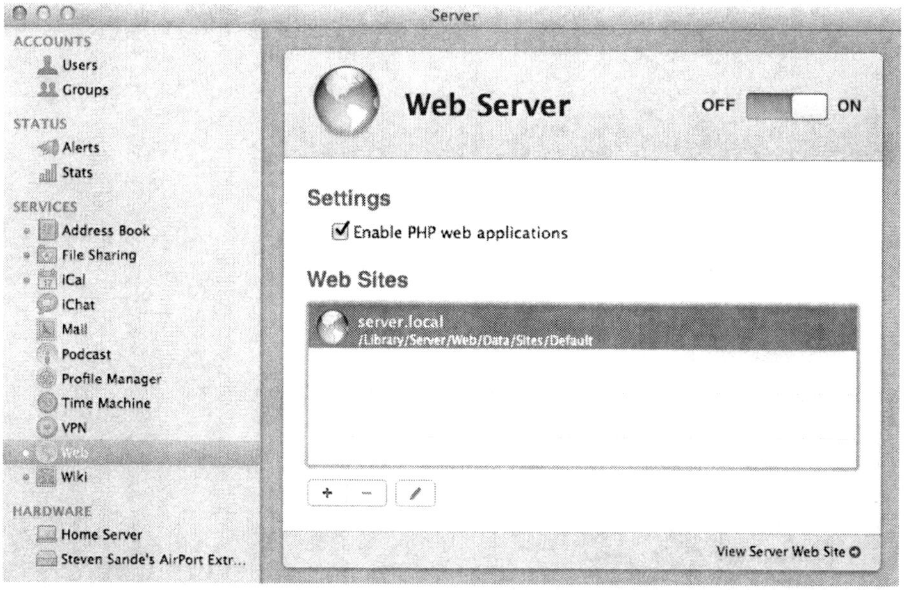

Figure 12–22. *The Lion Web Server, with the default web site displayed*

The files that make up that web site are stored in a hidden folder on your Mac that is accessible by double-clicking the default web site name or clicking the pencil-like edit icon below the list of web sites. Once the details of the site are revealed, clicking the View Document Root Contents link opens a Finder window containing the web site files.

Just about any Web design tool can be used to create your own web site, from Apple's sadly neglected iWeb and similar apps, such as RapidWeaver ($79.99, www.realmacsoftware.com) and Sandvox ($77.00, www.karelia.com), to powerful content management systems like WordPress (free, http://wordpress.org) and Drupal (free, http://drupal.org/). For workgroups or families, using Lion Server's wiki service in concert with the web service may be just the answer.

Wiki

A wiki is a web site that allows the authoring of interlinked web pages via a web browser. Like the other tools in Lion Server, the wiki service is enabled with a click of the wiki service in the Server App sidebar and another click on the On/Off switch.

Once the service is displaying the traditional green light to show that it is running, a visit to the server from a web browser displays a welcome page describing what can be done with the combination of the web and wiki services (Figure 12–23).

Figure 12–23. *The Lion Server web/wiki welcome page*

Note that in Figure 12–23 there's a "Log in" link. Clicking that link displays a server sign-in screen, and once a user name (the short name described earlier in this chapter) and valid password are entered, a profile page for the user is displayed (Figure 12–24).

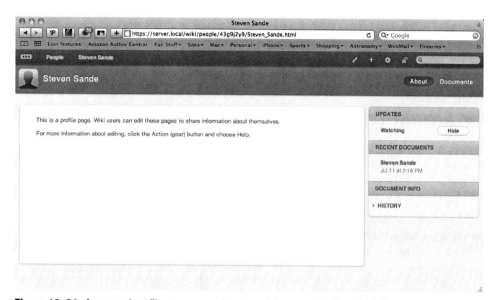

Figure 12–24. *A personal profile page created by the wiki server. This is editable by users to add additional pages, documents, and personal information.*

Apple made the wiki pages easy to edit. By clicking the action button at the top of this page (it looks like a gear), it's possible to add a personal blog page, an e-mail link, and even add a tiny photo thumbnail to the About page. There's a fully functional text editor that appears when you click the edit button (looks like a pencil), and the resulting web pages are very professional-looking. Figure 12–25 displays a personal blog page that took less than a minute to add and edit.

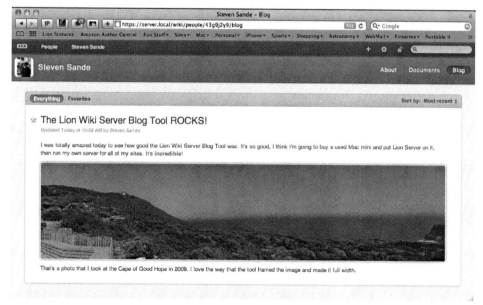

Figure 12–25. *A blog page created in OS X Lion Server's wiki server*

The Documents link on the wiki page is a wonderful place to store documents that you want to publicly share with others. Clicking the Create New Content button (the + sign at the top of the page), files of any type are uploaded to the wiki server and made available to others on your network with a single click.

Server Admin Tools

If your server is "headless" (doesn't have a monitor attached) or you need to tweak a setting or add a user while you're away, Apple's Server Admin Tools can be a big help. The tools are a free download from http://support.apple.com/downloads#macosxserver and not only provide a way to administer a server from another Mac but are also much more in-depth than the Lion Server app.

Once the disk image file containing the Server Admin Tools installer is downloaded, double-click the installer icon. The installer places a folder containing six different applications—Server Admin, Server Monitor, Workgroup Manager, Podcast Composer, System Image Utility, and Xgrid Admin—into the Applications folder of your server.

For those who have administered Mac OS X Server in the past, you already know about the Server Admin Tools because they're what you've used for day-to-day server administration. In this section, I'll introduce the rest of you to the Server Admin Tools and explain how they're used to configure and maintain OS X Lion Server.

Server Admin

Probably the most widely used of the Server Admin Tools is Server Admin. After launching the app, a list of all the servers on your network appears. To monitor what's going on with a specific server or to change settings, log into each server with an administrative user name and password.

Once Server Admin is logged into a specific server, six separate buttons provide a view into the server (Figure 12–26). Overview lists important information about the hardware that the server is running on. In this example, OS X Lion Server has been installed on a MacBook Air with 4GB of RAM and 120GB of storage that is about half full.

Administrators sometimes need access to the log files that are captured by the Unix underpinnings of Mac OS X. The Logs button reveals second-by-second updates of any information logged into the system log, kernel log, secure log, or software update log of the server.

If a server seems to be running slowly, administrators often look at the performance graphs available by clicking the Graphs button. The graphs display CPU usage or network traffic vs. time, which can show an administrator whether network traffic or a busy server was causing an issue.

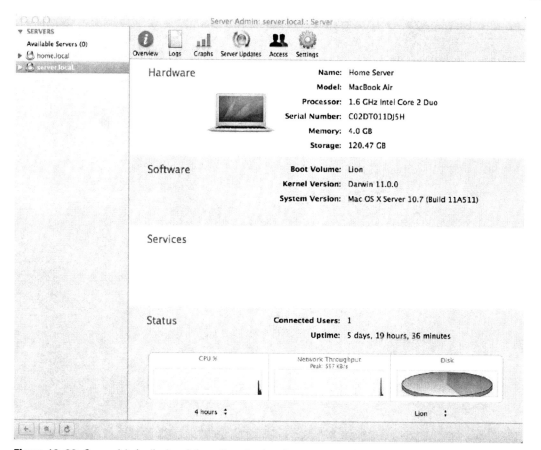

Figure 12–26. *Server Admin displays information about each server, as well as providing visibility to log files and performance graphs, the ability to install server updates, and the ability to set up access to different services.*

Server Updates displays information about updates to OS X Lion Server and makes the updates available for installation. Access determines which services on your server are available to various users and groups. The last button, Settings, gives access to five different tabs that are used to fine-tune server management protocols, network settings and host names, date and time settings, alerts, and other services that are not controlled by the Server app.

Workgroup Manager

Another widely used administrative tool is Workgroup Manager. As with Server Admin, a single administrator can create and maintain user accounts on more than one server through this tool (Figure 12–27).

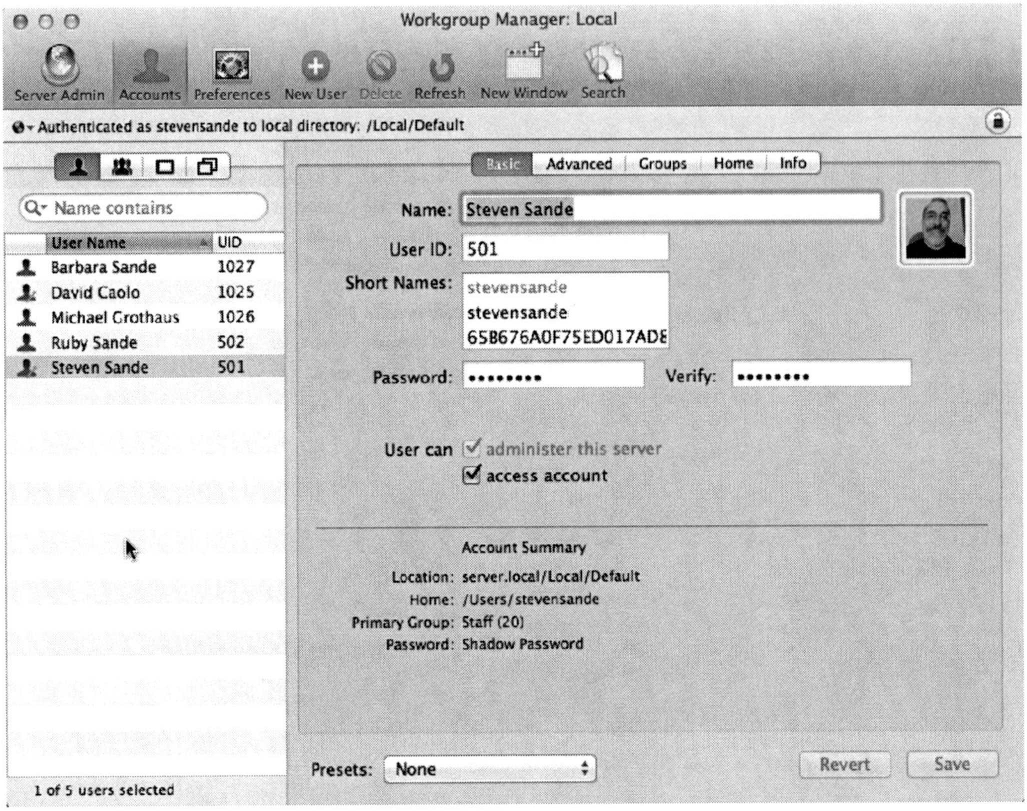

Figure 12-27. *Workgroup Manager is used to control the details of users and groups on a server.*

Once an administrator is logged into Workgroup Manager, all of the users and groups on the server are visible along with information about them. The Advanced tab can be used to set up password options such as requiring users to change their passwords every 30 days or making certain password keywords unusable.

Workgroup Manager can be used to add extensive contact information about each user on a server, which is then included in the Address Book Server directory. The Home tab is used to create a user home directory on the server, which is useful in terms of providing fast backups of the user's documents from a single location, namely, the server.

In locations with many Macs, administrators often use Workgroup Manager to set global preferences for all users by clicking the Preferences button. Since Server Admin and Workgroup Manager are often used together, there's a Server Admin button at the top of the window that launches Server Admin with a single click.

Server Monitor

Server Monitor is another of the tools that is primarily useful in locations that have many Mac servers. The interface of this tool provides a list of the status of all monitored servers, updated as often as every 10 seconds. Each server displays a green light if everything is running perfectly, and detailed status messages are listed or e-mailed to administrators when something seems to be going wrong with a server.

This tool was primarily developed for use in organizations with many Apple Xserve servers. The Xserve was a rack-mounted enterprise-quality server that was eliminated from Apple's product line in early 2011 due to low sales. Server Monitor is still useful with other Mac-based server installations, but many of the more powerful features such as lights-out management were available only with the Xserve.

Podcast Composer

When I described the many uses of OS X Lion Server at the beginning of the chapter, one of the services listed was Podcast Server. Podcast Composer is the third component of a Apple's podcasting solution, along with Podcast Server and Podcast Capture.

While Podcast Server is used to essentially "broadcast" recorded video or audio podcasts and Podcast Capture is used to record or import raw content, Podcast Composer has one purpose, which is creating podcasting workflows from import to editing, exporting, and publishing.

System Image Utility

For administrators who need to keep multitudes of Macs up-to-date with the same software, there's the System Image Utility. Through this utility, admins create system images containing licensed software and settings that can be pushed to individual Macs for hands-off loading of software.

There's usually a lot of scripting involved, so this is one utility that you'll want to study before you work with it. Apple provides a certification for system administrators (http://training.apple.com/certification/), and System Image Utility is one of the tools you'll need to know intimately to gain this valued certification.

Xgrid Admin

The final member of the Server Admin Tools family is Xgrid Admin. Xgrid is Apple's proprietary software program and distributed computing protocol that allows networked computers to all work on a single processor-intensive task. With the tool, administrators can create computing clusters made up of Mac OS servers and workstations. All Macs come with an Xgrid client that must be running for the computer to become part of a computing cluster.

What is Xgrid used for? In the scientific community, it's used to run calculations on a network of Macs that formerly required a supercomputer to process. The entertainment industry can use a Mac cluster for distributed rendering of sophisticated computer graphics.

Summary

OS X Lion Server brings a new level of power and simplicity to Mac OS X. While previous versions of the Server operating system were expensive and difficult to configure, OS X Lion Server is an inexpensive app available through the Mac App Store that is remarkably simple to set up and run.

Although OS X Lion Server could easily be the topic of a separate book, this chapter described how to set up a Mac as a home or small-office stand-alone server and how to use some of the most widely used services. Key points to remember include the following:

- OS X Lion Server is purchased and installed through the Mac App Store and will run on any Mac capable of running OS X Lion.

- The Server app is the control panel used to enable or disable services, add or edit users and groups, and make many configuration changes to the services.

- Address Book Server provides a common repository for contacts for workgroups or families.

- File Sharing creates share points that require user authentication for browsing, editing, or deleting files and folders.

- iCal Server enables workgroups to share calendars from Macs and iOS devices.

- Time Machine Server makes it possible to send backups of multiple Macs on a network to a single repository.

- OS X Lion Server's web server is useful both for hosting standard web sites and content management systems.

- Wiki Server works together with the web server to let any user build and edit their own personal site containing web pages, links to documents, and a personal blog.

- Server Admin Tools is a set of powerful administration tools for the configuration and maintenance of your OS X Lion Server.

Index

M